A Systematic Approach to Examination, Diagnosis & Manual Therapy of the Shoulder

IAOM Course Objectives:

A Systematic Approach to Examination, Diagnosis & Manual Therapy of the Shoulder

Through a combination of lecture and lab, participants will…

- Perform a systematic clinical examination to determine the most efficient course of treatment.

- Perform joint specific mobilization techniques to address capsular restrictions with limitations to 90 degrees and at end-range.

- Perform testing and treatment of limitations at the AC and SC joints.

- Understand the difference in clinical presentation between clients with external and internal impingement.

- Assess the integrity of the rotator cuff musculature, identify bursal irritation, and perform special tests related to impingement and instability.

- Develop and understanding of muscle groups to emphasize with shoulder rehabilitation using the most current research.

UE Shoulder Course Outline

Day 1

8:00-8:15 am	Introductions: instructors and course participants	
8:15-9:45 am	Anatomy and pathoanatomy of the shoulder	Lecture
9:45-10:15 am	Surface anatomy: bony surface anatomy of the shoulder complex	Lab
10:15-10:30 am	**BREAK**	
10:30-11:00 am	Complete surface anatomy	Lab
11:00-11:45 am	History	Lecture
11:45-12:30 pm	Clinical examination of the shoulder	Lab
12:30-1:30 pm	**LUNCH**	
1:30-2:00 pm	Complete clinical examination	Lab
2:00-2:30 pm	Adhesive Capsulitis	Lecture
2:00-3:15 pm	Treatment of capsular pattern of the glenohumeral joint (GHJ): addressing limitations below 90°	Lab
3:15-3:30 pm	**BREAK**	
3:30-4:00 pm	Complete joint-specific treatment below 90°	Lab
4:00-5:00 pm	Treatment of GHJ: end-range techniques	Lab
5:00-5:15 pm	**BREAK**	
5:15-6:00 pm	Shoulder Impingement	Lecture
6:00-6:30 pm	Clinical examination: extra tests for impingement	

Day 2

8:00-8:30 am	Interpretation of examination findings	Lecture
8:30-10:45 am	Bursal massage, joint-specific treatment for non-capsular pattern of the GHJ: posterior capsule tightness	Lab
10:15-10:30 am	**BREAK**	
10:30-11:30 pm	Sternoclavicular joint (SCJ) & Acromioclavicular joint (ACJ): joint-specific testing and treatment and scapular taping	Lab
11:30-12:30 pm	Soft tissue techniques: transverse friction massage, eccentric loading	Lab
12:30-1:00 pm	**LUNCH**	
1:00-2:15 pm	Instability with additional clinical tests	Lecture & Lab
2:15-2:30 pm	Exercise considerations	Lecture
2:30-2:45 pm	Case studies: tying together all the concepts presented	Lecture
2:45-3:00 pm	**QUESTIONS & CLOSING REMARKS**	

General Information

International Academy of Orthopedic Medicine – US PO
Box 65179
Tucson, Arizona 85728
520.318.4266 ph
866.426.6101 toll
866.698.4832 fax
www.iaom-us.com
info@iaom-us.com

FACULTY

Gail Apte, PT, ScD, OCS, FAAOMPT graduated from the Mayo School of Health Related Sciences, Minnesota in 1981. She completed certification by the IAOM in Orthopedic Medicine and Manual Therapy in 1992 and the Fellowship in 2008. In 2006, Dr. Apte completed her Doctorate of Science in Physical Therapy through Texas Tech University Health Sciences Center (TTUHSC). Dr. Apte is an assistant professor at TTUHSC, and maintains a clinical practice in Orthopedic Manual Therapy with a special interest in Chronic Pelvic Pain in Eugene, OR.

Esteban Azevedo, PT, ScD, COMT, graduated from the University of Arizona with a Bachelor's of Science in Exercise and Sports Science. He received his Master's Degree in Physical Therapy from Northern Arizona University in 2000. He completed IAOM-US certification in 2004, and completed his Doctorate of Science (ScD) from Texas Tech University Health Sciences Center in 2011. Esteban and his wife, Amy, own an outpatient physical therapy clinic, Modern Physical Therapy, in Kansas City, Missouri. www.modernpt.com Esteban has presented lectures on combining physical therapy with interventional pain management at pain conferences (Society for Pain Practice Management) on physical therapist and interventional pain physician teamwork. He has been teaching for the IAOM since 2005.

Nicolas Bellot, PT, COMT graduated in 2010 from a Physiotherapy School (IFMK) in Strasbourg, France. He completed his certifications in orthopaedic manual therapy with the IAOM-US in 2015. He contributes to the development of IAOM concepts in France and became assistant faculty for IAOM courses in 2015. Furthermore, he is a reviewer for the Journal of Manual & Manipulative Therapy and is enrolled in the Master of Science in Neuromusculoskeletal Physiotherapy at Brighton University in Great Britain. He assesses and treats patients with neuromusculoskeletal conditions in a private practice in Strasbourg, France.

Jamie Bergner, OTD, OTR/L, CHT, COMT, graduated from the University of Wisconsin-La Crosse with a Bachelor of Science degree in Occupational Therapy in 2000. She received her post-professional doctorate in occupational therapy with an elective track in education from Rocky Mountain University of Health Professions in 2016. She became a certified hand therapist in 2010, and obtained her certification through IAOM as a COMT in the upper extremity in 2015. She currently specializes in hand trauma at Vanderbilt University Medical Center, a level I trauma center in Nashville, Tennessee.

Jean-Michel Brismée, PT, ScD, OCS, FAAOMPT is professor in the Doctorate of Science Program of Physical Therapy at Texas Tech University Health Sciences Center (TTUHSC) in Lubbock, Texas. Dr. Brismée graduated from the Catholic University of Louvain-la-Neuve in Belgium with Bachelor of Science degrees in Physical Education (1982) and Physical Therapy (1985). He graduated from Texas Tech University in 1996 with a Master of Sciences in Sports Health and earned a Doctorate of Science degree in Physical Therapy from TTUHSC in 2003. He is the Director of the Fellowship Program and Chair of the Research Committee of the International Academy of Orthopedic Medicine, Editor-in-Chief of the Journal of Manual & Manipulative Therapy and maintains clinical practice in outpatient orthopedics at University Medical Center in Lubbock, TX.

John E. Cain, OTR, CHT, COMT graduated from the University of Wisconsin, Milwaukee in 2001. He became a Certified Leduc Trained Lymphedema Therapist in 2004, a Certified Hand Therapist in 2007 and earned his COMT in 2010. Currently, John works with the Lakeshore Medical Clinic in Milwaukee where he specializes in upper extremity orthopaedic injuries and lymphedema patients. John has been an assisting instructor for the Hand and Upper Extremity Track with the IAOM-US since 2010.

Frédéric Froment, PT, COMT graduated in 2000 from a Physical Therapy School in Paris, France with a bachelor degree. He pursed his educational curriculum at the "Conservatoire des Arts et Métiers" in bioengineering, and at the Rene Descartes University Paris V and obtained a University Diploma in Pediatric Physical therapy in 2009. He is involved in the development of Orthopedic Manual Therapy in France with the IAOM-US and began assisting courses as assistant faculty in 2015. Additionally, he is pursuing a doctor of science (ScD) degree in physical therapy at Texas Tech University Health Sciences Center. Currently, Frédéric is Vice-President of the French Society of Physiotherapy and is member of the executive committee of OMT-France (RIG). He is associate editor of the Journal of Manual & Manipulative Therapy and maintains his private clinical practice in outpatient orthopedics in Chartres (France).

Josué Gan, PT, COMT, MSc student graduated in 2010 from a Physical Therapy School (IFMK) in Strasbourg, France. He completed his first year of master of science at the University "Joseph Fournier" of Grenoble (France). He earned his certification in orthopedic manual therapy with Manual Concepts (Australia) and IAOM-US in 2015. He is involved in the development of Orthopaedic Manual Therapy in France with the IAOM-US and began assisting courses as assistant faculty in 2015. Currently, Josué is member of the executive committee of OMT-France (RIG) and pursues his Master of Science (MSc) degree in Physiotherapy (Musculoskeletal specialty) at the University of Applied Sciences of Zürich (Switzerland). He lectures at the Physical Therapy School in Strasbourg and assesses/treats patients with neuromusculoskeletal disorders in a private practice in Strasbourg (France).

Dale Gerke, PT, ScD, OCS, FAAOMPT, earned his Bachelor's Degree from Wisconsin Lutheran College in 1996, his Master of Physical Therapy from Concordia University Wisconsin in 2000 and his Doctor of Science in Physical Therapy from Texas Tech University Health Sciences Center in 2009. He currently serves as Assistant Professor and staff Physical Therapist at Concordia University in Wisconsin. Dale became an Orthopedic Certification Specialist in 2012 and a Certified Orthopedic Manual Therapist of the complete extremities in 2006. Dale completed his fellowship in 2017. He is an active contributor to multiple peer reviewed publications and presentations.

Amy Hay, PT, ScD, COMT, graduated from Northern Arizona University with a Bachelor's of Science in Exercise and Sports Science. She received her Master's Degree in Physical Therapy from Northern Arizona University in 2000. She completed IAOM-US certification in 2004. Amy completed her Doctorate of Science (ScD) from Texas Tech University Health Sciences Center in 2011. Amy and her husband, Esteban, own an outpatient physical therapy clinic, Modern Physical Therapy, in Kansas City, Missouri. www.modernpt.com

Amy Houchens, PT, CHT, COMT, graduated from the University of Wisconsin-Madison in 1996. After 9 years of general orthopedic and neurological outpatient practice, she began to specialize in hand therapy becoming a Certified Hand Therapist in 2010. She earned her COMT in 2013. Amy works full time for Therapeutic Associates in Bend, OR—a PT owned outpatient clinic. Her caseload is primarily hand and upper extremity with a mixture of post-operative and non-operative conditions. She began as an assistant instructor for IAOM in 2014.

Mary Kremer, PT, ScD, MOMT graduated from the Mayo School of Health Related Sciences, Minnesota in 1977. Ms. Kremer was certified by the IAOM in Orthopedic Medicine and Manual Therapy in 1991. She completed a Clinical Masters with Ola Grimsby in 1993. She is currently a senior therapist at the Institute for Athletic Medicine in Minneapolis, MN. www.athletic-medicine.org

Haley Main, PT, DPT, COMT, graduated from Harding University and received a Doctorate in Physical Therapy in 2017. She completed her IAOM-US certification in 2018. Haley is the Director of Clinical Education at Searcy Physical therapy which involves teaching therapists how to organize patient profiles and how to create comprehensive treatment programs. Haley is specialized in treating chronic pain patients at an orthopedic outpatient clinic in Searcy, Arkansas.

Omer Matthijs, PT, ScD, MOMT graduated from the Higher Institute for Medical Professions, Gent, Belgium in 1975 and received his Doctorate in Physical Therapy from Texas Tech University in 2011. He has become a recognized researcher, practitioner, author and teacher specializing in non-surgical orthopedic medicine and manual therapy. He continues to treat patients in private practice in Austria & provides consultation services to physicians & PTs. He is co-director of the IAOM-EUR. ww.iaom.de.

Mike McGalliard, PT, ScD, graduated from Texas Tech University Health Sciences Center (TTUHSC) with a Masters of Physical Therapy in 1997. In 2006, he completed IAOM certification and in 2008, Mike received his Doctorate of Science in Physical Therapy from TTUHSC. Dr. McGalliard is now the Physical Therapy Program Director at Harding University in Searcy, Arkansas.

Kasey Miller, PT, DPT, COMT, graduated from McPherson College with a Bachelor's in Biology. He received his doctorate of physical therapy from Kansas University Medical Center in 2016. He completed IAOM-US certification for the spine in 2017, and is currently a fellow candidate in the IAOM-US Fellowship program. Kasey works as a therapist at Modern Physical Therapy in Kansas City, MO.

Robert Moss, PT, ScD, OCS, FAAOMPT, graduated from Texas Tech University Health Sciences Center (TTUHSC) with a Masters in Physical Therapy in 1998 and graduated from the Doctorate of Sciences Program in Physical Therapy in 2007. Dr. Moss certified with the IAOM-US in 2002 and completed the IAOM-US Fellowship Program in 2007. He owns Moss Rehabilitation Center in Springtown, Texas. www.springtownphysicaltherapy.com

Patty Nelson, PT, ScD, OCS, FAAOMPT graduated from the University of Minnesota with a Bachelor's of Science in Exercise Physiology and then completed her Bachelors of Science in Physical Therapy. She achieved her IAOM-US certification in Orthopedic Manual Therapy in 1993 and 1995.In 2008 she completed her ScD in Advanced orthopedic manual therapy from Texas Tech University and went on to earn her Fellowship in manual therapy in 2009. Currently she teaches in the Doctor of Physical Therapy Program at Eastern Washington University and pursues research related to women's health conditions.

Mirka Normand, OTR, MA, CHT, COMT, graduated with a Bachelor of Science in Occupational Therapy from Laval University in Quebec, Canada, 1991. She attended the Hand Therapy Fellowship program of Texas Women's University and Baylor College of Medicine in 1999 and obtained her hand therapy certification (CHT) that same year. She completed her Advanced Master's degree in Occupational Therapy with Hand Therapy Specialty in 2003 at Texas Women's University. In 2006, she achieved the IAOM-US Manual Therapy Certification for the upper quadrant (COMT). She is one of the creators and lead instructors of the IAOM-US Hand and Upper Extremity Track.

Thomas Osinski, PT, MSc, COMT graduated in 2009 from a Physical Therapy School in Paris (EFOM), France. He pursed his educational curriculum in orthopedic manual therapy with the COMT of Manual Concepts (Australia) and IAOM-US. He completed the first year of his master of science at the University "Joseph Fournier" of Grenoble (France) and obtained his MSc at the University "Pierre et Marie Curie "of Paris (France). He is currently pursuing his PhD on pain related to spinal cord injured patients. He is involved in the development of Orthopedic Manual Therapy in France with the IAOM-US and became assistant faculty in 2015. Presently, Thomas is Vice-President of the association OMT-France (RIG of IFOMPT). He teaches in two Physical Therapy Schools and maintains clinical practice in outpatient orthopedics in his private practice.

Valerie Phelps, PT, ScD, OCS, FAAOMPT graduated with a Degree in Physical Therapy from the University of Minnesota in 1981. She became an international instructor for the IAOM in 1994; at that time she also received recognition as a specialty instructor in manual therapy education by the German Physical Therapy Association. Along with being the Founder and current Education Director of the IAOM-US, she also instructs for IAOM courses in the USA and Europe. She is the Practice Director of an employee owned practice: Advanced Physical Therapy in Anchorage, the Mat-Su Valley, and Fairbanks, Alaska. www.aptak.com

Theresa Parry, OTR, BS, MS, COMT, is a 2012 graduate from University of Wisconsin – La Crosse with a Master of Science Degree in Occupational Therapy and a Bachelor's degree in Psychology. Theresa completed the IAOM-US COMT of the upper quadrant in 2015. Theresa is a practicing therapist at the Hand to Shoulder Center of Wisconsin in Appleton, WI where she specializes in both conservative and post-operative treatment of orthopedic conditions of upper quadrant.

Ann Porretto-Loehrke, PT, DPT, CHT, COMT graduated from Marquette University in 1994. She became a CHT in 2002 and completed IAOM-US certification for the upper quadrant in 2003. In 2007, Ann completed a (DPT) degree with a specialty in hand and upper quarter rehabilitation from Drexel University in Philadelphia, PA. Ann is the therapy manager at the Hand to Shoulder Center of Wisconsin, located in Appleton, WI. She has previously served as an item writer for the Hand Therapy Certification Commission and been a member of the Examination Committee. Ann is one of the creators and lead instructors of the Hand and Upper Extremity Track. She has presented at ASHT annual conferences, Wisconsin Hand Experience, Canadian Hand Conferences, Philadelphia Hand Conference, and Teton Hand Conference.

Becky Sherwin, MPT, COMT graduated from Louisiana State University with a Masters in Physical Therapy in 1998. She completed her Spine Certification in 2012 and her Extremity Certification in 2017. She is currently a Fellow candidate in the IAOM Fellowship program. She is also enrolled in the ScD program at TTUHSC. She is employed by Melanie Massey Physical Therapy and is Director of the Adult Clinic in West Monroe, LA.

Dustin Silhan, PT, ScD, COMT, earned his Bachelor of Science in Health Services degree in 2005, his Master of Physical Therapy in 2007 and his Doctor of Science in Physical Therapy in 2012 from Texas Tech University Health Sciences Center. Currently, Dustin is a Therapist with BSA Outpatient Therapy Services in Amarillo, TX and working on a Doctoral teaching project: Diagnosis and Management of the Overhead Throwing Athlete: An Investigation of the Shoulder Complex and Kinematic Chain.

Phillip S. Sizer, Jr., PT, PhD, OCS, FAAOMPT graduated in 1985 from the University of Texas, Medical Branch in Galveston TX. He received a MEd in exercise science from Texas Tech University in 1993. He received a PhD with an emphasis in Motor Control from Texas Tech University in 2002. Along with serving as a Senior Clinician in an outpatient orthopedic clinic, he is a Distinguished Professor and Program Director of the Doctorate of Science Program in Physical Therapy, as well as Associate Dean of Research and Director of the Clinical Musculoskeletal Research Laboratory at Texas Tech University Health Sciences Center in Lubbock TX. Dr. Sizer is a reviewer for numerous peer-reviewed journals and serves as an Associate Editor for 2 peer reviewed journals: Journal of Manual & Manipulative Therapy and Pain Practice.

Didi van Paridon, PT, MOMT has been an instructor for the IAOM-EUR since 1980. Besides her private practice in Antwerp, Belgium, she teaches throughout Europe and the United States. She is co-author of the reference book series Manual Therapy of the Peripheral Joints [German, Dutch]. She has been president of the IAOM-EUR since 2005 when the founder, Dos Winkel, retired.

Tiffany Tang, OTD, MBA, OTR/L, CHT, COMT, CEAS, CFCE, has been a practicing occupational therapist since graduation from Hong Kong Polytechnic University in 1988. She became a certified hand therapist in 1995 and earned her Master in Business Administration in 2002. She received her post professional doctoral degree in occupational therapy in 2011, and completed IAOM-US certification in orthopedic manual therapy in 2015. She is also a certified ergonomics assessment specialist and a certified functional capacity evaluator. She is a Level IV clinician at California Pacific Medical Center and also teaches dental ergonomics in University of the Pacific Dugoni School of Dentistry in San Francisco.

Megan Vaught, PT, ScD, OCS, graduated from Texas Woman's University. Ms. Vaught was certified by the IAOM-US in Orthopedic Medicine and Manual Therapy in 1995. She works in outpatient physical therapy at Abbott Northwestern Hospital/Sister Kenny Institute, Minneapolis, Minnesota.

John Woolf, MS, PT, ATC, COMT, received his Bachelor of Science in Physical Therapy from Northern Arizona University and his Masters of Science from the University of Arizona in Exercise Science with an emphasis in Biomechanics and Motor Control. He is the former Director of Medical Services for Athletics at the University of Arizona and currently the owner of ProActive Physical Therapy in Tucson, AZ. www.proactivept.com He serves as a clinical instructor in the University of Arizona Sports Medicine Fellowship Program and is the Administrative Director of IAOM-US.

INTERNATIONAL ACADEMY OF ORTHOPEDIC MEDICINE

If patients are not one-dimensional, how can a single course of therapy deliver healing? It can't. That realization brought great minds in medicine and physical therapy together to create a powerful partnership for patient care.

The *International Academy of Orthopedic Medicine* (IAOM) was founded in 1978 by pioneering physicians and physical therapists in Europe and the UK who shared a vision that teamwork could transform orthopedic care for patients with non-surgical problems. The group organized dynamic courses, workshops, and lectures to explore an advanced method of clinical examination that employed selective tissue testing (via compression or tension), followed by establishing the most efficient treatment (of injection and/or manual therapy/exercise) based on specific patient selection.

Pain: a success story

The philosophy of the *International Academy of Orthopedic Medicine* continues to support a systematic approach to clinical diagnosis today, with the foundational paradigm that each structure of the musculoskeletal system has individual properties that do not change and are unique to that structure. Thus, when that structure is injured, the trauma causes pain in a certain region, often resulting in misleading symptoms in other locations. We have learned, however, that specific tests will evoke pain in a consistent pattern that clinicians can use to accurately diagnose their patients. Understanding pain as a diagnostic tool empowers both the clinician and the patient to take control of the healing process.

Healing without borders

In 1988, the *International Academy of Orthopedic Medicine* expanded to the USA, (*IAOM-US*), where research and instruction continue to build on the foundation of establishing an accurate clinical diagnosis that empowers clinicians to create the most effective plan of care. Taught at strategic locations throughout the USA, courses sell out quickly as the industry evolves and word of their demonstrated benefits spreads. Annual national and international forums draw bigger crowds each year, and cutting-edge techniques that improve patient outcomes continue to emerge. Fueled by this incredible momentum, the *IAOM-US* is bringing the methodology of clinical practice to Latin America and India in the near future.

Science + human interest

We teach healthcare professionals to go beyond orthopedic manual therapy, to reach past pain and treat people. *IAOM* courses give clinicians the tools they need to develop evidence-based treatment plans to manage or overcome pain and increase mobility, but it doesn't end there. Using biopsychosocial and sensorimotor control models, we help visionary healthcare professionals to move patients further down the road to recovery - toward sustainable health and active, joyful living.

Help for the healer

What makes the *IAOM* different? In short, we feel your pain. We understand the unique challenges you face, and we are dedicated to providing solutions that enable you to grow and flourish in your practice. We'll help you navigate the sea of literature by synthesizing the most critical information and providing it to you in a simple, dynamic format – so you can immediately and effectively apply it. More than a provider of continuing education, we are balm for today's busy healer—a strategic partner you can count on for the life of your career.

Evolving together

As the industry continues to evolve, the *IAOM* is committed to keeping healthcare professionals ahead of the curve through certification opportunities, interactive courses on emerging techniques, and a robust menu of learning aides including textbooks, DVDs, and

Healers Edge—a compelling, click-able newsletter available to healthcare professionals worldwide. We'll help you organize a wealth of must-have tools, so you're always on top of your game. We share your passion for providing patients with differentiated care and optimized outcomes—imagine what we can do together!

It is well known that MRI, CT scan, and radiographs often depict "abnormalities" that are misleading: surgery is performed, and the pain remains unchanged afterward. Several studies have confirmed that the clinical examination is more effective that imaging. For instance, using simple but specific tests (some compiled, some developed by the IAOM), it is possible to differentiate between a muscle lesion, a bursal irritation, a labral tear, a tenosynovitis of the biceps, or an arthropathy of the shoulder joint, as being the source of an individual's pain.

Following the same philosophy (of staying true to anatomical findings and recent research), IAOM instructors have developed and refined treatment techniques that consist of manual therapy and appropriate affliction-specific exercise programs. This affords the clinician an effective, comprehensive, and diagnosis-specific treatment plan for every non-operative orthopedic disorder.

RESOURCES:
A **DVD series** (set of 12) by IAOM-US faculty is now available. Authored by Phil Sizer, Jean-Michel Brismeé, Greg Dedrick, and Valerie Phelps, each DVD will address examination techniques, surface anatomy, and soft tissue and joint mobilization treatments for a specific joint.
In addition to several books in Dutch and German, Dos Winkel, Omer Matthijs, Didi van Paridon, and Valerie Phelps have published the following books in English:
Diagnosis and Treatment of the Spine. Aspen Publishers; 1996.
Diagnosis and Treatment of the Upper Extremity. Aspen Publishers; 1997. (No longer in print.)
Diagnosis and Treatment of the Lower Extremity. Aspen Publishers; 1997. (No longer in print.)
Diagnosis-Specific Orthopedic Management of the Hip OPTP 2007
Diagnosis-Specific Orthopedic Management of the Knee OPTP 2009
They have also created a video series of *Nonoperative Orthopedic Medicine and Manual Therapy of the Extremities*. Gustav Fischer Verlag; 1995.
All of the above resources are available from OPTP (1-800-367-7393) or via www.optp.com.

Book Chapter
Owens SC, Gerke DA, Brismeé JM*. **Ergonomic Impact of Spinal Loading and Recovery Positions on Intervertebral Disc Health: Strategies for Prevention and Management of Low Back Pain, Ergonomics. 2012 - A Systems Approach**, Dr. Isabel L. Nunes (Ed.), ISBN: 978-953-51-0601-2, InTech, Available from:
http://www.intechopen.com/books/ergonomics-a-systems-approach/ergonomic-impact-of-spinal-loading-and-recovery-positions-on-intervertebral-disc-health-and-preventi

Radelet M. **Chapter 12: Special Considerations for Specific Sports. In: Emergency Care of Sports Injuries** (Blanc, Feld, Gorse, eds.). FA Davis, 2007.

King P, Boissonnault W, Erhard D, Flynn T, Olson K, Paris S, Patla C, Rowe R, Sanders B, Sizer P, Swift M, Wainner R, Wolff-Burke M. **Manipulation Education Manual**. AlexandriaVA: APTA Manipulation Task Force. 2004

Orbegoza M, Sizer PS **Facet Block and Denervation**. In Raj P. (Ed). *Textbook of Regional Anesthesia* (3rd Ed). New York, NY: Churchill Livingstone, 2002, pp.703-732

Gokeler A, Knopf E, Lehmann M, & Freiwald J **Neue Erkenntnisse in der physiotherapeutischen Behandlung beim akuten Inversionstrauma des Sprunggelenks**. In: M. Engelhardt, J. Freiwald & L. Zichner (Eds.), Sprunggelenk und Fuß - Verletzungen und Überlastungsschäden (pp. 199-224). Nürnberg: Novartis Pharma. 2002.

Racz GB, Anderson SR, Sizer PS, Phelps V **Atlantooccipital and Atlantoaxial Injections in the Treatment of Headache and Neck Pain**. In Waldman S (Saunders) *Interventional Pain Management* (2nd Ed) 2000, 20, pp.295-305.

Peer Reviewed Journal Articles

Yamato T, Maher C, Saragiotto B, Moseley A, Hoffmann T, Elkins M, Petersen S, Riley SP, Brismée JM. **Improving Completeness and Transparency of Reporting in Clinical Trials Using the Template for Intervention Description and Replication (TIDieR) Checklist will Benefit the Physiotherapy Profession**. *Journal of Manual and Manipulative Therapy.* 2016;24(4):183-184.

Sizer PS, Mauri MV, Learman K, Jones C, Gill N, Showalter CR, Brismée JM. **Should Evidence or Sound Clinical Reasoning Dictate Patient Care?** *Journal of Manual and Manipulative Therapy.* 2016;24(3):117-119.

Brismée JM, Yang S, Lambert M, Chyu MC, Tsai P, Zhang Y, Han J, Hudson C, Chung E, Shen CL. **Differences in Musculoskeletal Health due to Gender in a Rural Multiethnic Cohort: a Project FRONTIER study**. *BMC Musculoskeletal Disorders.* 2016;17:181.

Sobczak S, Dugailly PM, Gilbert KK, Hooper T, Sizer PS, James RC, Matthijs O, Brismée JM. **Intra/Inter Rater Reliability and Accuracy of Lumbar Spine Height Using Musculoskeletal Ultrasound: A preliminary investigation**. *Journal of Back and Musculoskeletal Rehabilitation.* 2016;29:171-82.

Anwer S, Alghadir A, Brismée JM. **Effect of Home Exercise Program In Knee Osteoarthritis: A Systematic Review And Meta-Analysis**. *Journal of Geriatric Physical Therapy.* 2016;39(1):38-48.

Riley SP, Swanson B, Brismée JM. Re:"**Determining The Level Of Evidence For The Effectiveness Of Spinal Manipulation In The Upper Limb: A Systematic Review Meta-Analysis**". *Manual Therapy.* 2015;20(6):e15-6.

Gilbert KK, Smith M, Sobczak S, Sizer PS, James CR, Brismée JM. **Effects of Lower Limb Neurodynamic Mobilization on Intraneural Fluid Dispersion of the Fourth Lumbar Nerve Root: An Unembalmed Cadaveric Investigation**. *Journal of Manual and Manipulative Therapy.* 2015;23:5:239-245.

Riley SP, Swanson B, Brismée JM. Re:"**Determining The Level Of Evidence For The Effectiveness Of Spinal Manipulation In The Upper Limb: A Systematic Review Meta-Analysis**". *Manual Therapy.* 2015;20(6):e15-6.

Nagar VR, Sawyer SF, James CR, Brismée JM, Hooper TL, Sizer PS. **The Effects of Volitional Preemptive Abdominal Contraction on Postural Control Responses in Healthy Subjects**. *Physical Medicine and Rehabilitation.* 2015;7(11):1142-51.

Lohman CM, Gilbert KK, Sobczak S, Brismée JM, James CR, Day M, Smith MP, Taylor L, Dugailly PM, Pendergrass T, Sizer PS. **2015 Young Investigator Award Winner: Cervical Nerve Root Displacement and Strain During Upper Limb Neural Tension Testing: Part 2: Role of Foraminal Ligaments in the Cervical Spine.** *Spine* (Phila Pa 1976). 2015;40(11):801-808.

Lohman CM, Gilbert KK, Sobczak S, Brismée JM, James CR, Day M, Smith MP, Taylor L, Dugailly PM, Pendergrass T, Sizer PS. **2015 Young Investigator Award Winner: Cervical Nerve Root Displacement and Strain During Upper Limb Neural Tension Testing: Part 1: A Minimally Invasive Assessment in Unembalmed Cadavers.** *Spine* (Phila Pa 1976). 2015;40(11):793-800.

Brismée JM, Sizer PS. **Orthopaedic Manual Physical Therapists-Champions in Education, Manipulative Therapy and Movement Control Restoration.** *Journal of Manual and Manipulative Therapy.* 2015;23(4):171.

Riley SP, Cote MP, Leger RR, Swanson BT, Tafuto V, Sizer PS, Brismée JM. **Short-term Effects of Thoracic Spinal Manipulations and Message Conveyed by Clinicians to Patients with Musculoskeletal Shoulder Symptoms: A Randomized Clinical Trial.** *Journal of Manual and Manipulative Therapy.* 2015;23(1):3-11.

Riley SP, Bialosky J, Cote MP, Swanson BT, Tafuto V, Brismée JM. **Thoracic Spinal Manipulation for Musculoskeletal Shoulder Pain: Can an Instructional Set Change Patient Expectation and Outcome?** *Manual Therapy.* 2015;20(3):469-74.

Alghadir A, Anwer S, Brismée JM. **The Reliability and Minimal Detectable Change of Timed Up and Go Test in Individuals with Grade 1–3 Knee Osteoarthritis.** *BMC Musculoskeletal Disorders.* 2015;16:174.

Jonely H, Brismée JM, Desai MJ, Reoli R. **Chronic Sacroiliac Joint And Pelvic Girdle Dysfunction In a 35-Year-Old Nulliparous Woman Successfully Managed With Multimodal and Multidisciplinary Approach.** *Journal of Manual and Manipulative Therapy.* 2015;23(1):20-26.

Riley SP, Cote MP, Swanson B, Tafuto V, Sizer PS, Brismée JM. **The Shoulder Pain and Disability Index: Is it Sensitive and Responsive to Immediate change?** *Manual Therapy.* 2015;20(3):494-8.

Lazzarini M, Brismée JM, Dedrick GS, Sizer PS. **Spinal Height Change in Response to Sustained and Repetitive Prone Lumbar Extension After A Period Of Spinal Unloading.** *Journal of Manipulative and Physiological Therapeutics.* 2014;37(8):586-92.

Loyd BJ, Gilbert KK*, Sizer PS, Atkins LT, Sobczak S, Brismée JM, Pendergrass TJ. **The Relationship Between Various Anatomical Landmarks Used for Localizing the First Rib During Surface Palpation.** *Journal of Manual and Manipulative Therapy.* 2014;22(3):129-133.

Stump MD, Sizer PS, Brismée JM. **Rehabilitation Including Manual Therapy Management Following Complicated Immobilized Radial Head Fracture and Elbow Stiffness: A Case Report.** *International Journal of Clinical Medicine.* 2014;5:498-506. http://dx.doi.org/10.4236/ijcm.2014.59069

Atkins LT*, James CR, Sizer PS, Jonely H, Brismée JM. **Reliability and Concurrent Criterion Validity of a Novel Technique for Analyzing Hip Kinematics During Running.** *Physiotherapy Theory and Practice.* 2014;30(3):210-217.

Kitani LJ, Apte GG, Dedrick GS, Sizer PS, Brismée JM. **Effect of Variations in Forced Expiration Effort on Pelvic Floor Activation in Asymptomatic Women.** *Journal of Women's Health Physical Therapy.* 2014;38(1):19-27.

Shaffer SM, Brismée JM, Sizer PS Jr, Courtney CA. **Temporomandibular Disorders. Part 1: Anatomy and Examination/Diagnosis.** *Journal of Manual and Manipulative Therapy.* 2014;22(1):2-12.

Shaffer SM, Brismée JM, Sizer PS Jr, Courtney CA. **Temporomandibular Disorders. Part 2: Conservative Management.** *Journal of Manual and Manipulative Therapy.* 2014;22(1):13-23.

Matthijs OC, Dedrick G, James CR, Brismée JM, Hooper TL, McGalliard MK, Sizer PS*. **Co-Contractive Activation of the Superficial Multifidus During Volitional Preemptive Abdominal Contraction.** *Physical Medicine and Rehabilitation.* 2014;6(1):13-21.

Lohman CM*, Smith MP, Dedrick GS, Brismée JM. **Validity of Musculoskeletal Ultrasound for Identification of Humeroradial Joint Chondral Lesions: A Preliminary Investigation.** *Journal of Athletic Training.* 2014;49(1):7-14.

Nagar VR, Hooper TL, Dedrick GS, Brismée JM, Sizer PS Jr*. **Effect of Recurrent Low Back Pain History on Volitional Pre-emptive Abdominal Activation During a Loaded Functional Reach Activity.** *Spine* (Phila Pa 1976). 2014;39(2):E89-96.

Zhang Y, Shen CL, Peck K, Brismée JM, Doctolero S, Lo D, Lim SY, Lao L. **Training Self-administered Acupressure Exercise among Postmenopausal Women with Osteoarthritic Knee Pain: A Feasibility Study and Lesson Learned.** *Evidence-Based Complementary and Alternative Medicine.* 2012; 570431.

Manning DM, Dedrick GS, Sizer PS, Brismée JM*. **Reliability of a Seated Three-Dimensional Passive Intervertebral Motion Test for Mobility, End-Feel and Pain Provocation in Patients with Cervicalgia.** *Journal of Manual and Manipulative Therapy.* 2012; 20(3):135-141.

Shen CL, Chyu MC, Yeh JK, Zhang Y, Pence BC, Felton CK, Brismée JM, Doctolero S, Wang JS. **Effect of Green Tea and Tai Chi on Bone Health in Postmenopausal Osteopenic Women: A 6-month Randomized Placebo-Controlled Trial.** *Osteoporosis International.* 2012; 23(5):1541-52.

White CE, Dedrick GS*, Sizer PS, Apte GG, Brismée JM. **The Effect of Isometric Shoulder Internal and External Rotation on the Acromiohumeral Distance.** *American Journal of Physical Medicine and Rehabilitation.* 2012;91(3):193-199.

Pennell PL, Owens SC*, Brismée JM, Dedrick GS, James CR, Sizer PS. **Inter-tester and Intra-tester Reliability of a Clinically Based Spinal Height Measurement Protocol.** *Journal of Spine.* 2012; 1(2):1-4.

Apte G, Nelson P, Brismée JM, Dedrick G, Justiz R 3rd, Sizer PS Jr*. **Chronic Female Pelvic Pain--Part 1: Clinical Pathoanatomy and Examination of the Pelvic Region.** *Pain Practice.* 2012;12(2):88-110.

Nelson P, Apte G, Justiz R 3rd, Brismee JM, Dedrick G, Sizer PS Jr*. **Chronic Female Pelvic Pain--Part 2: Differential Diagnosis and Management.** *Pain Practice.* 2012;12(2):111-41.

Jonely H, Brismée JM, Sizer PS, James CR*. **Relationships Between Clinical Measures of Static Foot Posture and Plantar Pressure During Static Standing and Walking.** *Clinical Biomechanics (Bristol, Avon).* 2011;26(8):873-9. 2011.

Dedrick GS, Sizer PS, Sawyer BG, Brismee JM, Smith MP*. **Immunohistochemical Study of Human Costotransverse Joints: A Preliminary Investigation.** *Clinical Anatomy.* 2011;24(6):741-7.

Simmerman SM, Sizer PS, Dedrick GS, Apte GG, Brismée JM*. **Immediate Changes In Spinal Height And Pain Following Aquatic Vertical Traction In Patients With Persistent Low Back Symptoms: A Crossover Clinical Trial.** *Physical Medicine and Rehabilitation.* 2011; 3(5):447-57.

Domenech MA*, Sizer PS, Dedrick GS, McGalliard MK, Brismée JM. **The Deep Neck Flexor Endurance Test: Normative Data Scores in Healthy Adults.** *Physical Medicine and Rehabilitation.* 2011; 3(2):105-10.

Chyu MC, von-Bergen V, Brismée JM, Zhang Y, Yeh JK, Shen CL. **Complementary and Alternative Exercises for Management of Osteoarthritis,** *Arthritis.* 2011;1-10.

Vaught MS, Brismée JM*, Dedrick GS, Sizer PS, Sawyer SF. **Association of Disturbances in the Thoracic Outlet in Subjects with Carpal Tunnel Syndrome: A Case-Control Study**. *Journal of Hand Therapy*. 2011; 24(1):44-52.

Brown CL*, Gilbert KK, Brismée JM, James CR, Sizer PS, Smith MP. **The Effects of Neurodynamic Mobilization on Fluid Dispersion Within the Tibial Nerve at the Ankle: An Unembalmed Cadaveric Study**. *Journal of Manual and Manipulative Therapy*. 2011; 19(1):24-32.

Chyu MC, James CR, Sawyer SF, Brismée JM, Xu KT, Poklikuha G, Dunn DM, Shen CL*. **Effects Of Tai Chi Exercise On Posturography, Gait, Physical Function And Quality Of Life In Postmenopausal Women With Osteopaenia: A Randomized Clinical Study**. *Clinical Rehabilitation*. 2010; 24:1080-1090.

Gerke DA, Brismée JM*, Sizer PS, Dedrick GS, James CR. **Change In Spine Height Measurements Following Sustained Mid-Range And End-Range Flexion Of The Lumbar Spine**. *Applied Ergonomics*. 2011; 42:331-336.

Hooper TL, Denton J, McGalliard MK, Brismée JM, Sizer PS*. **Thoracic Outlet Syndrome: a Controversial Clinical Condition. Part 2: Non-Surgical and Surgical Management**. *Journal of Manual and Manipulative Therapy*. 2010; 18(3):132-138.

Rutland M, O'Connell D, Brismée JM, Sizer P, Apte G, O'Connell J. **Clinical Commentary: Evidence –Supported Rehabilitation of Patellar Tendinopathy**. *North American Journal of Sports Physical Therapy*. 2010; 5(3):166-178.

Hooper TL, Denton J, McGalliard MK, Brismée JM, Sizer PS*. **Thoracic Outlet Syndrome: a Controversial Clinical Condition. Part 1: Anatomy, and Clinical Examination/Diagnosis**. *Journal of Manual and Manipulative Therapy*. 2010; 18(2):74-83.

McGalliard MK*, Dedrick GS, Brismée JM, Cook CE, Apte GG, Sizer PS. **Changes in Transversus Abdominis Thickness With Use of the Abdominal Drawing-in Maneuver During a Functional Task**. *Physical Medicine and Rehabilitation*. 2010; 2(3):187-194.

Cook CE*, Brismée JM, Pietrobon R, Sizer PS, Hegedus E, Riddle DL. **Development of a Quality Checklist Using Delphi Methods for Prescriptive Clinical Prediction Rules: the QUADCPR**. *Journal of Manipulative and Physiological Therapeutics*. 2010; 33(1):29-41.

Brismée JM*, Smith TM, Sizer PS, Sawyer SF. **Cyclists - ulnar nerve and double crush**. *Clinical Journal of Sport Medicine*. 2010; 20(1):author reply 70-71.

Cook CE*, Brismée JM, Courtney CA, Hancock MJ, May S. **Clinimetrics Corner: Publishing a Scientific Manuscript on Manual Therapy**. *Journal of Manual and Manipulative Therapy*. 2009; 17(3):141-147.

Owens SC, Brismée JM*, Pennell PN, Dedrick GS, Sizer PS, James CR. **Changes In Spinal Height Following Sustained Lumbar Flexion And Extension Postures: A Clinical Measure of Intervertebral Disc Hydration Using Stadiometry**. *Journal of Manipulative and Physiological Therapeutics*. 2009; 32(5):358-63.

Brismeé JM, Sizer PS*, Dedrick GS, Sawyer BG, Smith MP. **Immunohistochemical And Histological Study Of Human Uncovertebral Joints: A Preliminary Investigation**. *Spine* 2009; 34(12):1257-63.

Lewis NL, Brismée JM, James CR, Sizer PS, Sawyer SF. **The Effect of Stretching on Muscle Responses and Postural Sway Responses during Computerized Dynamic Posturography in Women and Men**. *Archives of Physical Medicine and Rehabilitation*. 2009; 90(3):454-62.

Brismée JM*, Sizer P. **Potential Pitfalls of Clinical Prediction Rules**. *Journal of Manual and Manipulative Therapy*. 2008;16(3):182.

Goode A, Hegedus EJ, Sizer PS, Brismée JM, Linberg A, Cook CE*. **Three-Dimensional Movements Of The Sacroiliac Joint: A Systematic Review Of The Literature and Assessment of Clinical Utility**. *Journal of Manual and Manipulative Therapy*. 2008;16(1):25-38.

Shen CL*, James CR, Chyu MC, Bixby WR, Brismée JM, Zumwalt MA, Poklikuha G. **Effects of Tai Chi on Gait Kinematics, Physical Function, and Pain in Elderly with Knee Osteoarthritis - a Pilot Study**. *American Journal of Chinese Medicine*. 2008;36(2):219-232.

Poorbaugh K, Brismée JM, Phelps V, Sizer PS Jr*. **Late Whiplash Syndrome: A Clinical Science Approach To Evidence-Based Diagnosis And Management**. Pain Practice. 2008;8(1):65-87.

Smith TM, Sawyer SF, Sizer PS, Brismée JM*. **The Double Crush Syndrome: A Common Occurrence In Cyclists With Ulnar Nerve Neuropathy – A Case-Control Study**. *Clinical Journal of Sport Medicine*. 2008;18(1):55-61.

Dedrick GS*, Sizer PS, Merkle JN, Hounshell TR, McComb-Robert JJR, Sawyer SF, Brismée JM, James CR. **Effect of Sex Hormones on Neuromuscular Control Patterns During Landing**. *Journal of Electromyography and Kinesiology*. 2008;18:68-78.

Brismée JM, Paige RL, Chyu, MC, Boatright JD, Hagar JM, McCaleb JA, Quintela MM, Feng, D, Xu KT, Shen CL*. **Effects of Tai Chi for Knee Osteoarthritis Were Not Sustained After Detraining**. *Focus on Alternative and Complementary Therapies*. 2007;12(4):281-283.

McGaugh JM*, Brismée JM, Dedrick G, Jones E, Sizer PS. **Comparing The Anatomical Consistency Of The Posterior Superior Iliac Spine To The Iliac Crest As Reference Landmarks For The Lumbopelvic Spine: A Retrospective Radiological Study**. Clinical Anatomy. 2007; 20(7):819-25.

Smith TM, Sawyer SS, Sizer PS, Brismée **The Double Crush Syndrome: A Common Occurrence in Cyclists with Symptoms of Ulnar Nerve Neuropathy.** *Clinical Journal of Sports Medicine* 2007, Submitted

Brismée JM, Paige RL, Chyu MC, Boatright JD, Hagar JM, McCaleb JA, Quintela MM, Feng D, Xu KT, Shen CL. **Group and Home-Based Tai Chi in Elderly Subjects with Knee Osteoarthritis: A Randomized Controlled Trial.** *Clinical Rehabiliation* 2007; 21(2):99-111.

Sizer PS Jr., Brismée JM, Cook C **Coupling Behavior of the Thoracic Spine: A Systematic Review of the Literature.** *Journal of Manipulative and Physiological Therapeutics* 2007 Jun;30(5):390-9.

Sizer PS Jr., Felstehausen V, Sawyer S, Dornier L, Matthews P, Cook C **Eight Critical Skill Sets Required for Manual Therapy Competency: A Delphi Study and Factor Analysis of Physical Therapy Educators of Manual Therapy.** *Journal of Allied Health* 2007;36(1):30-40. ABSTRACT

Childs JD, Whitman JM, Pugia ML, Sizer PS Jr., Flynn TW, Delitto A **Knowledge in Managing Musculoskeletal Conditions and Educational Preparation of Physical Therapists in the Uniformed Services.** *Military Medicine* 2007; 172(4):440-5. ABSTRACT

Cook C, Sizer PS, Brismée JM, Showalter C, Huijbregts P **Does Evidence Support the Existence of Lumbar Spine Coupled Motion? A Critical Review of the Literature.** *Journal of Orthopeadic & Sports Physical Therapy* 2007; 37(7):412. No abstract available

Gilbert KK, Brismée JM, Collins D, James CR, Shah RV, Sawyer SF, Sizer PS **Lumbosacral Nerve Root Displacement and Strain: Part 2- A Comparison of Two Straight Leg Raise Conditions in Unembalmed Cadavers.** *Spine* 2007; 32(14):1521-1525. (Young Investigator Award Winner-2006).;ABSTRACT

Gilbert KK, Brismée JM, Collins D, James CR, Shah RV, Sawyer SF, Sizer PS **Lumbosacral Nerve Root Displacement and Strain; Part 1-A Novel Measurement Technique During Straight Leg Raise in Unembalmed Cadavers.** *Spine,* 2007; 32(14):1513-1520. (Young Investigator Award Winner-2006). ABSTRACT

Sizer PS, Brismée JM, Cook C **Medical Screening for Red Flags in the Diagnosis and Management of Musculoskeletal Spine Pain.** *Pain Practice,* 2007; 7(1):53-71. ABSTRACT

Cook C, Hegedus E, Showalter C, Sizer PS Jr. **Coupling Behavior of the Cervical Spine: a Systematic Review of the Literature.** *Journal of Manipulative and Physiological Therapeutics* 2006; 29(7):570-5. ABSTRACT

Cook C, Brismée JM, Sizer PS. **Subjective and Objective Descriptors of Clinical Lumbar Spine Instability: A Delphi Study.** *Manual Therapy.* 2006; 11(1):11-21. ABSTRACT

Brismée JM, Gipson D, Ivie D, Lopez A, Matthijs O, Moore M, Phelps V, Sawyer S, Sizer P **Interrater Reliability of a Passive Physiological Intervertebral MotionTest in the Mid-Thoracic Spine.** *Journal of Manipulative and Physiological Therapeutics* 2006; 29(5):368-73. ABSTRACT

Cook C, Brismée JM, Fleming R, Sizer PS Jr **Identifiers Suggestive of Clinical Cervical Spine Instability: a Delphi Study of Physical Therapists.** *Physical Therapy.* 2005 Sep;85(9):895-906 ABSTRACT

Brismée JM, Atwood K, Fain M, Hodges J, Sperle A, Swaney M, Phelps V, Van Paridon D, Matthijs O, Sizer P **Interrater Reliability of Palpation of Three-Dimensional Segmetal Motion of the Lumbar Spine.** *Journal of Manual & Manipulative Therapy,* 2005; 13(4):216-221. ABSTRACT

Cook C, Brismée JM, Sizer P **Factors Associated with Physiotherapist's Confidence During Assessment of Clinical Cervical and Lumbar Spine Instability.** *Physiotherapy Research International* 2005:10(2):59-71. ABSTRACT

Sizer P, Phelps V, Azevedo E, Hay A, Vaught M **Diagnosis and Management of Cervicogenic Headache.** *Pain Practice* 2005. ABSTRACT

Brismée JM, Atwood K, Fain M, Hodges J, Sperle A, Swaney M, Phelps V, van Paridon D, Matthijs O, Sizer P **Interrater Reliability of Palpation of Three-Dimensional Segmental Motion of the Lumbar Spine.** *Journal of Manual and Manipulative Therapy,* 2005;13(4):216-221. Full article.

Childs JD, Whitman JM, Sizer PS, Pugia ML, FlynnTW, Delitto A **A Description of Physical Therapists' Knowledge in Managing Musculoskeletal Conditions.** BMC Musculoskeletal Disorders. 2005;17;6:32. ABSTRACT

Brismée JM, Sizer PS, Phelps V **Differential Diagnosis and Treatment of Chronic Neck and Upper Trapezius Pain and Upper Extremity Paresthesia: A Case Study Involving the Management of an Elevated First Rib and Uncovertebral Joint Dysfunction.** *Journal of Manual & Manipulative Therapy,* 2005;13(2):79-90. Full article.

Cook C, Brismée JM, Sizer P **Psychosocial Variables Associated with Back Pain in the Elderly: A Retrospective Analysis.** *Journal of Geriatric Physical Therapy.* 2004;27:75-81. ABSTRACT

Sizer P, Phelps V, Brismée JM, Cook C, Dedrick L **Ergonomic Pain Part 2: Differential Diagnosis and Management Considerations.** *Pain Practice.* 2004; 4(2):136-162. ABSTRACT

Sizer P, Brismée JM, Cook C, Dedrick L, Phelps V **Ergonomic Pain, Part 1: Etiology, Epidemiology & Prevention.** *Pain Practice* 2004; 4:41-52. ABSTRACT

Sizer PS, Poorbaugh K, Phelps V **Whiplash Associated Disorders: Pathomechanics, Diagnosis, and Management.** *Pain Practice.* 2004;4(3):249-266. ABSTRACT

Brismée JM, Gilbert KK, Isom K, Hall R, Leathers B, Sheppard N, Sawyer S, Sizer PS **The Rate of False Positive Using the Cyriax Release Test for Thoracic Outlet Syndrome in an Asymptomatic Population.** *Journal of Manual & Manipulative Therapy* 2004; 12(2):73-81. Full Article ABSTRACT

Sizer P, Phelps V, Gilbert K **Diagnosis and Management of the Painful Shoulder. Part 2: Examination, Interpretation and Management**. *Pain Practice* 2003;3(2)152-85. ABSTRACT

Sizer P, Phelps V, Gilbert K **Diagnosis and Management of the Painful Shoulder. Part 1: Clinical Anatomy and Pathomechanics**. *Pain Practice,* 2003; Mar;3(1):39-57. ABSTRACT

Gokeler A, Lehmann M, Knopf E, Freiwald J **Current Concepts in the Diagnosis and Rehabilitation of the Shoulder in Overhead Athletes**. Sportverletz Sportschaden. 2003; 17(1):15-20. ABSTRACT

Gokeler A, Van Paridon-Edauw GH, DeClercq S, Matthijs O, Dijkstra PU **Quantitative Analysis of Traction in the Glenohumeral Joint. In Vivo Radiographic Measurements**. *Manual Therapy*. 2003; 8(2):97-102. ABSTRACT

Sizer P, Phelps V, Dedrick G, James R, Matthijs O **Diagnosis and Management of the Painful Ankle/Foot. Part 2: Examination, Interpretation, and Management** *Pain Practice,* 2003; 3:343-374. ABSTRACT

Sizer P, Phelps V, James R, Matthijs O **Diagnosis and Management of the Painful Ankle/Foot. Part 1: Clinical Anatomy and Pathomechanics**. *Pain Practice,* 2003; 3:238-262. ABSTRACT

James CR, Sizer P, Starch DW, Lockhart L, Slauterbeck J **Effects of Gender on Knee Kinematic and Ground Reaction Force Characteristics During a Rapid Sprint and Cut Maneuver**. *Research Quarterly for Exercise & Sport*, 2004;75:31-38.

Brismée J, Gilbert K, Sizer P, Sawyer S, Isom K, Hall R, Leathers B, Sheppard N **The Rate of False Positives Using the Cyriax Release Test for Thoracic Outlet Syndrome in an Asymptomatic Population**. *Journal of Manual & Manipulative Therapy,* 2002; 10(3):156.

Sizer P, Brismée J, Gilbert K, Sawyer S, Call D, Branscum S, Finger E, Maness J, Redman N **The Incidence of Positive Cervical Rotation-Lateral Flexion Tests for Elevated First Ribs in Asymptomatic Subjects and Correlations with Cervical Range of Motion Measurements**. *Journal of Manual & Manipulative Therapy* 2002; 10(3):166-7. ABSTRACT

Coffey TG, James CR, Sizer PS, Williams JS **Effects of Gender and Fatigue on Lower Extremity Mechanics**. *Medicine and Science in Sports & Exercise,* 2002; 34(5) S473.

James CR, Sizer PS, Poklikuha G, Elliott L, Coffey T, Davis J **Effects of Jumping Fatigue on GRF Impact Characteristics During Landing**. *Medicine and Science in Sports & Exercise* 2002; 34(5) S1246.

Sizer P, Phelps V, Brismée J **Diagnosis and Management of Cervicogenic Headache and Local Cervical Syndrome with Multiple Pain Generators**. *Journal of Manual & Manipulative Therapy,* 2002; 10(3):136-152.

Halverson L, Maas R **Shoulder Joint Capsule Distention (Hydroplasty): A Case Series of Patients with "Frozen Shoulders" Treated in a Primary Care Office**, *Journal of Family Practice*. January 2002; 51(1), 61-63. ABSTRACT

Clark R, Sizer P, Marchessault J, Slauterbeck J **Isolated Traumatic Rupture of the Subscapularis Tendon**. *Journal of the American Board of Family Practice*, 2002; 15(4):304-308. ABSTRACT

Clark R, Sizer P, Slauterbeck J **Stress Fracture of the Ulna in a Male Competitive Polo Player**. *American Journal of Sports Medicine*. 2002; 30(1), 130-132.

Sizer P, Phelps V, Dedrick G, Matthijs O **Differential Diagnosis and Management of Spinal Nerve Root-Related Pain**. *Pain Practice* 2002; 2(2),98-121. ABSTRACT

Sizer P, Phelps V, Thompsen K **Disorders of the Sacroiliac Joint**. *Pain Practice,* 2002; 2(1),17-34. ABSTRACT

Brooks T **Madelung Deformity in a Collegiate Gymnast: A Case Report**, *Journal of Athletic Training,* 2001; 36 (2), 170-173. ABSTRACT

Sizer P, Phelps V, Matthijs O **Pain Generators of the Lumbar Spine**. *Pain Practice,* 2001; 1(3),255-273. ABSTRACT

Sizer P, Phelps V, Azevedo E **Disc Related and Non-Disc Related Disorders of the Thoracic Spine**. *Pain Practice,* 2001; 2:136-149. ABSTRACT

Sizer P, Phelps V, Brismée J **Differential Diagnosis of Local Cervical Syndrome as Compared to Cervico-Brachial Syndrome**. *Pain Practice,* 2001; 1(1), 21-35.

Sizer P, Starch S, James R, Slauterbeck J **Kinematic and Ground Reaction Force Comparison of Male and Female Athletes Performing a Rapid Cut**. *Medicine and Science in Sports & Exercise,* 2000; 32:S146.

Sizer P, James CR, Schot PK **ACL Injury Risk Goes Beyond Gender**. *BioMechanics,* 2000; 7:45-56.

Sizer P, Matthijs O, Phelps V **Influence of Age on the Development of Spinal Pathology**. *Current Review of Pain,* 2000; 4:362-373. ABSTRACT

Taylor R, Marshall P, Dunlap R, Gable C, Sizer P **Knee Position Error Detection in Closed and Open Kinetic Chain Tasks During Concurrent Cognitive Distraction**. *Journal of Orthopaedic & Sports Physical Therapy,* 1998; 28: 88-96. ABSTRACT

Electronic Publications
Sizer P, Phelps V, Hay A, Azevedo E **Thoracic Spine Disorders Part I: History, Inspection and Clinical Examination**. *MD Consult* 2005; In press.

Sizer P, Phelps V, Hay A, Azevedo E **Upper Cervical Disorders Part II: Differential Diagnosis and Management**. *MD Consult* 2004

Hay A, Azevedo E, Phelps V, Sizer P **Upper Cervical Disorders Part I: History, Inspection and Clinical Examination**. *MD Consult* 2004

Sizer P, Phelps V, Vaught M **Lower Cervical Disorders: Differential Diagnosis and Management**. *MD Consult* 2003

Sizer P, Phelps V, Vaught M **Lower Cervical Disorders: Inspection and Clinical Examination**. Published in Clinical Insights at mdconsult.com. Accessed 7-23-03.

For abstracts of the above-listed IAOM publications, visit www.iaom-us.com, click on "Resources" and then "Research".

Print Publications
Winkel D, Aufdemkampe G, Matthijs O, Meijer O, Phelps V **Diagnosis and Treatment of the Spine**. PRO-ED, Inc. 1996

Sizer P, Phelps V, Brismée JM, vanParidon D, Matthijs O **Diagnosis-Specific Orthopedic Management of the Hip**. OPTP 2007

Brismée JM, Phelps V, Sizer P, Matthijs O, vanParidon D **Diagnosis-Specific Orthopedic Management of the Knee**. OPTP 2009

To purchase the above-listed IAOM publications, visit www.optp.com/

IAOM-US CERTIFICATION IN
ORTHOPEDIC MEDICINE AND MANUAL THERAPY

The International Academy of Orthopedic Medicine – United States (IAOM-US) offers certifications in Nonoperative Orthopedic Medicine and Manual Therapy for physical and occupational therapists ("COMT"). Certifications are offered in the areas of the Upper and Lower Spine, Upper and Lower Extremities, and the Hand and Upper Extremity (UE) Track.

The IAOM-US has created the Hand and Upper Extremity Specialty Track for certified hand therapists (CHTs), occupational therapists and physical therapists specializing in the upper extremity. Courses in this track are two-day intensive, and the IAOM-US is now happy to offer certification upon completion of all UE track courses.

Individuals certified in the Upper or Lower Spine, Upper or Lower Extremities, or UE Track, and obtaining their COMT (Certification in Orthopedic Manual Therapy) will be able to thoroughly diagnose and treat patients with orthopedic problems. Because of increased understanding of pathoanatomy, joint-specific biomechanics, and their inter-relationships, certified clinicians are able to make precise recommendations for conservative treatment and for individualized home programs. Although there can be no guarantee, certified clinicians (and their clinical sites) have reported increased treatment efficiency and decreased number of patient visits secondary to successful restoration of function.

I. IAOM-US COURSES LEADING TO CERTIFICATIONS IN ORTHOPEDIC MANUAL THERAPY

To become certified through the IAOM-US in Orthopedic Medicine and Manual Therapy an individual must meet the following requirements:

1. Upper Extremity Certification (3 Hybrid courses: Shoulder, Elbow, Wrist & Thumb)

2. Lower Extremity Certification (3 Hybrid courses: Hip, Knee, Ankle & Foot)

3. Complete Extremity Certification (6 Hybrid courses: Shoulder, Elbow, Wrist & Thumb, Hip, Knee, Ankle & Foot)

4. Upper Spine Certification (3 Hybrid courses: Upper Cervical & Headache, Lower Cervical, Thoracic Outlet Syndrome and Cervicothoracic Junction)

5. Lower Spine Certification (3 Hybrid courses: Acute Lumbar and Sacroiliac Joint, Recurrent Lumbar and Root Related Pain, Thoracic Spine & Ribs)

6. Complete Spine Certification (6 Hybrid courses: Upper Cervical & Headache, Lower Cervical, Thoracic Outlet Syndrome and Cervicothoracic Junction, Acute Lumbar and Sacroiliac Joint, Recurrent Lumbar and Root Related Pain, Thoracic Spine & Ribs)

7. UE Track Certification I (3 two day courses: UE Hand, UE Wrist Part 1, UE Wrist Part II)

8. UE Track Certification II (3 two day courses: UE Elbow, UE Shoulder, UE TOS/CTJ)

Successful completion of certification for a minimum of three courses (67.5 contact hours) results in a "COMT" Certification. The Certification will become official within two months of the examination date. You will then be entitled to use the initials "COMT" following your name and credentials.

II. MODULAR ASSESSMENT

To ensure adequate learning of course-material, IAOM offers the participant modular-based competency assessments that are applicable to completed courses. The examinations are completed during set times and locations throughout the year.

A. Content of the Modular Examinations

In undergoing the modular examinations, participants have the following choices:

1. **Modular Examination for any 3 courses**: Participants working toward certification of the Spine and the Extremities are eligible to sit for written and practical examinations for any combination of three Hybrid IAOM-US courses. After successfully completing the examinations for each module, participants will be officially notified by mail within 2 months of passing the module.

2. **Modular Examination for Upper Extremity Track courses**: Participants working toward certification for the UE track are eligible to sit for written and practical examinations after they have taken either of the two three-course sequences. After successfully completing the examinations for each module, participants will be officially notified by mail within 2 months of passing the module.

The following modular examinations are available:
1. Modular Examination Upper Extremity (Shoulder, Elbow, Wrist/Thumb)
2. Modular Examination Lower Extremity (Hip, Knee, Ankle/Foot)
3. Modular Examination Upper Spine (Upper Cervical, Lower Cervical, TOS/CTJ)
4. Modular Examination Lower Spine (Acute Lumbar & SI Joint, Recurrent Lumbar, and Thoracic Spine & Ribs)
5. Modular Examination All Extremities
6. Modular Examination All Spine
7. Modular Examination UE I (UE Hand, UE Wrist Level I, UE Wrist Level II)
8. Modular Examination UE II (UE Elbow, UE Shoulder, UE TOS/CTJ)

B. Application for the Modular Examinations

Applications for any Modular Examination should be made to the IAOM-US office no later than 1 month prior to the requested date of testing.

Applications may be submitted by
1. Mail: IAOM-US, P.O. Box 65179, Tucson, AZ 85728
2. e-mail: info@iaom-us.com
3. Phone:866-426-6101
(from outside the US, phone: 520-318-4266)

C. Fee for Applications for the Modular Examinations for Physical Therapists and Occupational Therapists

1. Modular Examination for 1 through 9 Above $450
2. Modular Examination for All Extremities $900
3. Modular Examination for All Spine $900
4. Modular Examination for All UE $900

The examination fee is due at the time of the examination request. In the event the individual cancels the test within 2 weeks of the scheduled date, IAOM-US will refund the individual for the examination fee minus a 15% administrative fee.

Colleagues failing one portion (written or practical) of the examination are allowed to re-take the failed portion within one-year of the date of their examination. If they schedule a re-take after one-year, they are required to re-take the entire examination (both written and practical). In the event of **failure to pass a module, retake of the examination is ½ price** of the modular original price (if modular exam is $200, retake of the full examination is $100; retaking the written examination only is $50 and the practical examination only is $50).

III. <u>EXAMINATION PROCESS</u>

The IAOM-US schedules each year a set of dates and locations in the United States for clinicians to take their examinations. Information about dates and testing sites are available at the IAOM-US Website. IAOM-US reserves the right to cancel any certification due to insufficient registrations. We will inform candidates of cancellation within 5 weeks of any scheduled certification. For more information, contact the IAOM-US at 1-866-426-6101.

To best prepare for the examination, we recommend you study the material in the course manuals provided at the courses. We also recommended that you purchase the DVDs (for OMT) as the practical examination comprises the material from the DVDs as well as the course manuals and textbooks. Written examinations are generally scheduled for the morning of the testing date. Colleagues registering to take the IAOM-US certification examination are required to take both the written and practical examination on the same day (or on 2 consecutive days in cases of an unusually large group taking the examination).

A. <u>Examination of Physical Therapists and Occupational Therapists</u>

The examinations for each module consist of two parts (please note that NO books, notes, manuals or electronic media may be used or accessed during any part of the examination process):

1. **Written Examination**
   - Scheduled for a maximum of 2 hours for 3 module examination or 3 hours for 6 module examination
   - Test taken on a scantron (provided); bring a #2 Pencil
   - Consists of multiple choice and true/false questions
   - Material for the examination consists of the IAOM-US course manuals and the course textbooks, and online course video modules.
   - Includes questions regarding:
     - a) Pathoanatomy
     - b) Surface anatomy
     - c) Pathology
     - d) Biomechanics, osteo- & arthrokinematics
     - e) Differential diagnosis
     - f) Manual Therapy
     - g) Other treatment approaches

2. **Practical Examination**
   - Follows the written examination
   - Scheduled for 1 hour 30 minutes for each group of two (in case of groups of 3, time will be extended)
   - Practical Exam will be videotaped
   - Includes the following*:

a) 1 basic clinical or local segmental exam   35%
b) Surface anatomy locations (10% each)   20%
c) 2 mobilization techniques (15% each)   30%
d) 1 high velocity manipulative technique   15%
* The following format applies for modular examinations of 2 or 3 IAOM-US courses. Modular examinations for the 4 (Upper Quadrant) or 6 IAOM-US courses, often includes a greater number of techniques.

Passing Score
- **Written Examination: 70%**
- **Practical Examination: 70%**
- **Overall score: 70%**

*Note: The practical examination counts twice the written examination. For example, a grade of 70% on the written examination and a grade of 80% for the practical exam results in an overall score of 77%, as illustrated: $70 + (80 \times 2) = 230/3 = 77\%$

IV. CERTIFICATION IN ORTHOPEDIC MANUAL THERAPY (COMT)

To obtain Certification in Orthopedic Manual Therapy, individuals are required to submit proof of:
- **Current membership of the IAOM-US.**
- **PT, OT licensure in the state of practice.**

Please note: To align IAOM-US with the American Physical Therapy Association and American Academy of Orthopaedic Manual Physical Therapists stance regarding physical therapist assistants performing joint mobilization/manipulation, effective January 1, 2006, IAOM-US no longer offers a certification process for physical therapist assistants nor occupational therapist assistants.

Each school or academy of manual therapy has its OWN certification process for manual therapy. This is the initial recognition of completing an education and passing a "certification" examination by that particular organization, and it is termed COMT.

For many schools or academies of manual therapy, this certification process is a step toward even greater acknowledgment after study and clinical contact, via the Fellowship program. Fellowship programs are recognized by the APTA. The IAOM has a Fellowship program that has been recognized by the APTA and successful completion of this program allows the individual to apply for fellowship status with the AAOMPT. The IAOM certification process is also part of the Doctor of Science program in physical therapy for Texas Tech University.

Currently, the AOTA does not have fellowship recognition, and Texas Tech does not have a doctoral program in occupational therapy. The latter is in current stages of development.

The IAOM-US Certification in OMT is a career-defining achievement. Because this process can transform the clinician from novice to musculoskeletal specialist, the ongoing learning that follows this achievement is strongly encouraged and supported through various IAOM-US resources including membership, fellowship and doctoral education.

Stay on the transformational journey! Witness the journey in the Connection. Study the content and gain the skills through the courses. Be challenged in the Certification Exam. Become a Master in the Fellowship. Become a Leader through Doctoral Education.

V. **FELLOWSHIP PROGRAM**

International Academy of Orthopedic Medicine - US Fellowship in Clinical Diagnostics and Orthopedic Manual Therapy is accredited by the American Board of Physical Therapy Residency and Fellowship Education of the American Physical Therapy Association as a post-professional clinical fellowship program for physical therapists in Orthopedic Manual Physical Therapy.

The mission statement for IAOM-US Fellowship Program is based on a commitment to excellence in clinical practice and professional development. In response, the IAOM-US Fellowship Program is committed to advancing physical therapy practitioners in evidence-based clinical diagnostics and orthopedic manual therapy.

Call the IAOM-US office or go to our website at http://www.iaom-us.com/ for more details.

IAOM-US Glossary Signs & Symbols

GLOSSARY FOR TERMS USED IN THE IAOM ORTHOPEDIC MEDICINE AND MANUAL THERAPY COURSES

1. **Actual resting position:** with respect to the pathological condition of the intra- and extra-articular structures, the actual position where the capsule is most relaxed or the position were the least nociceptive afference occurs

2. **Anatomical axis:** the anatomical axes lie in the line created when two anatomical planes bisect each other. Therefore, every axis lies in two planes.
   - Frontal axis: lies in the frontal and transverse planes (runs right-left)
   - Sagittal axis: lies in the sagittal and transverse planes (runs dorsal-ventral)
   - Vertical axis: lies in the sagittal and frontal planes (runs cranial-caudal)

3. **Anatomical osteokinematics:** active or passive rotations around a defined axis. The movements start from the zero position and occur in an anatomical plane.
   These anatomical bone movements (osteokinematics) are used in order to describe and measure motions of the joint.
   - Flexion-extension: movements in the sagittal plane around a frontal axis
   - Abduction-adduction: movements in the frontal plane around a sagittal axis
   - Internal - external rotation: movements in the transverse plane around a vertical axis

4. **Anatomical joint:** two bony joint partners with the joint capsule, ligaments and intra-articular structures

5. **Anatomical planes:** three traditional planes, perpendicular to each other, which divide the body. The planes are used to describe and measure anatomical bone movements.
   - Sagittal plane: divides the body into right and left halves. Planes that are parallel to the midline sagittal plane are called parasagittal planes.
   - Frontal planes: divide the body into anterior/ventral and posterior/dorsal parts
   - Transverse planes: divide the body into superior/cranial and inferior/caudal parts

6. **Arcuate swing:** a "curved" swing. The swing of a bone which occurs in more than one plane. The swing occurs with an accompanying spin.

7. **Arthritis:** an inflammation of the joint due to trauma, systemic causes, etc. Clinical examination will show a limitation of motion in the capsular pattern.

8. **Arthrokinematics:** describes the relationship between two articulation joint surfaces when the bones move. The four basic movements in arthrokinematics consist of:
   - rock (concave) or roll (convex)
   - glide (concave) or slide (convex)
   - spin
   - translation

9. **Arthrosis = Osteoarthrosis = Osteoarthritis:** the "degenerative" aging process of a joint. The clinical examination will show a limitation of motion in the capsular pattern.

10. **Basic clinical examination**: a series of tests that will give the evaluator the most information in the shortest period of time, enabling the evaluator to be able to determine the most likely lesion. Often one must add specific extra test(s) to determine the diagnosis

11. **Capsular pattern**: a specific sequence of limitations of passive motions in a specific relation which is specific for each joint. It always indicates an arthritis or an arthrosis (osteoarthrosis / osteoarthritis)

12. **Cardinal swing**: a "hinge" type swing. The swing of a bone which occurs in one plane, without an accompanying spin. This is theoretical, it does not occur in the human body.

13. **Curved gliding mobilization**: performed as a dynamic mobilization in very curved congruent joints (such as the humero-ulnar joint and the hip) in which traction is applied in an equal amount as the gliding force.

14. **End-feel**:at the end of every passive movement (whether angular or translatory) one tests the quality of that movement by giving overpressure. The type of structures (and their integrity) restricting that motion determine the end-feel.
One can differentiate between a physiological or "normal" end-feel and a pathological end-feel. Every joint has a characteristic end-feel for each motion depending on the structure(s) restricting that motion. In general there are three different qualities of end-feel: soft, firm, and hard.
Due to pathology or changes in a collagenous structure, the end-feel can change.

15. **Glide**: between two surfaces, when a new point on one surface comes into contact with a new point on the other joint surface. Pure gliding occurs between CONGRUENT surfaces. There are two types of gliding: straight (no axis) and curved (has an axis).

16. **Hypermobility**: more than normal mobility (in comparison to the "normal side")

17. **Hypomobility**: less than normal mobility (in comparison to the "normal side")

18. **Instability**: (Functional instability) a hypermobility with pathology

19. **Joint play**: the quantity (amount) and the quality (end-feel) of movement that a joint capsule allows in translatory directions of traction and gliding

20. **Joint specific examination**: a series of tests used to determine and/or evaluate a hypermobility or hypomobility in a joint. The tests consist of performing joint play of traction and gliding/sliding in which the quantity and quality (end-feel) of each direction is determined and always compared to the non-affected side. Occasionally the tests consist of angular movements in joints where translatory movements are impossible or too impractical to perform, such as in the patellofemoral joint and the subtalar joint.

21. **Kennedy's Stages of Tendinitis**:
    - STAGE I: Pain after activity
    - STAGE II: Pain at the beginning and after activity
    - STAGE III: Pain at the beginning, during and after activity, but the performance is not affected
    - STAGE IV: Pain at the beginning, during and after activity and the performance is affected

22. **Maximal close-packed position**:
    Position of the joint in which:
    - joint surfaces have the most contact

- joint capsule and ligaments are most taut
- joint partners cannot be separated through traction and translatory gliding is minimal

23. **Neuromuscular Reeducation or Training**: (after a session of mobilization)
As a part of every joint specific mobilization session, proprioceptive training consists of moving the joint within the newly gained range of motion with respect to the osteokinematic and arthrokinematic behavior of the joint. Therapist performs the osteokinematic rotation and the arthrokinematic gliding/sliding. This is done in three parts: first passively, then active-assisted, then the patient is asked to perform an isometric contraction of the agonist at the end of the newly gained range of motion.

24. **Osteoarthritis**: see ARTHROSIS

25. **Osteokinematics**: describes movement of bone in space. The two basic movements are rotation and translation.

26. **Physiological joint**: anatomical joint with all of the surrounding structures to include innervation, blood supply, etc.

27. **Physiological movements**: movements in the joints during daily activities do not occur around the rigid anatomical axes. Movements occur simultaneously around many axes and similarly the movements take place in many planes (not only in one anatomical plane).

28. **Physiological osteokinematics:** a coordinate system for each joint specific to the position of the concavity in space. For example: an anatomical osteokinematic shoulder flexion is a physiological osteokinematic shoulder flexion, abduction and external rotation.

29. **Radicular pain**: projected pain originating from irritation of a nerve root.

30. **Referred pain**: pain felt in an area of the body different from the local area from which the pain originates.
Except for the organs and dura mater:
- the pain does not cross the midline
- the deeper the lesion the further the pain radiates
- the more severe the lesion the further the pain radiates
- the more distal in the extremity the lesion lies, the less referred pain
- pain can be felt in the whole dermatome or in part of the dermatome
- the kind of structure determines the amount of referred pain e.g. skin has minimal referred pain whereas nerves give a large amount of referred pain
- pain is usually referred distally from the affected structure and not proximally

31. **Resting position = maximal loose-packed position**:
- capsule most relaxed and therefore has the most volume
- joint surfaces have least contact with each other
- joint play is the greatest in this position

33. **Roll**: the name for the arthrokinematic movement that occurs between two surfaces, when a new point on one surface comes into contact with a new point on the joint surface. Rolling occurs between two INCONGRUENT surfaces. The convex surface rolls, and the concave surface 'rocks'. When the convex surface moves, the rolling and the gliding occur in opposite directions. When the concave joint partner moves, the rolling and the gliding occur in the same direction.

35. **Rotation**: all active and passive motions, which occur around one axis. There is always one point of the moving bone that does not move. The two basic osteokinematic rotations are SPIN and SWING.

36. **Slack**: the amount of movement that a joint capsule allows during a passive translatory movement. After that point the fibers of the capsule are stretched.

38. **Spin**: Osteokinematic spin: the rotation about the longitudinal axis of the bone
Arthrokinematic spin: the rotation about one axis that is perpendicular to the contact point of the articulation (both perpendicular to the concavity and to the convexity)

39. **Swing**: all osteokinematic rotations outside of a spin. There are two kinds of swing: CARDINAL SWING and ARCUATE SWING.

40. **Traction**: distraction or separation of the two joint partners in the direction that is perpendicular to the treatment plane

41. **Translation**: between two surfaces, when all the points of one surface move in a straight line the same distance, at the same speed, and in the same direction:
    - the movement does not occur around an axis
    - can move perpendicular to the treatment plane = traction
    - can move parallel to the treatment plane = glide
    - are always passive movements; do not occur actively in a joint

42. **Transverse friction**: local massage technique transverse to the running of the fibers of the affected structure with local pain relief and transverse mobilization as the two main goals:
    - therapist's finger and patient's skin move as one over the affected structure
    - pressure is exerted to patient's tolerance and can be increased after about 2 minutes when the local anesthetic effect has occurred. When a tendon sheath is being treated, the stretch is increased after approximately 2 minutes when the local anesthetic effect has occurred.
    - pressure is exerted only in one direction. This prevents a local ischemia

43. **Treatment plane**: the plane perpendicular to the line connecting the actual contact point and the center of the curved surface of the joint or plane formed by the concavity

44. **Visual Analog Scale**: Patient rating of pain and/or symptoms on a scale of 0 to 100 with 0 being no pain/symptoms and 100 being the most (or worst) pain/symptoms imaginable. (Patient is given a 10cm long line without markings on which to indicate pain/symptoms. Patient does not have access to ratings from previous days.) Pain is rated daily and at approximately the same time each day. Therapist measures and records the daily markings on a graph. This is an objective way to rate pain/symptoms and the effects of treatment and/or daily activities.

45. **Zero position** = null position = neutral position: internationally recognized positions of each joint which are used as starting positions from which to measure bone movements

Signs & Symbols Used in IAOM Orthopedic Medicine And Manual Therapy Courses

+/- = approximately

RPT = resting position traction (traction from the maximal loose packed position)

PPT = prepositioned traction
- **P₁PT** = prepositioned in one dimension
- **P₂PT** = prepositioned in two dimensions
- **P₃PT** = prepositioned in three dimensions

RPG = resting position gliding

PPG = prepositioned gliding
- **P₁PG** prepositioned in one dimension
- **P₂PG** = prepositioned in two dimensions
- **P₃PG** = prepositioned in three dimensions

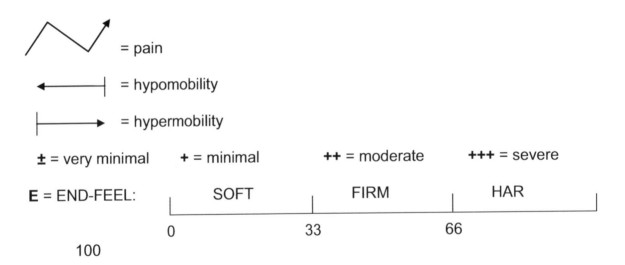

= pain

= hypomobility

= hypermobility

± = very minimal   **+** = minimal   **++** = moderate   **+++** = severe

E = END-FEEL:

	SOFT	FIRM	HAR
0		33	66

100

Documented as follows: E healthy side/E affected side.
e.g. elbow extension: E 80/50, elbow flexion: E 30/60

Ω = resisted

A = active

P = passive

Extension:

Flexion:

Sidebending Left and Right:

Axial Rotation Right:

Axial Rotation Left:

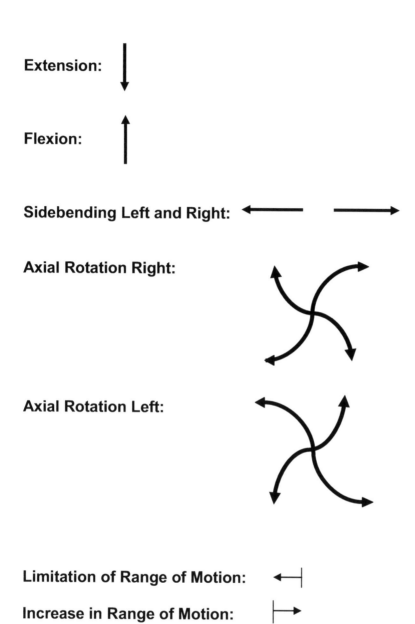

Limitation of Range of Motion:

Increase in Range of Motion:

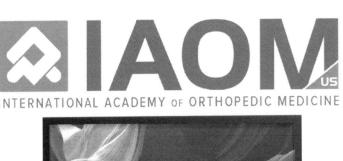

Welcome!

Who we are

- Founded in the 70's by physicians and physical therapists who recognized the importance of working in an integrative fashion

Who we are

- Today
  - 30 faculty members
  - 200 + members
  - Over 6000 therapists have taken our courses
  - 300+ published articles in the literature
- APTA accredited Fellowship for PTs
- ScD Program for PTs
- IAOM-Europe
- IAOM-LA (Latin America)
- International Forums
- Collaborative research & authorship

What we teach

- Diagnosis-specific Orthopedic management

  - Least amount of testing for the most amount of information
  - A systematic approach to diagnosis-specific management

Materials

- Manuals

- **IAOM-US-Free App (Library of Awesome)**

- IAOM-US Surface Anatomy App

- IAOM-US Dry Needling App

- Textbooks reference guides and tools

- Website http://www.iaom-us.com/

Hand & Upper Extremity Track

- This specialty track is a committee composed of certified hand therapists within the IAOM-US that offers coursework for OTs & PTs specializing in the upper quadrant intervention.

- Started in 2005

Hand & Upper Extremity Track

- 77 UE Track Courses over past 10 years

- 1977 UE Track Course registrations

IAOM

Hand & Upper Extremity Track

Lead instructors:
Mirka Normand, MA, OTR, CHT, COMT
Ann Porretto-Loehrke, PT, DPT, CHT, COMT

IAOM

Hand & Upper Extremity Track

Our instructors!

Tiffany, Theresa, John, Ann, Mirka, Amy, Jamie

IAOM

Hand & Upper Extremity Track

Six 2-day courses

A Systematic Approach to Examination, Diagnosis & Manual Therapy of the Hand

-addresses joint and soft tissue mobilization techniques for the thumb CMC, and MP and IP joints of all digits

A Systematic Approach to Examination, Diagnosis & Manual Therapy of the Wrist-Part I

-introduces a systematic approach to evaluating and treating joint and soft tissue disorders of the wrist as well as forearm rotation limitations

A Systematic Approach to Examination, Diagnosis & Manual Therapy of the Wrist-Part II

-addresses wrist instability and more advanced manual therapy techniques

IAOM

Hand & Upper Extremity Track

A Systematic Approach to Examination, Diagnosis & Manual Therapy of the Elbow

-utilizes a systematic approach to evaluating and treating post-operative and conservative management of joint and soft tissue disorders affecting the elbow

A Systematic Approach to Examination, Diagnosis & Manual Therapy of the Shoulder

-addresses the evaluation and treatment of shoulder impingement, adhesive capsulitis and instability

A Systematic Approach to Examination, Diagnosis & Manual Therapy of the Thoracic Outlet/Cervicothoracic Junction

-provides a specific systematic approach to evaluate and treat the shoulder and upper thoracic region

---

Hand & Upper Extremity Track

Certification for the Upper Quadrant!

<u>COMT</u>: Certified Orthopedic Manual Therapist for the Upper Quadrant

What does the test involve?

- written & practical examination covering the content of all 6 courses of the track
- can be taken in 2 modules: Hand, Wrist-Part I, and Wrist-Part II & Elbow, Shoulder, TOS/CTJ

Congratulations to our Newest COMTs!

- Eric Curnutte, OTR, CHT, COMT from Clinton, Missouri
- Mike Dal Molin, PT, DPT, CSCS, COMT from Manchester, Connecticut
- Kim Taylor, OTR, CHT, COMT from Peterborough, New Hampshire
- Janine Thomas, OTR, CHT, COMT from Lynchburg, Virginia

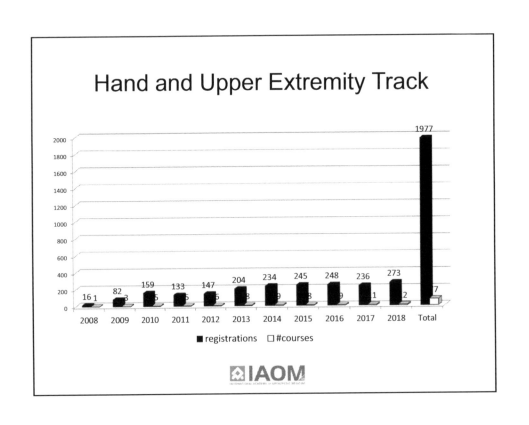

Hand and Upper Extremity Track

Involvement with MedBridge

A new collaboration for IAOM!

- Ann has courses on the following topics: TOS, Peripheral Nerve Compressions of the UE, Differential Diagnosis and Treatment of Lateral Elbow Pain, Manual Therapy to Address Stiffness at the Elbow, Wrist, and Thumb
- Mirka has courses on: Understanding Carpal Instability, Testing & Treatment for Carpal Instability

The Best Experience

- Ask questions!
  - There is no such thing as a stupid question!
  - "We may not have the answer – but we will work with you to get one"

IAOM's Hand & Upper Extremity Track presents..

A Systematic Approach to Examination, Diagnosis & Manual Therapy of the
Shoulder

Course developed by:

Mirka Normand, MA, OTR, CHT, COMT &

Ann Porretto-Loehrke, PT, DPT, CHT, COMT

Shoulder Anatomy

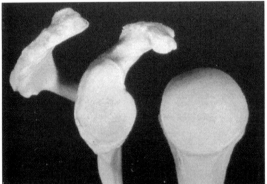

Acromion

Coracoid Process

Humeral Head

Glenoid fossa

Bony Structure

Shoulder Anatomy

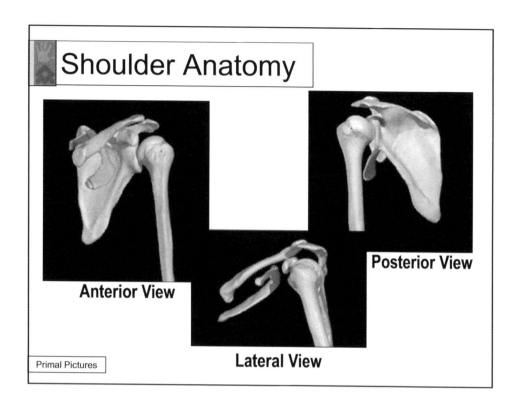

Anterior View

Lateral View

Posterior View

Primal Pictures

Shoulder Anatomy

Bony Structure

• only 1/3 of the humeral head articulates with the glenoid in any given position

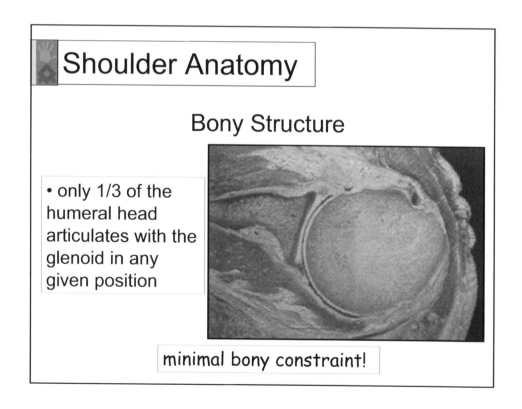

minimal bony constraint!

Shoulder Anatomy

Orientation of the Glenoid: TILT

- Range of tilt
  7° inferiorly to
  15.8° superiorly
- slight outwardly-
  rotated position

Churchill RS et al. Glenoid size,
inclination & version. An anatomic
study. *J Sh Elbow Surg* 2001;
10:327-32.

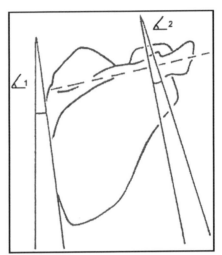

Shoulder Anatomy

Orientation of the Glenoid: VERSION

Angle between
plane of scapula
and glenoid
center line

9.5 ° anteversion to
10.5 ° retroversion

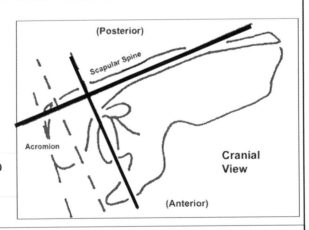

Churchill RS et al. Glenoid size, inclination & version. An anatomic study. J Sh
Elbow Surg 2001; 10:327-32.

Shoulder Anatomy

Orientation of the Glenoid

with arm at side:

- **Anterior**: slightly medial & slightly inferior

- **Posterior**: slightly superior & slightly lateral

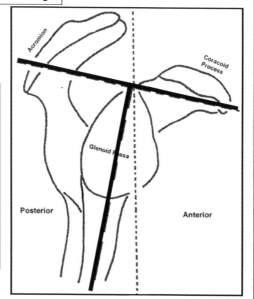

Shoulder Anatomy

Orientation of the Glenoid

- **Inferior**: slightly lateral and slightly posterior

(perpendicular to a line connecting the coracoid process and posterior acromion and perpendicular to the scapular spine)

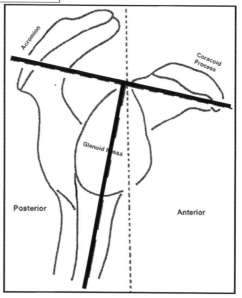

Shoulder Anatomy

Acromion morphology

Shoulder Anatomy

Acromion morphology

Outlet view

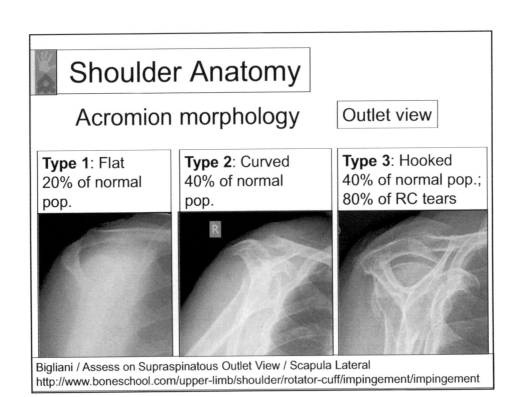

| **Type 1**: Flat 20% of normal pop. | **Type 2**: Curved 40% of normal pop. | **Type 3**: Hooked 40% of normal pop.; 80% of RC tears |

Bigliani / Assess on Supraspinatous Outlet View / Scapula Lateral
http://www.boneschool.com/upper-limb/shoulder/rotator-cuff/impingement/impingement

Shoulder Anatomy

Acromion morphology

Purpose: analyzed the relationship between age, gender, the side of the shoulder, acromion type and severity of rotator cuff tear using magnetic resonance arthrography (MRA); N=277

Results: the severity of supraspinatus tear and multiple RTC tears were statistically significant with old age, being female, the right shoulder, but *not* with a specific acromion type.

Kim JM, Kim YW, Kim HS, et al. The relationship between rotator cuff tear and four acromion types: cross-sectional study based on shoulder magnetic resonance imaging in 227 patients. Acta Radiol. 2018; Aug 15:284185118791211. [Epub ahead of print]

Shoulder Anatomy

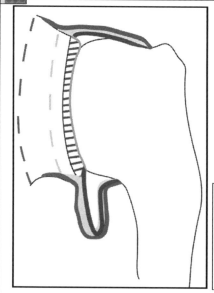

Variations in Capsule Attachments

- 30%: labrum only

- 30%: labrum/glenoid

- 30%: glenoid only

Hato Y, Saitoh S, Murakami N, et al. Shrinkage in the inferior pouch of the scapulohumeral joint is related to posterior pain after rotator cuff repair: Radiographic and arthrographic comparison between patients with postoperative pain and those without it. *J Shld Elbow Surg.* 2001, 10 (4): 333-339.

Shoulder Anatomy

Capsuloligamentous Structures

Anterior View

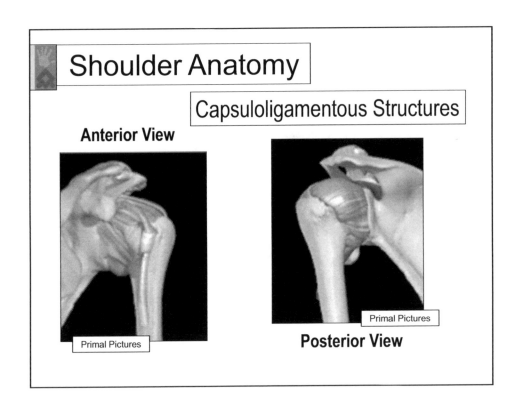

Primal Pictures

Primal Pictures

Posterior View

Shoulder Anatomy

Capsuloligamentous Structures

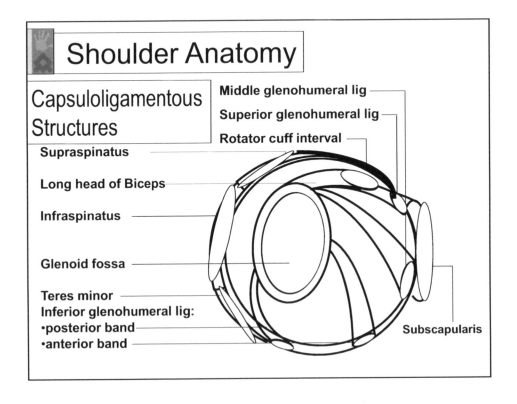

Middle glenohumeral lig

Superior glenohumeral lig

Rotator cuff interval

Supraspinatus

Long head of Biceps

Infraspinatus

Glenoid fossa

Teres minor

Inferior glenohumeral lig:
•posterior band
•anterior band

Subscapularis

Shoulder Anatomy

Rotator Cuff Interval

- area of weakness between the supraspinatus & subscapularis

- filled with ligaments!

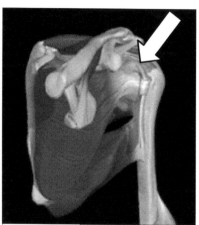

Primal Pictures

Shoulder Anatomy

Capsuloligamentous Structures

Rotator cuff interval

Rotator Cuff Interval

BICEPS PULLEY SYSTEM:

-coracohumeral ligament (CHL)

-superior GH ligament (SGHL)

At the entrance of the bicipital groove, the SGHL & CHL blend together, forming the reflection pulley

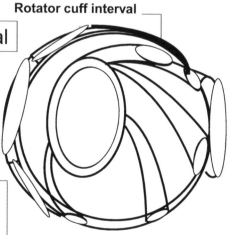

Shoulder Anatomy

Superior GH Ligament

• most important function: stabilizing the biceps within the groove

• contributes to stability with arm at side

• Sulcus test: evaluates the SGHL, CHL, and RTC interval

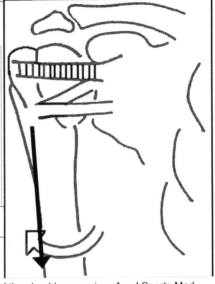

Van der Reis W, Wolf EM. Arthroscopic rotator cuff interval capsular closure. *Orthop* 2001; 24:657-61.

Itoi E, et al. Range of motion after Bankart repair - Vertical compared with horizontal capsulotomy. *Am J Sports Med* 2001; 29:441-45.

Bahk M, Keyurapan E, Tasaki A, et al. Laxity testing of the shoulder: a review. Am J Sports Med. 2007;35(1):131-144.

Shoulder Anatomy

Middle GH Ligament

• contributes to stability with arm at 45° of abd

• prevents anterior translation of humeral head

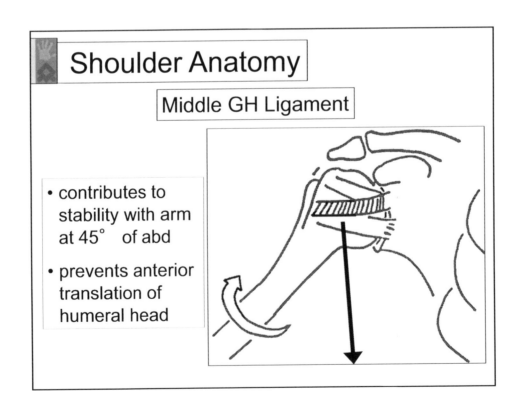

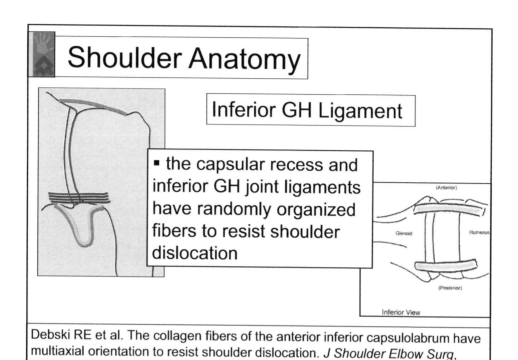

Shoulder Anatomy

Inferior GH Ligament

- the capsular recess and inferior GH joint ligaments have randomly organized fibers to resist shoulder dislocation

Debski RE et al. The collagen fibers of the anterior inferior capsulolabrum have multiaxial orientation to resist shoulder dislocation. *J Shoulder Elbow Surg*, 2003; 12: 247-52.

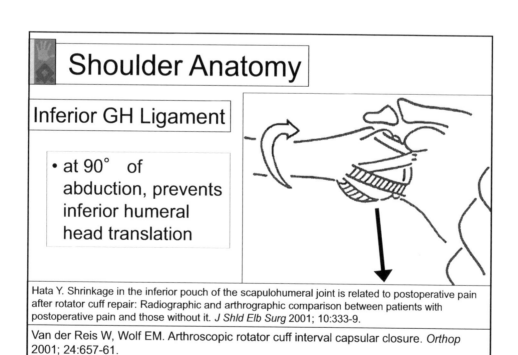

Shoulder Anatomy

Inferior GH Ligament

- at 90° of abduction, prevents inferior humeral head translation

Hata Y. Shrinkage in the inferior pouch of the scapulohumeral joint is related to postoperative pain after rotator cuff repair: Radiographic and arthrographic comparison between patients with postoperative pain and those without it. *J Shld Elb Surg* 2001; 10:333-9.

Van der Reis W, Wolf EM. Arthroscopic rotator cuff interval capsular closure. *Orthop* 2001; 24:657-61.

Bahk M, Keyurapan E, Tasaki A, et al. Laxity testing of the shoulder: a review. Am J Sports Med. 2007;35(1):131-144.

Shoulder Anatomy

Coracohumeral Ligament (CHL)

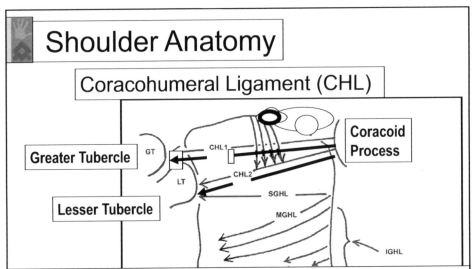

Cole BJ et al. The anatomy and histology of the rotator interval capsule of the shoulder. Clin Orthop Rel Res 2001;390:129-137.

Yang et al. An anatomic & histologic study of the coracohumeral ligament. *J Shoulder Elbow Surg.* 2009; 18: 305-310.

Jost B, Koch PP, Gerber C. Anatomy and functional aspects of the rotator interval. *J Shoulder Elbow Surg.* 2000; 9:336-41.

Shoulder Anatomy

CHL: most taught with shoulder flexion, adduction, & ER

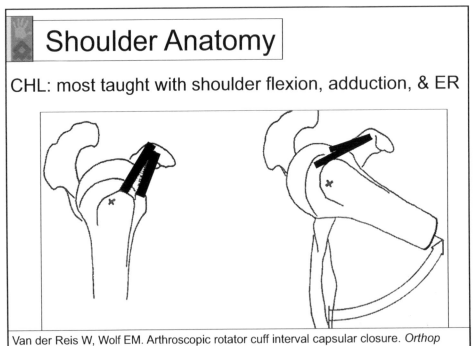

Van der Reis W, Wolf EM. Arthroscopic rotator cuff interval capsular closure. *Orthop* 2001; 24:657-61.

Shoulder Anatomy

Glenoid Labrum

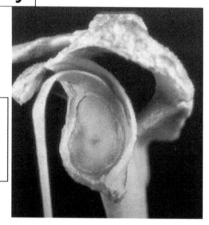

- ↑'s GHJ surface area contact
- Promotes GHJ stability

Habermeyer P, Schuller U. [Significance of the glenoid labrum for stability of the glenohumeral joint. An experimental study] *Unfallchirurg* 1990; 93:19-26.

Halder AM, Kuhl SG, Zobitz ME, Larson D, An KN. Effects of the glenoid labrum and glenohumeral abduction on stability of the shoulder joint through concavity-compression. *J Bone Joint Surg* 2001; 83-A 1062-9.

Shoulder Anatomy

Biceps Tendon

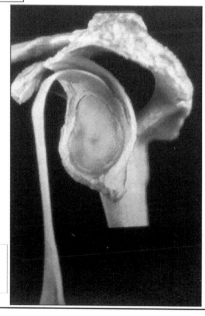

Architecture of the Groove:

higher incidence of biceps tenosynovitis with small or shallow grooves

Pfahler M et al. The role of the bicipital groove in tendopathy of long biceps tendop. J Shoulder Elbow Surg. 1999;8:419-24.

Shoulder Anatomy

Rotator Cuff Muscles

Subscapularis

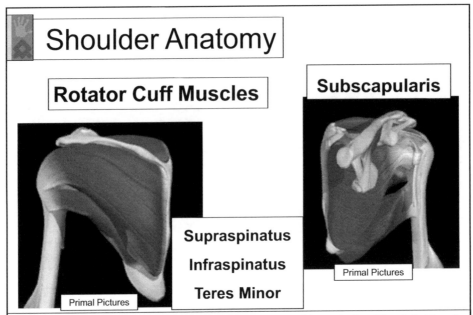

Supraspinatus

Infraspinatus

Teres Minor

Primal Pictures

Reddy AS, Mohr KJ, Pink MM, Jobe FW. Electromyographic analysis of the deltoid and rotator cuff muscles in persons with subacromial impingement. *J Shld Elbow Surg.* 2000;9:519-23.

Shoulder Anatomy

Rotator Cuff Muscles

Subscapularis (2)

Supraspinatus (1)

Infraspinatus (4)

Teres Minor (5)

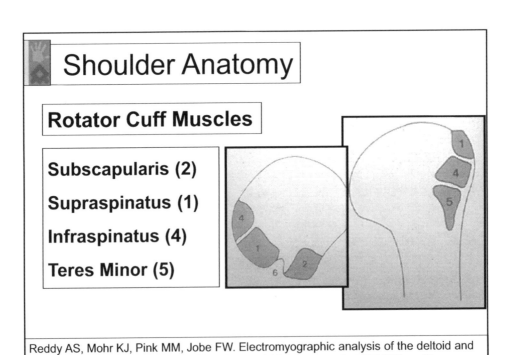

Reddy AS, Mohr KJ, Pink MM, Jobe FW. Electromyographic analysis of the deltoid and rotator cuff muscles in persons with subacromial impingement. *J Shld Elbow Surg.* 2000;9:519-23.

Shoulder Anatomy

Function of the Subscapularis

Primal Pictures

- most powerful muscle RTC muscle
- important anterior stabilizer, especially with eccentric function
- acts as a passive and active restraint to prevent anterior humeral translation

Halder, ME Zobitz, F Schultz, KN An. Structural properties of the subscapularis tendon. J Orthop Res, 2000;18: 829-834

Shoulder Anatomy

Function of the Supraspinatus

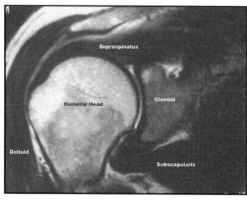

- The supraspinatus muscle has _both internal and external rotational actions_ depending on the shoulder position

Ihashi K, Matsushita N, Yagi R, Handa Y. Rotational Action of the Supraspinatus Muscle on the Shoulder Joint. J Electromyography and Kinesiology. 1998;8:337-346.

Shoulder Anatomy

Supraspinatus Vascular Supply

Wringing Out Phenomenon

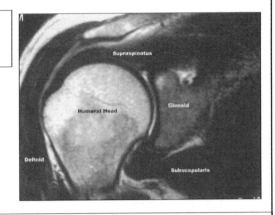

Determe D, Rongieres M, Kany J, Glasson JM, Bellumore Y, Mansat M, Becue J.
Anatomic study of the tendinous rotator cuff of the shoulder. *Surg Radiol Anat*.
1996;18:195-200.

Lohr JF, Uhthoff HK. The microvascular pattern of the supraspinatus tendon. *Clin Orthop*
1990; 254:35-8.

Shoulder Anatomy

Supraspinatus Vascular Supply

Wringing Out Phenomenon...

Relaxed Adducted position

Active Abduction

Shoulder Anatomy

Function of the Infraspinatus & Teres Minor

- <u>Purpose</u>: to measure the effect of rotator cuff muscle contraction on glenohumeral joint translation using real time US and EMG
- <u>Results</u>: contraction of the posterior rotator cuff muscles (infraspinatus & teres minor) appeared to tether anterior humeral head translation

Rathi S, Taylor NF, Green RA. The effect of in vivo rotator cuff muscle contraction on glenohumeral joint translation: an ultrasonographic and electromyographic study. J Biomech. 2016;49(16):3840-3847.

Shoulder Anatomy

Subacromial Bursa

- significantly richer supply of free nerve fibers in the bursa compared with the other tissues

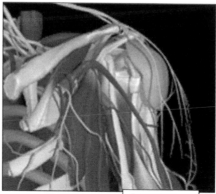

Primal Pictures

Soifer TB, Levy HJ, Soifer FM, Kleinbart F, Vigorita V, Bryk E. Neurohistology of the subacromial space. Arthroscopy. 1996;12:182-186

Shoulder Anatomy

Subacromial Bursa

- this may be responsible for the pain associated with impingement syndrome

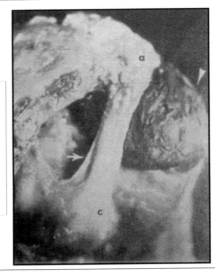

Soifer TB, Levy HJ, Soifer FM, Kleinbart F, Vigorita V, Bryk E. Neurohistology of the subacromial space. Arthroscopy. 1996;12:182-186

Shoulder Anatomy

Suprascapular nerve

Motor:
   Supraspinatus
   Infraspinatus

Sensory:
   ACJ

Shishido H, Kikuchi S. Injury of the suprascapular nerve in shoulder surgery: An anatomic study. J Shoulder Elbow Surg. 2001; 10: 372-376.

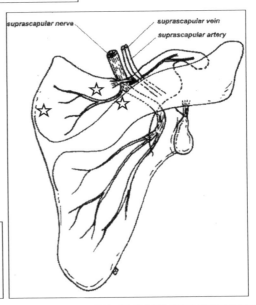

Shoulder Anatomy

Suprascapular Nerve Entrapment

Mechanical Etiologies

- Cocking
- Neural Tension
- Neuritis
- Iatrogenic

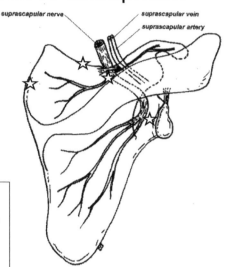

Antoniou J, Clin Orthop Rel Res. 2001; 386:131-8.

Shishido H, Kikuchi S. *J Shoulder Elbow Surg* 2001; 10:372-6.

Visser C, J Shoulder Elbow Surg. 2001; 10: 421-7.

Shoulder Anatomy

Suprascapular Nerve Entrapment Etiologies

- Transverse scapular ligament anomalies
- Compression from adjacent ganglia
- Abnormal osseous morphology of the supra notch
- Direct trauma or traction injury
- Rotator cuff rupture
- Trauma

Lafosse L, et al. Arthroscopic release of suprascapular nerve entrapment at the suprascapular notch: technique and preliminary results. Arthroscopy. 2007;23:34-42.

Lee BC, Yegappan M, Thiagarajan P. Suprascapular nerve neuropathy secondary to spinoglenoid notch ganglion cyst: case reports and review of literature. Ann Acad Med Singapore. 2007;36(12):1032-5.

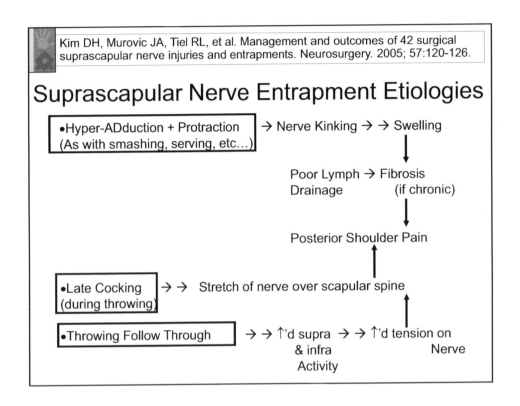

Kim DH, Murovic JA, Tiel RL, et al. Management and outcomes of 42 surgical suprascapular nerve injuries and entrapments. Neurosurgery. 2005; 57:120-126.

Suprascapular Nerve Entrapment Etiologies

- Hyper-ADduction + Protraction (As with smashing, serving, etc...) → Nerve Kinking → → Swelling

Poor Lymph → Fibrosis
Drainage   (if chronic)

Posterior Shoulder Pain

- Late Cocking (during throwing) → → Stretch of nerve over scapular spine

- Throwing Follow Through → → ↑'d supra & infra Activity → → ↑'d tension on Nerve

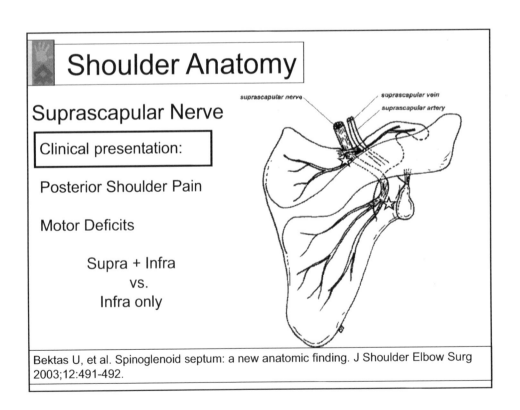

Shoulder Anatomy

Suprascapular Nerve

Clinical presentation:

Posterior Shoulder Pain

Motor Deficits

Supra + Infra
vs.
Infra only

suprascapular nerve

suprascapular vein

suprascapular artery

Bektas U, et al. Spinoglenoid septum: a new anatomic finding. J Shoulder Elbow Surg 2003;12:491-492.

Shoulder Anatomy

Suprascapular Nerve

| Clinical presentation: |

Posterior Shoulder Pain

Motor Deficits

Supra + Infra
vs.
Infra only

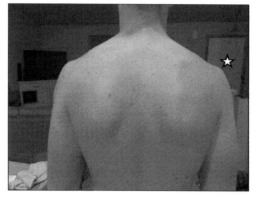

Bektas U, et al. Spinoglenoid septum: a new anatomic finding. J Shoulder Elbow Surg 2003;12:491-492.

Yukata K, et al. Intraarticular ganglion cyst (paralabral cyst) of the shoulder associated with recurrent anterior dislocation: A case report. J Shoulder Elbow Surg 2002; 11:95-7.

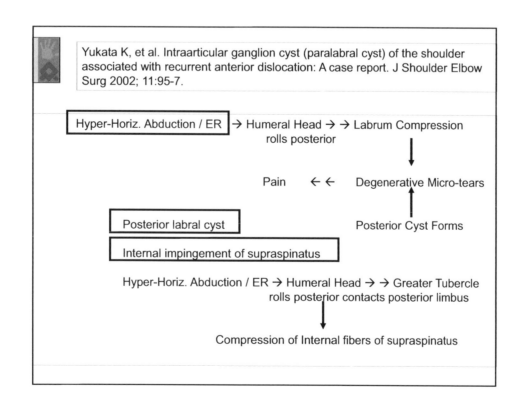

Hyper-Horiz. Abduction / ER → Humeral Head → → Labrum Compression
rolls posterior

Pain ← ← Degenerative Micro-tears

Posterior labral cyst   Posterior Cyst Forms

Internal impingement of supraspinatus

Hyper-Horiz. Abduction / ER → Humeral Head → → Greater Tubercle
rolls posterior contacts posterior limbus

Compression of Internal fibers of supraspinatus

Shoulder Anatomy

Suprascapular Nerve

73 Patients with Spinoglenoid notch cysts

65 of these patients had labral tears

52 men, 11 women; mean age = 39 (19-76)

25 Patients with infraspinatus atrophy

43 Patients with weakness in ER

30 Patients with posterior shoulder tenderness

Piatt BE, Hawkins RJ, Fritz RC, Ho CP, Wolf E, Schickendantz M. Clinical evaluation and treatment of spinoglenoid notch ganglion cysts. J Shoulder Elbow Surg. 2002; 11:600-604.

Shoulder Anatomy

Suprascapular Nerve

Group I: 19 pts; non operative Rx

Group II: 11 pts; needle aspiration of the cyst

Group III: 6 pts; Isolated arthroscopic labral repair/no cyst excision

Group IV: 27 pts; arthroscopic or open labral repair with cyst excision

Satisfaction rate:

Group I:	53%	Group II:	64%
Group III:	67%	Group IV:	97%

Piatt BE, Hawkins RJ, Fritz RC, Ho CP, Wolf E, Schickendantz M. Clinical evaluation and treatment of spinoglenoid notch ganglion cysts. J Shoulder Elbow Surg. 2002; 11:600-604.

Shoulder Anatomy | Axillary nerve

Quadrilateral/Quadrangular Space

- Humerus
- Triceps (long head)
- Teres minor
- Teres major

<u>Cause:</u>

Post band IGHL: extra-articular bone spur from repeated traction

Clinical presentation:

Posterior shoulder pain

Deltoid weakness

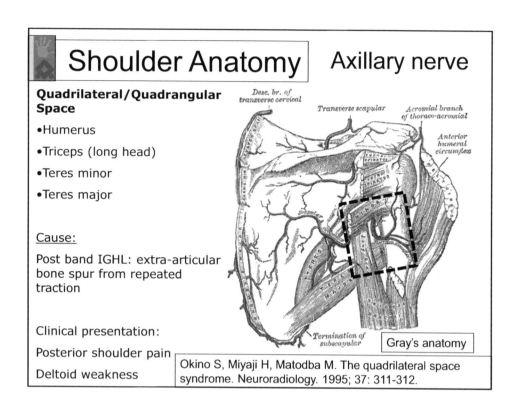

Gray's anatomy

Okino S, Miyaji H, Matodba M. The quadrilateral space syndrome. Neuroradiology. 1995; 37: 311-312.

Shoulder Anatomy

Quadrilateral Space Syndrome

- Point tenderness to the quadrilateral space

- Poorly localized shoulder pain and/or parathesias radiating nondermatomally to the lateral shoulder and arm

- Forced abduction and external rotation aggravate the symptoms

- Deltoid and teres minor weakness with possible atrophy

- Intermittent claudication symptoms

Hoskins WT, Pollard HP, McDonald AJ. Quadrilateral space syndrome: a case study and review of the literature. Brit J Sports Med. 2005; 39:E9.

Shoulder Anatomy

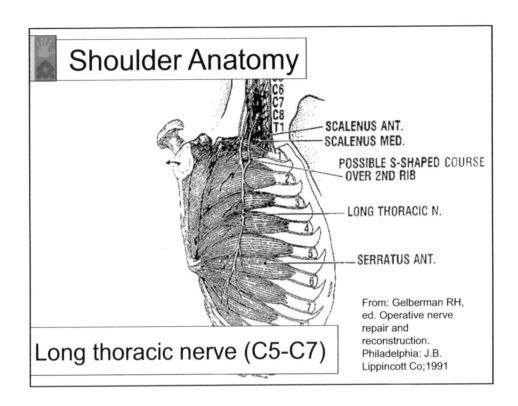

SCALENUS ANT.
SCALENUS MED.

POSSIBLE S-SHAPED COURSE
OVER 2ND RIB

LONG THORACIC N.

SERRATUS ANT.

From: Gelberman RH, ed. Operative nerve repair and reconstruction. Philadelphia: J.B. Lippincott Co;1991

Long thoracic nerve (C5-C7)

Shoulder Anatomy

Serratus Anterior Dysfunction

Etiology 1: Parsonage-Turner Syndrome
      Neuritis of suprascapular or long thoracic n.
      Possible link to viral infection history: 50%
      Generally occurs at night

Clinical:
-posterior pain (early, spontaneous)
-weakness
-Possible scapular winging

Misamore GW, et al. Parsonage turner syndrome (Acute brachial neuritis). J Bone Joint Surg. 1996; 78A: 1405-1408.

Shoulder Anatomy

Serratus Anterior Dysfunction

Etiology 2: Chronic Horizontal Add / Protraction

Due to: Activity, Sleep, Surgery**

Long Thoracic Nerve deforms →
        Winging / Tipping results →
           Deformity exaggerated

Result: More winging and attenuated healing
$2°$ to ↓'d axon / vascular flow

Shoulder Anatomy

Serratus Anterior Dysfunction

…most patients experience a return of serratus anterior function with conservative treatment, but recovery may take as many as 2 years.

IAOM Management: tape or brace to ↓ winging & & neuro-vascular deformity; scapular stabilization with unloading

Wiater JM, Flatow EL. Long thoracic nerve injury. Clinical Orthopaedics and Related Research, 1999; 368: 17-27.

Scapula

Functions:

• Optimizes glenoid position for concavity compression

• Adapts to task requirements in elevation (mobility vs. stability)

• Clears the acromion over the moving rotator cuff

• Proximal to distal link for sequencing velocity, energy & force

Forthomme B, Crielaard JM, Croisier JL. Scapular Positioning in Athlete's Shoulder : Particularities, Clinical Measurements and Implications. Sports Med. 2008;38(5):369-86.

Scapulohumeral rhythm

Author	0-30 degrees	90-180 degrees
Poppen	4 : 1	5 : 4
Doody	7 : 1	1 : 1
Bergman	GHJ > STJ	GHJ = STJ
Inman	2 : 1	
Saha	2 : 1	
Kent	3 : 2	
Jensen-Poppen	1.25 : 1	

Shoulder Anatomy

Scapulohumeral rhythm

Fifteen adults, 7 females, 25–37 years of age, and 14 children, 8 females, 4–9 years of age,

Results: Children have a greater contribution from the scapulothoracic joint, specifically upward rotation toward humeral elevation.

Ratios: Adults: 2.4 : 1

            Children: 1.3 : 1

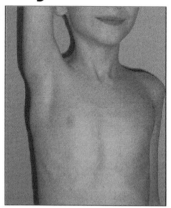

Dayanidhi S, Orlin M, Kozin S, Duff S, Karduna A. Scapular kinematics during humeral elevation in adults and children. Clin Biomech 2005; 20:600-606.

Shoulder Anatomy

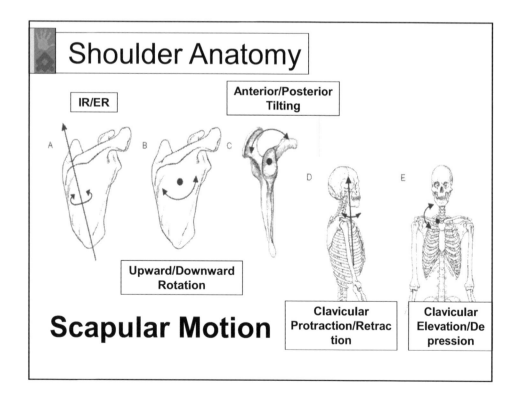

IR/ER

Anterior/Posterior Tilting

Upward/Downward Rotation

Scapular Motion

Clavicular Protraction/Retraction

Clavicular Elevation/Depression

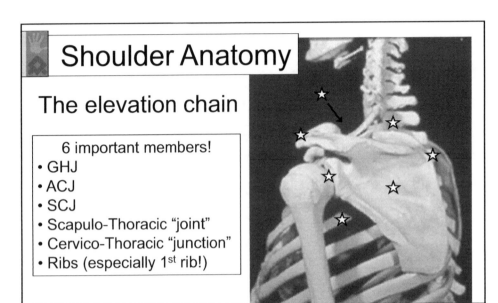

Shoulder Anatomy

The elevation chain

6 important members!
- GHJ
- ACJ
- SCJ
- Scapulo-Thoracic "joint"
- Cervico-Thoracic "junction"
- Ribs (especially 1st rib!)

Fung M, Kato S, Barrance PJ, et al. Scapular and clavicular kinematics during humeral elevation: A study with cadavers. J Shoulder Elb Surg. 2001, 10:278-285.

Jobe CM, Iannotti JP. Limits imposed on glenohumeral motion by joint geometry. J Shoulder Elbow Surg. 1995; 4:281-285.

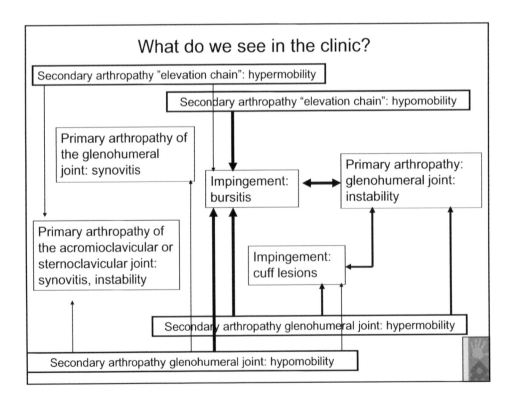

What do we see in the clinic?

Secondary arthropathy "elevation chain": hypermobility

Secondary arthropathy "elevation chain": hypomobility

Primary arthropathy of the glenohumeral joint: synovitis

Impingement: bursitis

Primary arthropathy: glenohumeral joint: instability

Primary arthropathy of the acromioclavicular or sternoclavicular joint: synovitis, instability

Impingement: cuff lesions

Secondary arthropathy glenohumeral joint: hypermobility

Secondary arthropathy glenohumeral joint: hypomobility

Surface Anatomy

Shoulder Region

Bony structures

Winkel D. Diagnosis and treatment of the upper extremities, pp. 12-41

Surface Anatomy

IAOM-US Suggestions:

- Use Index and Middle Fingers
- Soft Pressure
- Palpate perpendicular to structure
- Utilize positioning to make soft tissue structures more accessible
- SA palpation after BCE to confirm
- Systematic approach=consistency

Posterior shoulder

- Medial Border of scapula
- Lateral Border of scapula
- Spine of scapula***
- Posterior angle of acromion*
- Lateral border of acromion
- Superior angle of the scapula

Approximately at the level of T2 spinous process.

- Inferior angle of the scapula

Approximately at the level of T8 spinous process.

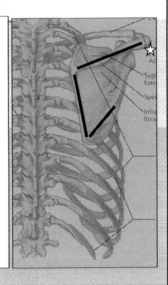

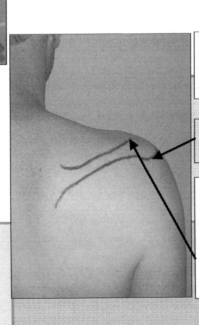

Palpate **scapular spine** from underneath and follow it to the posterior corner of the acromion.

Palpate the **posterior angle (corner) of the acromion**

Palpate the scapular spine from above, and follow it laterally to where it meets the clavicle. The two bones come together and form another "V" (**posterior "V"**)

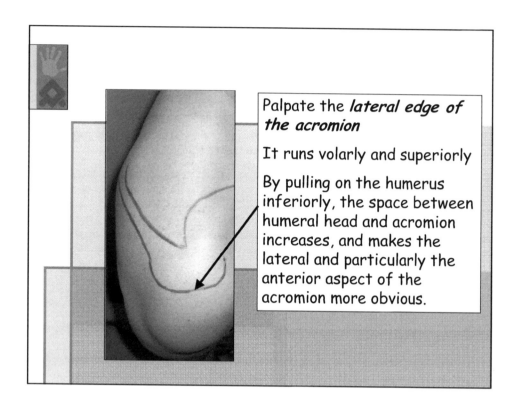

Palpate the *lateral edge of the acromion*

It runs volarly and superiorly

By pulling on the humerus inferiorly, the space between humeral head and acromion increases, and makes the lateral and particularly the anterior aspect of the acromion more obvious.

Anterior shoulder

Follow the acromion anteriorly to the anterior corner (where it meets the clavicle). From the lateral edge, this meeting point lies about 1.0 to 1.5cm medially and it makes a palpable "V" (*anterior "V"*)

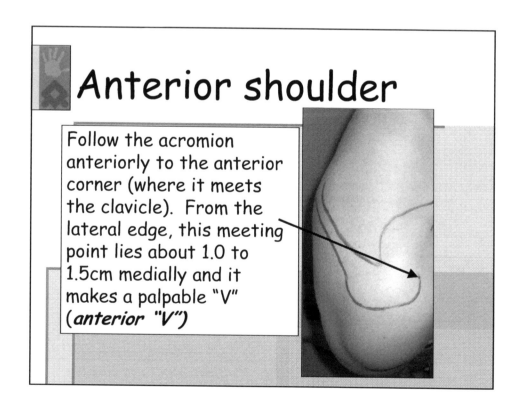

Medial End of the Clavicle and Sternoclavicular Joint (SCJ)

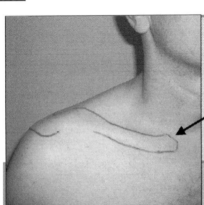

Find the most **medial aspect of the clavicle** at the region of the jugular notch. Take notice of the sharp ridge on the superior half of the medial clavicle.

Note that the medial aspect of the clavicle sits superior to the sternum and you can actually palpate about half of the articulating surface of the medial clavicle.

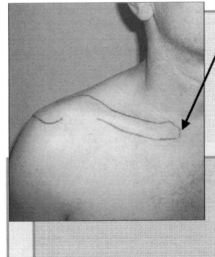

The inferior aspect of the bony clavicle is the region where the **true SCJ** lies. Notice its orientation from superior/medial/posterior to inferior/lateral/anterior. Remember that this portion of the clavicle articulates with the sternum of the axial skeleton at the **Sternoclavicular joint (SCJ)**.

Borders of the Clavicle:
From the medial clavicle, palpate the superior and inferior borders of the clavicle. Start by palpating from inferior to superior, pushing into the soft tissue of the pectoralis major, and then superior into the **inferior border of the clavicle**. Continue to follow the inferior border of the clavicle laterally until you run into the **anterior "V" notch**.

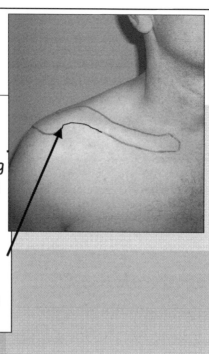

Palpate the **superior/posterior aspect of the clavicle**. Start by pushing into the soft tissue of the supraclavicular fossa, and then inferiorly and anteriorly, into the superior/posterior aspect of the clavicle.
Notice that as you follow this part of the clavicle laterally, the posterior border is partially covered by a portion of the trapezius muscle, making it difficult to palpate.
The posterior lateral aspect of the clavicle meets with the posterior "V" notch of the ACJ.

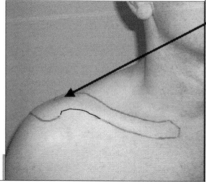

make sure to appreciate the "S" curve of the clavicle, the anterior concave lateral portion, as well as how wide the lateral portion of the clavicle really is

Connect the two "V's" with a slightly laterally convex line. Then palpate from posterior to anterior, perpendicular to this "helper's line."

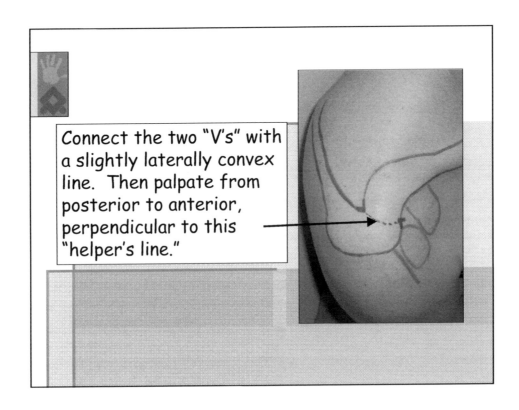

Along the posterior half of the "helper's line" one palpates an obvious bony step from acromion to clavicle. As one approaches the anterior portion of the "helper's line" the bony step suddenly becomes a smoother inclination. This area of smooth inclination from acromion to clavicle is the *acromioclavicular joint (ACJ)*. It is about 1cm long and lies in the area of the anterior half of the "helper's line."

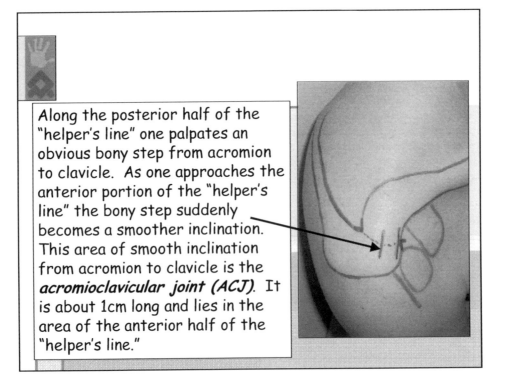

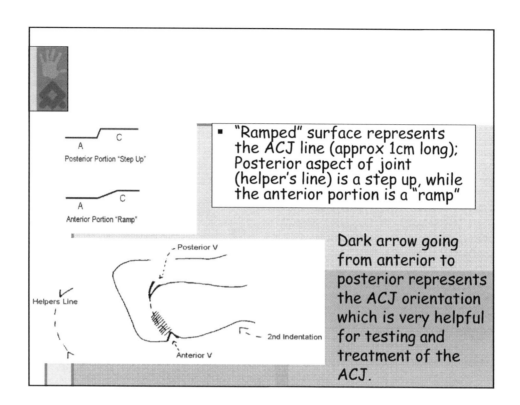

- "Ramped" surface represents the ACJ line (approx 1cm long); Posterior aspect of joint (helper's line) is a step up, while the anterior portion is a "ramp"

Dark arrow going from anterior to posterior represents the ACJ orientation which is very helpful for testing and treatment of the ACJ.

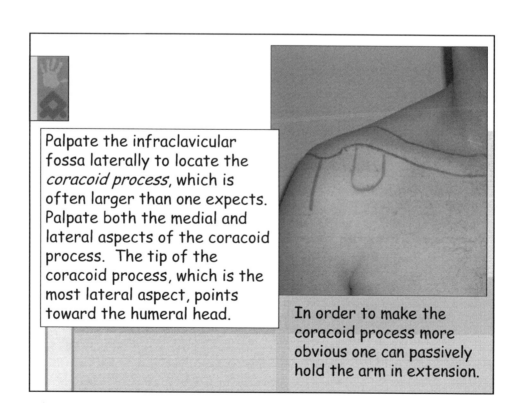

Palpate the infraclavicular fossa laterally to locate the *coracoid process*, which is often larger than one expects. Palpate both the medial and lateral aspects of the coracoid process. The tip of the coracoid process, which is the most lateral aspect, points toward the humeral head.

In order to make the coracoid process more obvious one can passively hold the arm in extension.

With the patient's shoulder/arm in physiological neutral position, place the middle finger of the contralateral hand on the tip of the coracoid process and move laterally until meeting a bony resistance = the medial aspect of the lesser tubercle. Then palpate with the index finger over the *lesser tubercle* until the finger "falls" into the **intertubercular sulcus.**

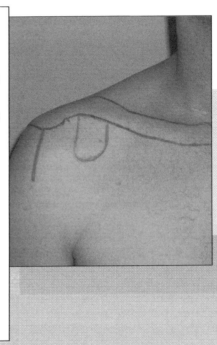

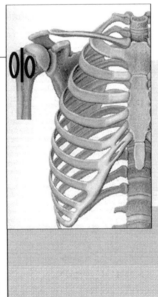

Confirmation of the *inter-tubercular sulcus* location:
> With the arm in the physiological neutral position, the intertubercular sulcus lies directly underneath the division between the anterior (clavicular) and medial (acromial) parts of the deltoid. When the patient makes an active abduction (in the plane of the scapula) without rotation, the finger falls between this division in the deltoid.

With the index finger in the intertubercular sulcus, perform slight passive internal and external rotation just on either side of physiological neutral position. The lesser tubercle (with ER) and the greater tubercle (with IR) come into contact with the index.

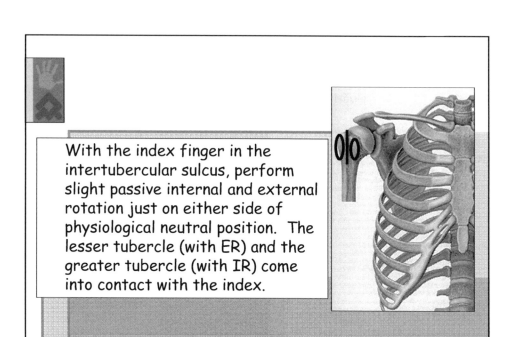

Between the tip of the coracoid process and the intertubercular sulcus lies the *lesser tubercle*. One can palpate it superiorly and inferiorly (upside down pear-shaped structure).

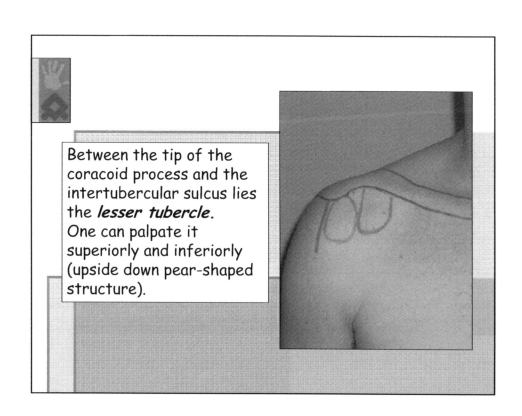

View from above:
-2 "V" notches of the ACJ
-Line from posterior angle of the acromion (*) to the coracoid process (**) is parallel to the glenoid

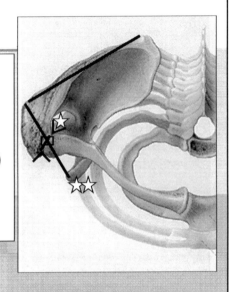

Basic Clinical Examination

> "...Experienced therapists using the Cyriax evaluation can be highly reliable in classifying patients with shoulder pain. ..."

Our clinical exam is essential!

Pellecchia GL. Intertester reliability of the Cyriax evaluation in assessing patients with shoulder pain. J Orth Sports Phys Ther. 1996;1:34-38.

Basic Clinical Examination

Principles of James Cyriax:

1. Referred pain- provocation tests
2. Capsular pattern- quantity of motion
3. End-feel- quality of motion

Our clinical exam is essential!

Basic Clinical Examination

Referred pain

❖ **C4 pain:**
AC and SC joint

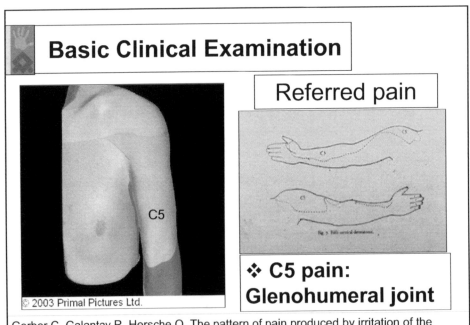

© 2003 Primal Pictures Ltd.

Gerber C, Galantay R, Hersche O. The pattern of pain produced by irritation of the acromioclavicular ioint and the subacromial space. J Shoulder Elbow Surg. 1998; 7: 352-355.

Basic Clinical Examination

Referred pain

© 2003 Primal Pictures Ltd.

❖ **C5 pain:**
Glenohumeral joint

Gerber C, Galantay R, Hersche O. The pattern of pain produced by irritation of the acromioclavicular ioint and the subacromial space. J Shoulder Elbow Surg. 1998; 7: 352-355.

Basic Clinical Examination

Referred pain

Distal vs Proximal

Ventral vs Dorsal

Superficial vs Deep

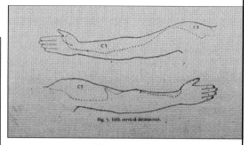

C5 pain

Jessell TM, Kelly DD. 1991. Pain and analgesia. In: Kandel ER, Schwartz JH, Jessell TM (Eds.) Principles of Neural Science (3rd ed.) Norwalk: Appleton & Lange, pp. 385-399.

Basic Clinical Examination

Patient History :

Age

Arthropathy: GH joint synovitis
- < 30: systemic synovitis
- 45: traumatic synovitis
- 40-60: idiopathic synovitis

Basic Clinical Examination

Patient History :

Age

Soft tissue lesions
- < 40: more deep cuff lesions
  (internal impingement)
- > 40: more superficial cuff lesions
  (external impingement)
- > 50: with h/o recent trauma: cuff
  tears in 50% of cases

Basic Clinical Examination

Patient History :

Gender

Female
- increased risk of developing
  idiopathic adhesive capsulitis

Basic Clinical Examination

Patient History :

Chief Complaint

- pain—where?
- limited range of motion?
- loss of strength?

Basic Clinical Examination

Patient History :

Chief Complaint

Where is the problem?
- C4 pain? –SCJ or ACJ
- C5 pain?
    -posterior pain with overhead activity
    -referred pain distal to the elbow

Basic Clinical Examination

Patient History :

Chief Complaint

When are the symptoms felt?
- With activity?
  - -rule out a cervical problem
  - -tendinopathy vs. tenosynovitis
- At rest: synovitis
  - -lying on the shoulder
  - -only at night

Basic Clinical Examination

Patient History :

Chief Complaint

How long?
- Chronic
  - -idiopathic adhesive capsulitis
  - -chronic bursitis
- Acute
  - -bursitis
  - -tendon injury

Basic Clinical Examination

Series of active and passive tests used to determine the pain generator!

Basic Clinical Examination

Passive Testing

- **Quantity**: How far do they go?

- **Quality**: What is the end feel?

- **Provocation**: Does the test provoke the patient's symptoms?

- Most important question:

Where is their pain?

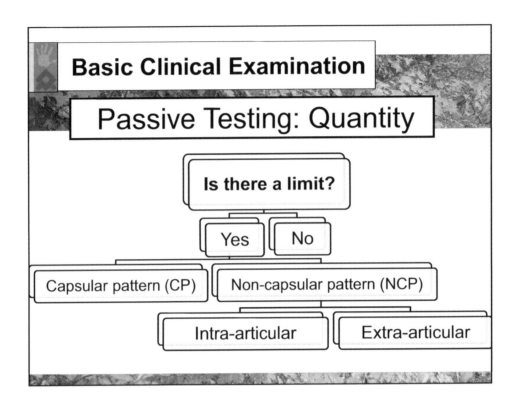

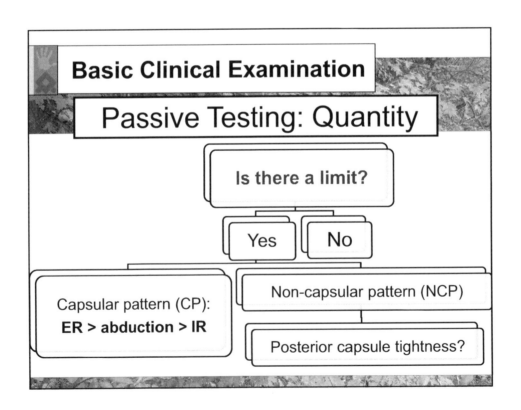

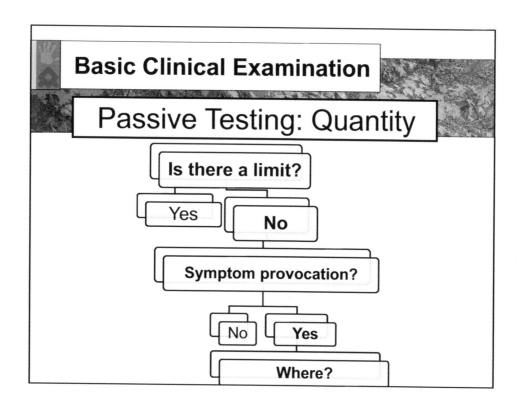

Basic Clinical Examination

Passive Testing: Quantity

Is there a limit?

Yes

No

Symptom provocation?

No

Yes

Where?

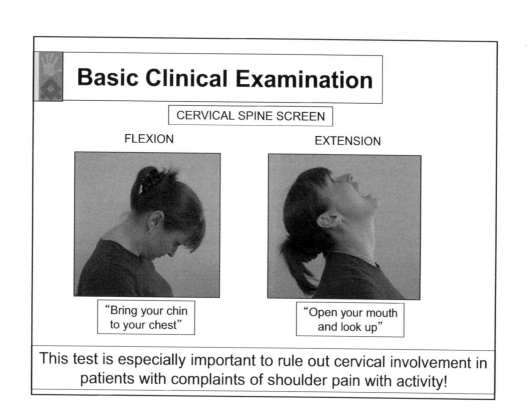

Basic Clinical Examination

CERVICAL SPINE SCREEN

FLEXION

EXTENSION

"Bring your chin to your chest"

"Open your mouth and look up"

This test is especially important to rule out cervical involvement in patients with complaints of shoulder pain with activity!

Basic Clinical Examination

CERVICAL SPINE SCREEN

ROTATION

SIDE BENDING

"Look to the right and left"

"Tip your ear toward your shoulder"

Basic Clinical Examination

Spurling's test

- Step #1: Patient performs cervical extension with ipsilateral sidebending. If pain or paresthesias occur in the arm in a dermatomal pattern, the test is **positive and no need to proceed with step 2.**
- Step #2: If no symptoms occur, redo the test with extension, ipsilateral sidebending, & rotation prior to applying gentle downward pressure on patient's head.

Anekstein Y, Blecher R, Smorgick Y, et al. What is the best way to apply the spurling test for cervical radiculopathy? Clin Orthop Relat Res. 2012; 470(9): 2566-72.

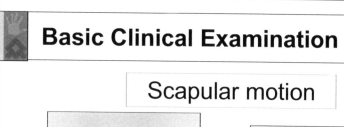

Basic Clinical Examination

Scapular motion

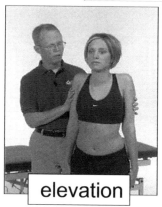

elevation

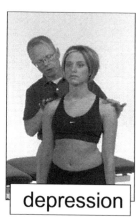

depression

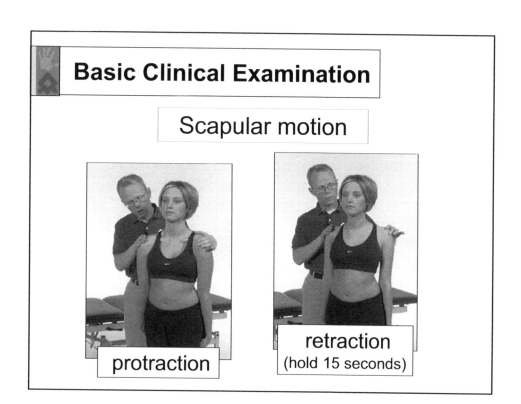

Basic Clinical Examination

Scapular motion

protraction

retraction
(hold 15 seconds)

Basic Clinical Examination

Scapular position at rest

- depression
- elevation
- downward rotation
- abduction

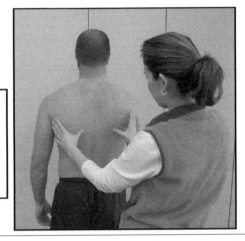

Scapular alignment can greatly contribute to the amount of space for the RTC beneath the acromion!

Basic Clinical Examination

Glenohumeral Joint alignment

- normal: humeral head located 1/3 of width anterior to roof of acromion
- is the humeral head translated anteriorly?

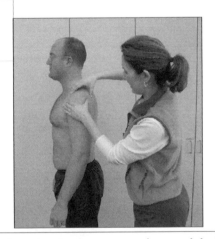

The humeral head translated anteriorly may give a hint that posterior capsule tightness is present!

Basic Clinical Examination

Scapulothoracic Junction

Tested in 3 static positions

- **"scolding position"**
- "sleepwalk position"
- arms abducted to 90°

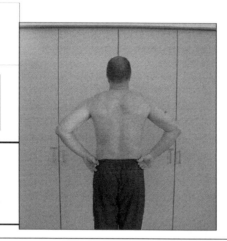

Kibler WB, Uhl TL, Maddux WQ, Brooks PV, Zeller B, McMullen J. Qualitative clinical evaluation of scapular dysfunction: A reliability study. J Shoulder Elbow Surg 2002; 11:550-6.

Basic Clinical Examination

Scapulothoracic Junction

- "scolding position"
- **"sleepwalk position"**
- arms abducted to 90°

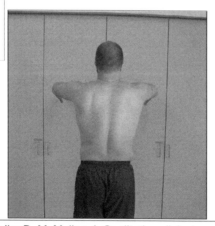

Kibler WB, Uhl TL, Maddux WQ, Brooks PV, Zeller B, McMullen J. Qualitative clinical evaluation of scapular dysfunction: A reliability study. J Shoulder Elbow Surg 2002; 11:550-6.

Basic Clinical Examination

Scapulothoracic Junction

- "scolding position"
- "sleepwalk position"
- **arms abducted to 90°**

Kibler WB, Uhl TL, Maddux WQ, Brooks PV, Zeller B, McMullen J. Qualitative clinical evaluation of scapular dysfunction: A reliability study. J Shoulder Elbow Surg 2002; 11:550-6.

Basic Clinical Examination

Scapulohumeral Rhythm

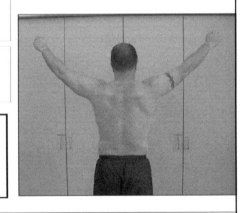

Tested in 3 planes: concentric & eccentric

- **through abduction**
- through flexion
- through scaption

Kibler WB, Uhl TL, Maddux WQ, Brooks PV, Zeller B, McMullen J. Qualitative clinical evaluation of scapular dysfunction: A reliability study. J Shoulder Elbow Surg 2002; 11:550-6.

Basic Clinical Examination

Scapulohumeral Rhythm

- through abduction
- **through flexion**
- through scaption

Is there a painful arc?

Kibler WB, Uhl TL, Maddux WQ, Brooks PV, Zeller B, McMullen J. Qualitative clinical evaluation of scapular dysfunction: A reliability study. J Shoulder Elbow Surg 2002; 11:550-6.

Basic Clinical Examination

Scapulohumeral Rhythm

- through abduction
- through flexion
- **through scaption**

Is there a painful arc?

Kibler WB, Uhl TL, Maddux WQ, Brooks PV, Zeller B, McMullen J. Qualitative clinical evaluation of scapular dysfunction: A reliability study. J Shoulder Elbow Surg 2002; 11:550-6.

Basic Clinical Examination

Passive Elevation Test

This test can be used as:

1- Mobility test

2- Provocation test

Basic Clinical Examination

Passive Elevation Test

1- Mobility testing: The therapist stabilizes the contralateral scapula

Contralateral scapular stabilization

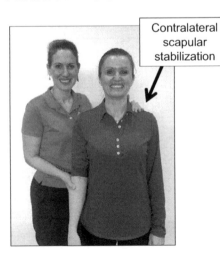

Basic Clinical Examination

Passive Elevation Test

1- Mobility testing: A firm end-feel indicates a limitation may be present at either the GH, SC, or AC joints

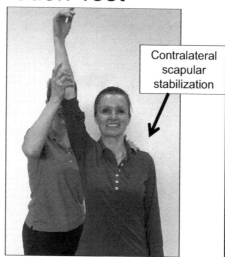

Contralateral scapular stabilization

Basic Clinical Examination

Passive Elevation Test

1- Mobility testing: The therapist stabilizes the ipsilateral scapula (not allowing contribution from the AC & SC joints)

Ipsilateral scapula stabilization

Basic Clinical Examination

Passive Elevation Test

1- Mobility testing:
If the GH range was found to be comparable to the unaffected side but the composite elevation (without scapular stabilization) was noted to be limited; this would suggest a limitation at either SC or AC joints.

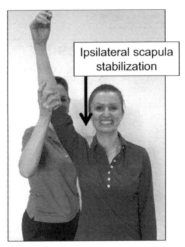

Ipsilateral scapula stabilization

Basic Clinical Examination

Passive Elevation Test

2- Provocation testing: The therapist passively brings the arm to about 120 degrees of elevation, then provide ipsilateral scapular stabilization.

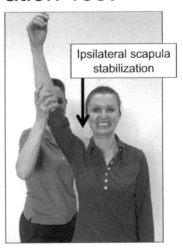

Ipsilateral scapula stabilization

Basic Clinical Examination

Passive Elevation Test

2- Provocation testing:

The therapist performs:

- passive medial overpressure (suggests internal impingement)
- passive posterior overpressure (suggests external impingement)

Pain with Posterior overpressure = **Neer Impingement Test**

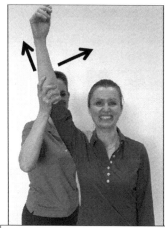

Ipsilateral scapula stabilization

Basic Clinical Examination

Passive GH Joint testing

- **external rotation**
- abduction
- internal rotation

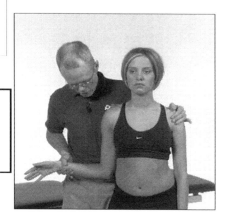

Basic Clinical Examination

Passive GH Joint testing

- external rotation
- **abduction**
- internal rotation

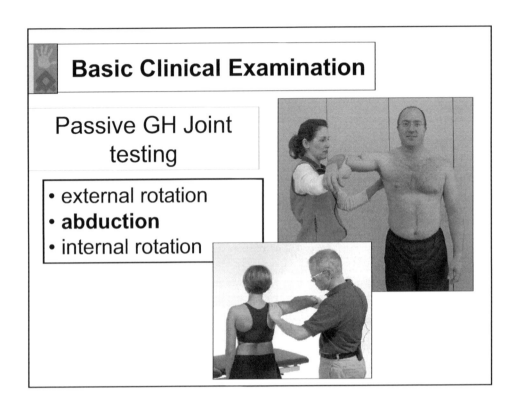

Basic Clinical Examination

Passive GH Joint testing

- external rotation
- abduction
- **internal rotation**

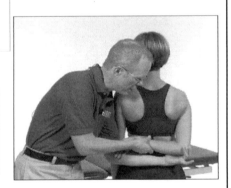

Basic Clinical Examination

Strength testing: resisted (Ω) Tests

- Isometric testing
- If resisted test is painful: tendinitis/tendinopathy
- Ω shoulder tests: adduction, abduction, IR, ER, elbow flexion & extension

Basic Clinical Examination

Strength testing: Ω Adduction

- Stabilize the patient's trunk
- attempt to pull the patient's elbow away from the body

Basic Clinical Examination

Strength testing: Ω Abduction

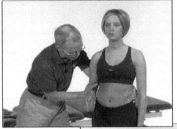

- Test in neutral
- May also test resisted Abduction eccentrically at 30° abduction

Basic Clinical Examination

Bursal Pull Test

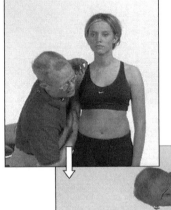

- If pain occurs with Ω abduction, IR, or ER, the bursal pull test is indicated
- If pain is relieved or strength improves with inferior pull on humerus, the test is (+)

Basic Clinical Examination

Bursal Pull Test

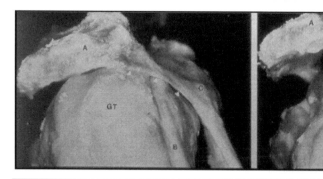

external impingement (painful arc 80-130°)

Neer CS. Impingement lesions. Clin Orthop 1983; 173:70.

Basic Clinical Examination

Strength testing: Ω External Rotation

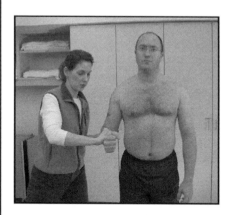

- Provide resistance just proximal to the patient's wrist on the dorsal aspect of the forearm

Basic Clinical Examination

Strength testing: Ω Internal Rotation

- Provide resistance on the volar aspect of the patient's forearm, just proximal to the wrist

Basic Clinical Examination

Strength testing: "Lift off" sign

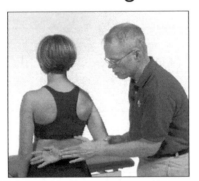

- This tests the integrity of the subscapularis

Alqunaee M, Galvin R, Fahey T. Diagnostic accuracy of clinical tests for subacromial impingement syndrome: a systematic review and meta- analysis. Arch Phys Med Rehabil. 2012;93:229–36.

Gerber C, Krushell RJ. Isolated rupture of the tendon of the subscapularis muscle. Clinical features in 16 cases. *J Bone Joint Surg* 1991 73-B:389-94.

Basic Clinical Examination

Strength testing: "Lift off" sign

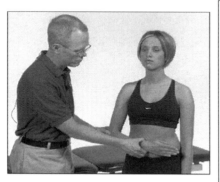

- Ask the patient to lift their hand off of the low back
- Alternate method: belly press test
- If unable to perform lift off test/belly press test, (+) for subscapularis rupture

Tokish JM, Decker MJ , Ellis HB, Torry MR, Hawkins RJ. The belly-press test for the physical examination of the subscapularis muscle: Electromyographic validation and comparison to the lift-off test. J Sh Elbow Surg 2003;12:427-430.

Basic Clinical Examination

Strength testing: Ω Elbow flexion

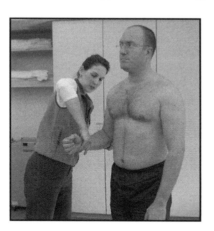

- Provide resistance at the distal forearm
- This tests the biceps integrity

Basic Clinical Examination

Strength testing: Ω Elbow extension

- Provide resistance at posterior aspect of distal forearm
- This tests the patient's scapular stabilizers!

Basic Clinical Examination

Extra Tests for Acromioclavicular joint (ACJ)

Passive Horizontal Adduction

ventral

dorsal

Basic Clinical Examination

Extra Tests for Acromioclavicular joint (ACJ)

ACJ Compression Test

- position patient's shoulder at 90° flexion with neutral rotation
- perform resisted horizontal abduction
- + test: reproduction of C4 pain

Basic Clinical Examination

Extra Tests for Acromioclavicular joint (ACJ)

Paxinos Sign

- for ACJ differential diagnosis
- Only performed when there is C4 pain.
- Place thumb on post-lat aspect of acromion and IF & MF at the mid-portion of clavicle. Apply pressure in an A-P direction (squeezing together)

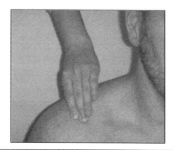

+ test: pain occurs or is increased at ACJ
- test: no change in pain level

Walton J, Mahajan S, Paxinos A, et al. Diagnostic values of tests for acromioclavicular joint pain. J Bone Joint Surg Am. 2004 Apr;86-A(4):807-812.

Basic Clinical Examination

Suprascapular Nerve Stretch Test

- In instance of posterior shoulder pain often there is atrophy of the supraspinatus and/or **infraspinatus**

1. Generally performed through ventral horizontal adduction followed by contralateral sidebend of the head

2. Can also be performed through dorsal horizontal adduction, followed by contralateral sidebend of the head

Basic Clinical Examination

Let's practice!

Clinical Examination of the Shoulder

Date:
Diagnosis:

CHIEF COMPLAINTS
INSPECTION & PALPATION
CERVICAL SPINE SCREEN
SCAPULAR MOTION - elevation - depression - protraction - retraction (15 second hold)
SCAPULAR POSITION AT REST - scapular alignment

SCAPULOTHORACIC JUNCTION
Observation of Scapular Position
 - prepositioned – the "scolding" position
 - prepositioned – arms abducted to 90°
 - prepositioned – the "sleepwalk position
 - concentric and eccentric full elevation
   o through abduction
   o through flexion
   o through scaption

ARM ELEVATION
AROM: Test for Painful Arc - through abduction - through flexion - through scaption

Passive Elevation Test
 - with contralateral scapular fixation
 - with ipsilateral scapula fixation
      & medial overpressure
 - with ipsilateral scapula fixation
      & posterior overpressure (Neer Impingement Test)

PASSIVE TESTS (Evaluating GHJ capsular mobility)
External Rotation
Glenohumeral Abduction

Internal Rotation

RESISTED TESTS (in physiological neutral rotation, except lift off sign)

Resisted Adduction	
Resisted Abduction - concentric in neutral	If needed: (Resisted Abduction eccentric, in 30° abduction & IR)

Resisted External Rotation

Resisted Internal Rotation
"Lift Off Sign"

Resisted Elbow Flexion

Resisted Elbow Extension

EXTRA TESTS

Painful Resisted Tests with Pull—Bursal Pull Test
- abduction
- external rotation
- internal rotation

ACJ
- Passive Horizontal Adduction from ventral & dorsal
- ACJ Compression Test
- Paxinos Sign

Suprascapular Nerve Test

Extra tests for Impingement
- Subacromial impingement (Hawkins-Kennedy) test
- Subcoracoid impingement
- Modified Relocation test

Test for Tight Posterior Capsule
- With arm at side, testing passive IR (tested with basic clinical exam)
- at 90° abduction, testing passive IR

Stretch for Long Head of Biceps

Labrum tests:
- Active Compression (O'Brien) test
- Modified Crank
- Modified Clunk
- Biceps Load I & II

STABILITY TESTS

Anterior & Posterior Laxity Tests
  - Drawer test (static, neutral position)
  - Load and Shift
      o Maximal loose packed position (MLPP)
      o Anterior: 90° abduction with maximal ER
      o Posterior: 90° flexion, IR, horizontal add

Anterior Instability Test
  - relocation test
  - reverse relocation test

Inferior Laxity Tests
  - Sulcus test
      o in neutral
      o in ER
      o in IR
  - in 90° abduction (neutral)

Adhesive Capsulitis

Frozen Shoulder

Consensus Definition from American Shoulder and Elbow Society (ASES):

"A condition characterized by functional restriction of both active and passive shoulder motion for which radiographs of the glenohumeral joint are essentially unremarkable except for the possible presence of osteopenia or calcific tendinitis."

Grant JA, Schroeder N, Miller BS, et al. Comparison of manipulation and arthroscopic capsular release for adhesive capsulitis: a systematic review. J Shoulder Elbow Surg. 2013;22:1135-1145.

Adhesive Capsulitis

"Primary"= Idiopathic

Not associated with a systemic condition or history of injury

"Secondary"

Defined by a relationship between a disease or pathology with 3 subcategories:
- Systemic: Hx of diabetes mellitus and thyroid disease
- Extrinsic: Pathology not directly related to the shoulder such as CVA, Myocardial Infarction, COPD, cervical disk disease, distal extremity fracture, self-imposed immobilization
- Intrinsic: Known pathology of the GHJ soft-tissues or structures

Kelley et al. Shoulder pain and mobility deficits: Adhesive capsulitis. Clinical practice guidelines linked to the international classification of functioning, disability, and health from the orthopedic section of APTA. J Orthop Phys Ther.2013;43(5):A1-A31

Adhesive Capsulitis

Commonly occurs in the anterior superior region of the glenohumeral joint capsule

Predictable Pattern of Limitation

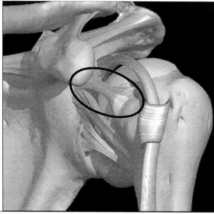

Primal
Pictures
2000

Ozaki J. Pathomechanics and operative management of chronic frozen shoulder. Ann Chir Gynaecol.1996; 85(2):156-8.

Adhesive Capsulitis

clinical presentation

○ Key feature: Capsular Pattern

- **External Rotation Limitation Greatest**

- **Abduction Limitation Less**

- **Internal Rotation Limitation Least**

- **3:2:1 Ratio**

"A Spirit of the Law verses the Letter of the Law"

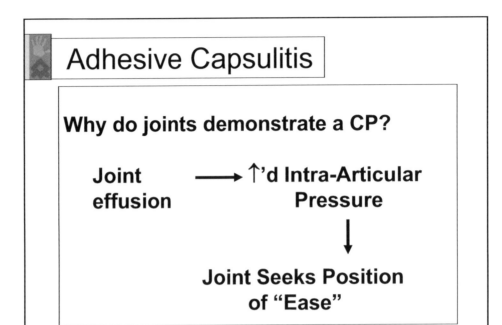

Adhesive Capsulitis

Why do joints demonstrate a CP?

Joint effusion $\longrightarrow$ **↑'d Intra-Articular Pressure**

$\downarrow$

Joint Seeks Position of "Ease"

Eyring EJ, Murray Wr. The effect of joint position on the pressure of intraarticular effusion. J Bone Joint Surg. 1964; 46-A:1235-1241.

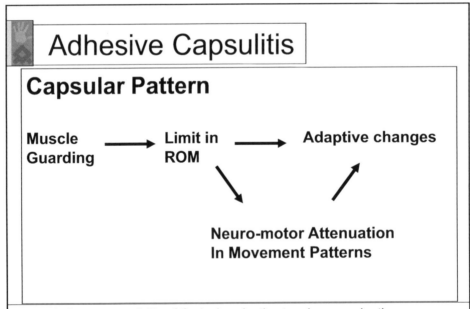

Adhesive Capsulitis

Capsular Pattern

Muscle Guarding $\longrightarrow$ **Limit in ROM** $\longrightarrow$ **Adaptive changes**

Neuro-motor Attenuation In Movement Patterns

Atkins E. Construct validity of Cyriax's selective tension examination: Association of end-feels with pain at the knee and shoulder; Invited commentary. JOSPT, 2000; 30:523-525.

Adhesive Capsulitis

- PROM Assessment
- 3:2:1 ratio of limitation
- **ER**>Abd>IR

Capsular pattern

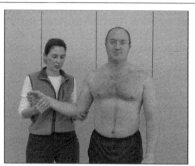

Normal External Rotation

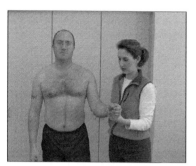

Limited External Rotation

Adhesive Capsulitis

- PROM Assessment
- 3:2:1 ratio of limitation
- ER>**Abd**>IR

Capsular pattern

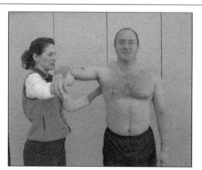

Normal Abduction

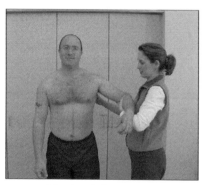

Limited Abduction

Adhesive Capsulitis

- PROM Assessment
- 3:2:1 ratio of limitation
- ER>Abd>**IR**

Capsular pattern

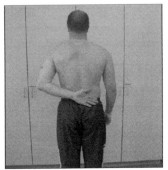

Normal Internal Rotation

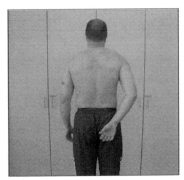

Mild limitation with IR

Primary Adhesive Capsulitis

Risk Factors

- Diabetes mellitus and thyroid disease
- Individuals between 40-65 years of age
- Individuals with previous episode of adhesive capsulitis in the contralateral arm.
- Significant relationship with Dupuytren's contracture

Kelley et al. Shoulder pain and mobility deficits: Adhesive capsulitis. Clinical practice guidelines linked to the international classification of functioning, disability, and health from the orthopedic section of APTA. J Orthop Phys Ther.2013;43(5):A1-A31

Primary Adhesive Capsulitis

Clinical Identifiers

- Impacts daily activities of middle-aged people
- Affects female more than males
- Characterized by shoulder pain, mainly at night, restriction of A/PROM
- Pain with end-range in all directions
- Caused by inflammation of the synovial lining and capsule leading to dense adhesions formation
- Typically evolves through 3-4 phases
- Can last 1-3 years

Walmsley S, Rivett D, Osmotherly P. Adhesive capsulitis: establishing consensus on clinical identifiers for stage 1 using the delphi technique. Physical Ther. 2009; 89(9): 906-916.

Eljabu W, Klinger HM, von Knoch M. Prognosis factors and therapeutic options for treatment of frozen shoulder: a systematic review. Arch Orthop Trauma Surg. 2016;136:1-7.

Primary Adhesive Capsulitis

Pathoanatomical Features

Multiregional *synovitis* (inflammation)

vs

Focal vascularity and *angiogenesis* (capillary growth) accompanied by nerve growth

Kelley et al. Shoulder pain and mobility deficits: Adhesive capsulitis. Clinical practice guidelines linked to the international classification of functioning, disability, and health from the orthopedic section of APTA. J Orthop Phys Ther. 2013;43(5):A1-A31

Primary Adhesive Capsulitis

Imaging

Radiography-Plain film

-Typically negative

-Possibly more useful for ruling out other pathologies in the differential diagnosis.

-Might reflect **osteopenia**

Primary Adhesive Capsulitis

Imaging

MR Arthrography
Comparison of 35 patients diagnosed with Adhesive capsulitis with 45 patients without.
Conclusion:
An abundance of enhancing tissue in the rotator interval and thickening and enhancement of the axillary recess are signs suggestive of adhesive capsulitis on indirect MR arthrography.

Song KD et al. Indirect MR arthrographic findings of adhesive capsulitis. AJR:197, December 2011.

Primary Adhesive Capsulitis

Imaging

MR Arthrography

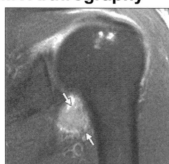

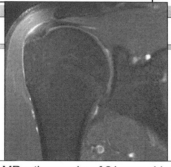

Oblique coronal gadolinium chelate–enhanced T1-weighted image shows enhancing portion of axillary recess (arrows).

Indirect MR arthrography of 21-year-old man without adhesive capsulitis who presented with shoulder pain but did not show restricted range of motion. There is no visible enhancing portion in axillary recess on oblique coronal gadolinium chelate–enhanced T1-weighted image.

Song KD et al. Indirect MR arthrographic findings of adhesive capsulitis. AJR:197, December 2011.

Primary Adhesive Capsulitis

Imaging

Diagnostic Ultrasound

The average thickness of the CHL was significantly greater in adhesive capsulitis (3 mm) than in the asymptomatic (1.34 mm) and painful (1.39 mm) shoulders. No significant difference was found between asymptomatic and painful shoulders.

.

Homsi C, Bordalo-Rodrigues M, da Silva JJ, et al. Ultrasound in adhesive capsulitis of the shoulder: is assessment of the coracohumeral ligament a valuable diagnostic tool? Skeletal Radiol. 2006; 35(9): 673-678.

Primary Adhesive Capsulitis

4 Stages

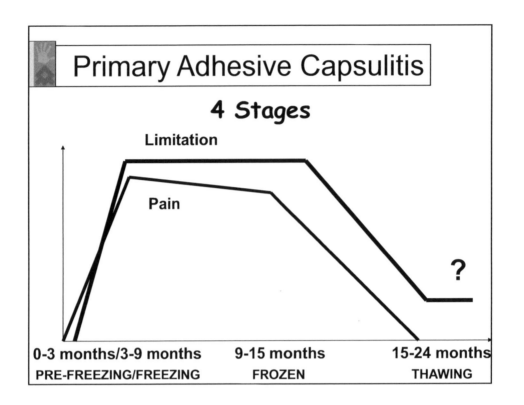

0-3 months/3-9 months	9-15 months	15-24 months
PRE-FREEZING/FREEZING	FROZEN	THAWING

Primary Adhesive Capsulitis

Stage 1: (0-3 months)
-Sharp pain at end range of motion
-Achy at rest
-Sleep disturbance
-Diffuse synovial reaction without contractures
-Early loss of external rotation

Kelley et al. Shoulder pain and mobility deficits: Adhesive capsulitis. Clinical practice guidelines linked to the international classification of functioning, disability, and health from the orthopedic section of APTA. J Orthop Phys Ther 2013;43(5):A1-A31

Primary Adhesive Capsulitis

Stage 2: (3-9 mos)

- "Painful or freezing" stage
- Gradual loss of motion in all directions due to pain
- Aggressive synovitis /angiogenesis

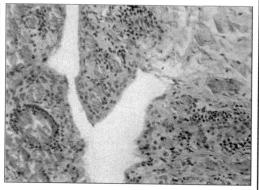

Hypervascular Synovial Tissue

Hannafin JA. Chiaia TA. Adhesive capsulitis. A treatment approach. Clin Orthop Rel Res. 2000; (372): 95-109.

Kelley et al. Shoulder pain and mobility deficits: Adhesive capsulitis. Clinical practice guidelines linked to the international classification of functioning, disability, and health from the orthopedic section of APTA. J Orthop Phys Ther 2013;43(5):A1-A31

Primary Adhesive Capsulitis

Stage 3: (9-15 mos)

- "Frozen" stage
- Pain and loss of motion
- Lessening of synovitis /angiogenesis
- Progressive capsuloligamentous fibrosis resulting in loss of axillary fold

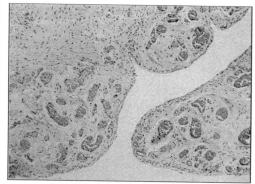

Perivascular Scar Formation & Extensive Fibrosis

Hannafin JA. Chiaia TA. Adhesive capsulitis. A treatment approach. Clin Orthop Rel Res. 2000; (372): 95-109.

Kelley et al. Shoulder pain and mobility deficits: Adhesive capsulitis. Clinical practice guidelines linked to the international classification of functioning, disability, and health from the orthopedic section of APTA. J Orthop Phys Ther 2013;43(5):A1-A31

Primary Adhesive Capsulitis

Stage 4: (15-24 mos)
-"Thawing" stage
-Resolving pain
-Capsuloligamentous complex fibrosis and receding synovial involvement

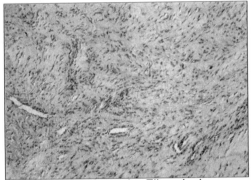

Extensive Capsular Fibroplasia
& Pericellular Matrix

Hannafin JA. Chiaia TA. Adhesive capsulitis. A treatment approach. Clin Orthop Rel Res. 2000; (372): 95-109.

Kelley et al. Shoulder pain and mobility deficits: Adhesive capsulitis. Clinical practice guidelines linked to the international classification of functioning, disability, and health from the orthopedic section of APTA. J Orthop Phys Ther 2013;43(5):A1-A31

Primary Adhesive Capsulitis

How do these patients respond to therapy?

...development of symptoms is directly correlated to anatomical deterioration, spontaneous recovery to normal levels of function is possible and standardized non-operative treatment programs are an effective alternative to surgery in most cases. However, patients with chronic symptoms and those who have risk factors such as diabetes mellitus or are affected bilaterally might benefit from earlier surgical intervention.

Eljabu W, Klinger HM, von Knoch M. Prognosis factors and therapeutic options for treatment of frozen shoulder: a systematic review. Arch Orthop Trauma Surg. 2016; 136:1-7.

Primary Adhesive Capsulitis

Management

- **Pre-Freezing/Freezing Stages:** Palliative and Injection Therapy
- **Frozen Stage:** Suprascapular N. Block and Distention Hydroplasty
- **Thawing Stage:**
  - Manipulation Under Anesthesia (MUA)
  - Arthroscopic Capsular Release (ACR)

Primary Adhesive Capsulitis

Freezing Stages: Palliative Management

Patient education: about the phases

Decrease sympathetic output:** T4-9 (soft tissue massage, myofascial techniques), TENS

Mild modalities: e.g. moist heat

Check JH, Cohen R. Complete resolution of frozen shoulder syndrome in a women treated with dextroamphetamine sulfate for chronic urinary urgency. Clin Exp Obsetet Gynecol. 2015;42(5):679-80.

Vanderwindt DAWM, Koes BW, Deville W, et al. Effectiveness of corticosteroid injections versus physiotherapy for treatment of painful stiff shoulder in primary-care - Randomized trial. *Br Med J.* 1998; 317:1292-1296.

Primary Adhesive Capsulitis

Freezing Stages: Palliative Management

Maintain range of motion, no pain

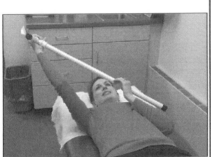

Check JH, Cohen R. Complete resolution of frozen shoulder syndrome in a women treated with dextroamphetamine sulfate for chronic urinary urgency. Clin Exp Obsetet Gynecol. 2015;42(5):679-80.

Primary Adhesive Capsulitis

Freezing Stages: Palliative Management

- Case study demonstrated a "top down approach" of addressing the central sensitization via pain neuroscience education, tactile discrimination (TD) and graded motor imagery (GMI) for 6 weeks was successful.

- Discussion: intensive PT in the freezing stage may be detrimental to long-term outcomes. Authors recommend a "top-down approach" to allow for a faster transition through the freezing stage of adhesive capsulitis.

Sawyer EE, McDevitt AW, Louw A, et al. Use of pain neuroscience education, tactile discrimination, and graded motor imagery in an individual with frozen shoulder. JOSPT. 2018; Dec 19:1-29. doi: 10.2519/jospt.2018.7716. [Epub ahead of print]

Primary Adhesive Capsulitis

Freezing Stages: Modalities

Short wave diathermy, ultrasound, or electric stimulation combined with mobility and stretching exercises to reduce pain and improve mobility is recommended based on weak evidence.

Kelley et al. Shoulder pain and mobility deficits: Adhesive capsulitis. Clinical practice guidelines linked to the international classification of functioning, disability, and health from the orthopedic section of APTA. J Orthop Phys Ther 2013;43(5):A1-A31

Primary Adhesive Capsulitis: Treatment

Freezing Stages: Modalities

Systematic Review
- **Electrotherapy can help in providing short-term pain relief**
- **CPM is recommended for short-term pain relief, but not for improving ROM or function**
- **Deep heat can be used for pain relief and improving ROM**
- **Ultrasound (US) for pain relief, improving ROM or function *is not recommended***

Jain TK and Sharma NK. The effectiveness of physiotherapeutic interventions in treatment of frozen shoulder/adhesive capsulitis: a systematic review. J Back and Musculoskeletal Rehab. 2014;27:247-273.

Primary Adhesive Capsulitis: **Treatment**

Freezing Stages: Ultrasound

- A pilot randomized double-blind clinical trial compared use of continuous 3 MHz, 1.5 w/cm2 US (versus sham US) in 50 patients with primary adhesive capsulitis in conjunction with semi supervised exercise and mobilization
- *Conclusion:* continuous US with primary adhesive capsulitis <u>did not</u> have any additional effect to placebo US on outcome measures.

Ebadi S, Forogh B, Fallah E, et al. Does ultrasound therapy add to the effect of exercise and mobilization in frozen shoulder? A pilot randomized double-blind clinical trial. Journal of Bodywork & Movement Therapies. 2017;21:781-787.

Primary Adhesive Capsulitis: **Treatment**

Dry Needling

Case Study

- 54 year-old patient, primary adhesive capsulitis, stage 2
- It was determined that the patient's pain was due in part to trigger points in the upper trap, levator scapula, deltoid, and infraspinatus muscles

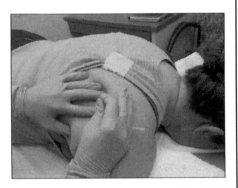

Clewey D, Flynn TW, Koppenhaver S. Trigger point dry needling as an adjunct treatment for a patient with adhesive capsulitis of the shoulder. J Orthop Sports Phys Ther. 2014;44(2):92-101.

Primary Adhesive Capsulitis: **Treatment**

Dry Needling

Case Study

- After dry needling the trigger points in these muscles (13 visits over 6 weeks), the patient had significant improvements in ROM and perceived disability on the QuickDASH and SPADI self-report questionnaires

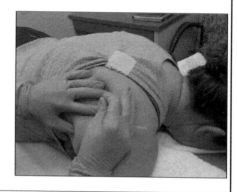

Clewey D, Flynn TW, Koppenhaver S. Trigger point dry needling as an adjunct treatment for a patient with adhesive capsulitis of the shoulder. J Orthop Sports Phys Ther. 2014;44(2):92-101.

Primary Adhesive Capsulitis: **Treatment**

Dry Needling

Case Study

- This rapid improvement suggests the surrounding muscles around the GH joint may be a significant source of pain in this condition
- Dry needling can be an effective treatment

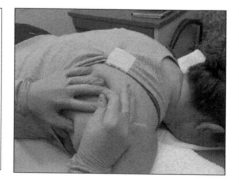

Clewey D, Flynn TW, Koppenhaver S. Trigger point dry needling as an adjunct treatment for a patient with adhesive capsulitis of the shoulder. J Orthop Sports Phys Ther. 2014;44(2):92-101.

Primary Adhesive Capsulitis

Freezing Stages: Intra-Articular Injection

- Intra-articular corticosteroid injection combined with shoulder mobility and stretching exercises are more effective in providing short-term (4-6 weeks) pain relief and improved function compared to shoulder mobility and stretching exercises alone.
- Recommendation based on strong evidence.

Kelley et al. Shoulder pain and mobility deficits: Adhesive capsulitis. Clinical practice guidelines linked to the international classification of functioning, disability, and health from the orthopedic section of APTA. J Orthop Phys Ther 2013;43(5):A1-A31

Primary Adhesive Capsulitis

Frozen: Suprascapular Nerve Block (SSNB)

produced a faster and more complete resolution of pain and restoration of ROM than a series of intra-articular injections
Significant difference in favor of SSNB from day 1 to day 3 after surgery.
Near-nerve electro-myographically guided ($P < 0.05$)** More successful at providing pain relief.
SSNB safe and well tolerated.

Kiliç Z, Filiz MB, Çakir T, Toraman NF. Addition of suprascapular nerve block to a physical therapy program produces and extra benefit to adhesive capsulitis: a randomized controlled trial. Am J Phys Med Rehabil 2015;94:912-920.

Jerosch J, Saad M, Greig M, Filler T. Suprascapular nerve block as a method of preemptive pain control in shoulder surgery. Knee Surg Sports Traumatol Arthrosc. 2008 Jun;16(6):602-607.

Karatas GK. Meray J. Suprascapular nerve block for pain relief in adhesive capsulitis: comparison of 2 different techniques. Archives of Physical Medicine & Rehabilitation. 2002; 83(5):593-597.

Primary Adhesive Capsulitis

Frozen: Distention Hydroplasty/ Hydrodilatation/Hydraulic distension/ Arthrographic distension

Kim K et al. Capsule preservation improves short-term outcome of hydraulic distension in painful stiff shoulder. J Orthop Res. 2011; 29:1688-1694.

Watson L, Bialocerkowski A, Dalziel R, et al. Hydrodilatation (distension arthrography): a long-term clinical outcome series. Br J Sports Med. 2007; 41: 167–173.

Halverson L, Maas R. Shoulder joint capsule distention (hydroplasty); A case series of patients with "frozen shoulders" treated in a primary care office. *J Fam Prac* 2002; 51:61-4.

Amoretti N, Grimaud A, Brocq O, et al. Shoulder distension arthrography in adhesive capsulitis. Clin Imaging. 2006; 30(4):254-256.

Calligan N et al. Effectiveness of hydroplasty and therapeutic exercise for treatment of frozen shoulder. J Hand Ther. 2003;16:219-224.

Primary Adhesive Capsulitis

Frozen: Distention Hydroplasty

Cochrane Collaboration's Conclusion:
• Silver level of evidence that arthrographic distension with saline, local anesthetic and steroid provides significant short-term benefits in terms of pain, function, and range of shoulder movement in people with adhesive capsulitis.
• Lack of reliable evidence to establish the comparative effectiveness of arthrographic distension with saline, local anaesthetic and steroid versus other treatments (steroid injection alone and distension with saline alone).

Cochrane Collaboration. Arthrographic distension for adhesive capsulitis (frozen shoulder) (Review) 2009.

Primary Adhesive Capsulitis

Thawing: Manipulation Under Anesthesia (MUA)

successful therapy in adhesive capsulitis stage III, or when limitation in the range of motion is the main symptom

MUA has been shown to improve ROM and pain, but repeat MUA may be necessary. Most common risk being failure to improve and most serious risk being humerus fracture.

Smitherman JA et al. Arthroscopy and manipulation versus home therapy program in treatment of adhesive capsulitis of the shoulder: a prospective randomized study. Journal of Surgical Orthopaedic Advances. 2015;24(1):69-74.

Pap G, Liebau C, Meyer M, et al. Results of mobilization under anesthesia in adhesive capsulitis in relation to stage of the disease. [German] Zeitschrift fur Orthopadie und Ihre Grenzgebiete. 1998; 136(1): 13-17.

Primary Adhesive Capsulitis

Thawing: Arthroscopic Capsular Release (ACR)

- represents a valuable therapeutic choice with minimal complications, to effectively reduce pain and improve movement in all planes of motion."
- early significant improvements in shoulder range of motion, pain frequency and severity, and function. These improvements were maintained and /or enhanced at seven years.

Smitherman JA et al. Arthroscopy and manipulation versus home therapy program in treatment of adhesive capsulitis of the shoulder: a prospective randomized study. Journal of Surgical Orthopaedic Advances. 2015;24(1):69-74.

Jerosch J et al. Mid-term results following arthroscopic capsular release in patients with primary and secondary adhesive capsulitis. Knee Surg Sports Traumatol Arthrosc 2012.

Le Lievre HMJ, Murrell GAC. Long-term outcomes after arthroscopic capsular release for idiopathic adhesive capsulitis. J Bone Joint Surg Am. 2012;94:1208-16.

Primary Adhesive Capsulitis

Arthroscopic Release vs MUA

Conclusion:

There is no clear difference in shoulder ROM or patient-reported outcomes when comparing a manipulation under anaesthesia to an arthroscopic capsular release for the treatment of recalcitrant idiopathic or secondary-systemic adhesive capsulitis.

Grant JA, Schroeder N, Miller BS, Carpenter JE. Comparison of manipulation and arthroscopic capsular release for adhesive capsulitis: a systematic review. J Shoulder Elbow Surg. 2013; 22:135-1145.

Primary Adhesive Capsulitis

Idiopathic Adhesive Capsulitis: Conclusion

- ❑ **Complex pathology**
- ❑ **Stage Specificity in Diagnosis**
- ❑ **Stage Specificity in Treatment**

Neviaser AS, Hannafin JA. Adhesive capsulitis: a review of current treatment. Am J Sports Med. 2010 Nov;38(11):2346-2356

Secondary Adhesive Capsulitis

History...

- **Trauma or immobilization (secondary)**
  - Shoulder stiffness develops when there is a known intrinsic, extrinsic, or systemic cause
  - Stiffness can develop after surgical intervention, traumatic events, & often in combination with prolonged immobilization
  - Symptoms appear 3 to 5 days later after trauma

Secondary Adhesive Capsulitis

...due to trauma or immobilization

- **Inactivity of the shoulder joints due to immobilizing the upper extremities of patients after acute aneurysm surgery seemed to cause the development of frozen shoulder**

- **The incidence of this complication was greatly reduced by keeping the patient's upper arms raised alternately to maintain their range of motion after acute aneurysm surgery.**

Tanishima T & Yoshimasu N. Development and prevention of frozen shoulder after acute aneurysm surgery. Surg Neurol. 1997;48:19-22

Secondary Adhesive Capsulitis

...due to trauma or immobilization

Irritability: Low

- **symptoms: C5 pain, proximal to the elbow**
- **pain occurs only with activity**
- **able to lie on affected shoulder**
- **end-feel: firm (occurs before pain)**

Responds well to joint specific mobilization!

Secondary Adhesive Capsulitis

...due to trauma or immobilization

Irritability: Moderate

- **symptoms: combination of low & high**
- **pain may occur with activity &/or at rest**
- **may/may not be able to lie on affected shoulder**
- **end-feel: end-feel and pain occur at the same time**

Secondary Adhesive Capsulitis

...due to trauma or immobilization

Irritability: High

- symptoms: C5 pain, distal to the elbow
- pain occurs at rest & with activity
- unable to lie on affected shoulder
- end-feel: pathological (first pain, then end-feel)

Intra-articular injection likely needed to bring patient to a stage favorable for joint specific mobilization!

Secondary Adhesive Capsulitis

Systematic Review

- <u>Therapeutic exercises</u> and <u>mobilization</u> are strongly recommended for reducing pain, improving range of motion (ROM) and function in patients with Stages 2 and 3 of frozen shoulder

Jain TK and Sharma NK. The effectiveness of physiotherapeutic interventions in treatment of frozen shoulder/adhesive capsulitis: a systematic review. J Back and Musculoskeletal Rehab. 2014;27:247-273.

Secondary Adhesive Capsulitis

The ideal therapy candidate!

- **Difficulty raising the arm**
- **Loss of shoulder motion, causing problems with daily activities**
- **History of trauma or immobilization or systemic disorder**

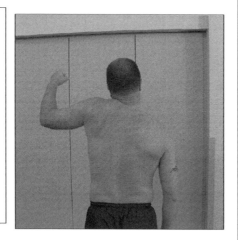

Secondary Adhesive Capsulitis

The ideal therapy candidate!

- **Pain in the C5 region, proximal to the elbow**
- **Able to lie on affected shoulder**
- **With clinical testing, the end-feel is firm (verses painful)**

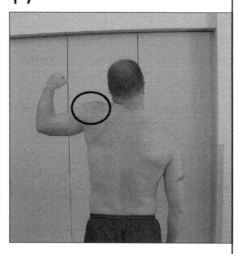

129

Secondary Adhesive Capsulitis

Joint Mobilization

2 types of mobilization techniques for the shoulder:

- **to improve motion below 90 degrees (abduction and flexion)**
- **to improve motion at end-range**

GHJ arthrokinematics

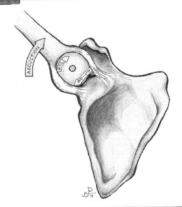

ABDUCTION:
- The humeral head rolls in superior direction and glides inferiorly.
- To improve abduction, perform glides in an inferior direction

Wuelker N, Schmotzer H, Tren K, et al. Translation of the glenohumeral joint with simulated active elevation. Clin Orth. 1994;309:193-200.
Kaltenborn FM. Manuelle mobilisation der extremitätengelenke. Olaf Norlis Bokhandel; 1985:25)

Neumann D. Kinesiology of the musculoskeletal system: foundations for rehabilitation. St. Louis: Elsevier 2017.

GHJ arthrokinematics

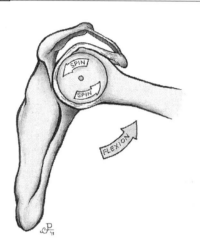

FLEXION:
- The humeral head spins and tightens the entire capsule
- To improve flexion, perform glides in an anterior, inferior, or posterior direction

Neumann D. Kinesiology of the musculoskeletal system: foundations for rehabilitation. St. Louis: Elsevier 2017.

GHJ mobilization: glide

- Parallel to the plane of treatment (concavity)
- In the opposite direction as the osteokinematic motion (rolling)

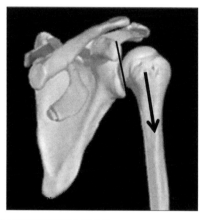

Wuelker N, Schmotzer H, Tren K, Korell M. Translation of the glenohumeral joint with simulated active elevation. Clin Orth. 1994;309:193-200.

GHJ mobilization: traction

Perpendicular and away from the plane of treatment (concavity)

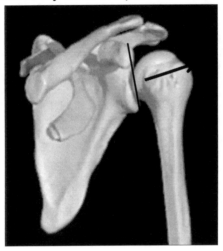

GHJ mobilization

GENERAL PRINCIPLES IN JOINT SPECIFIC MOBILIZATION OF THE GLENOHUMERAL JOINT

JOINT SPECIFIC TESTING

Should we test joint play? Not necessary, especially for large limits of capsular pattern because:

1. The motion is limited
2. If we test joint play: glides only.
3. No testing of traction because the **humeral head does not separate from the glenoid**

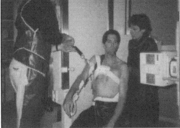

Gokeler A, van Paridon-Edauw GH, DeClercq S, Matthijs O, Dijkstra PU. Quantitative analysis of traction in the glenohumeral joint. In vivo radiographic measurements. Manual Therapy. 2003; 1-6.

GHJ mobilization

TRACTION

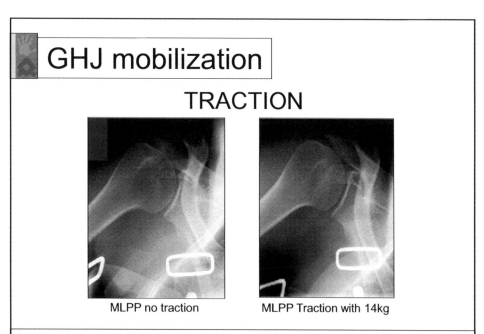

MLPP no traction   MLPP Traction with 14kg

Gokeler A, van Paridon-Edauw GH, DeClercq S, Matthijs O, Dijkstra PU. Quantitative analysis of traction in the glenohumeral joint. In vivo radiographic measurements. Manual Therapy. 2003; 1-6.

Principles of joint mobilization

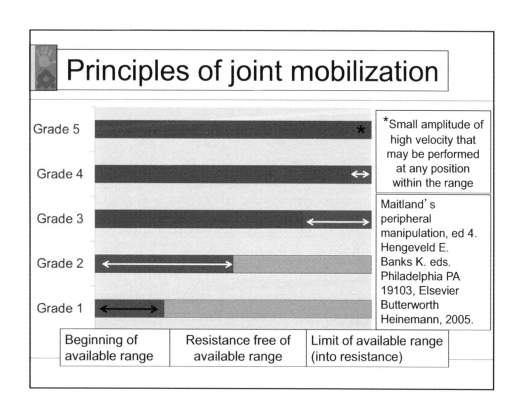

Grade 5			*Small amplitude of high velocity that may be performed at any position within the range
Grade 4			
Grade 3			Maitland's peripheral manipulation, ed 4. Hengeveld E. Banks K. eds. Philadelphia PA 19103, Elsevier Butterworth Heinemann, 2005.
Grade 2			
Grade 1			
Beginning of available range	Resistance free of available range	Limit of available range (into resistance)	

Principles of joint mobilization

Arthrokinematics

	Pain Dominant	Stiff Dominant
Position of the shoulder for the Mobilizations	*Maximum Loose Packed Position* (Resting Position of Joint)	*End Range* of available ROM to be restored (then 2-D or 3-D to increase tissue stretch)
Type of Mobilizations	*Traction* (glides)	*Glides* (tractions)
Grade of Mobilization	*Grades 1-2* (up to the resistance of the tissue)	*> Grade 2* (into the resistance of the tissue)
Qualitative	*Oscillations* – rhythmic	*Hold* the position (may also do rhythmic)

Hsu AT, Hedman T, Chang JH, et al. Changes in abduction and rotation range of motion in response to simulated dorsal and ventral translational mobilization of the glenohumeral joint. Phys Ther. 2002 Jun;82(6):544-56.

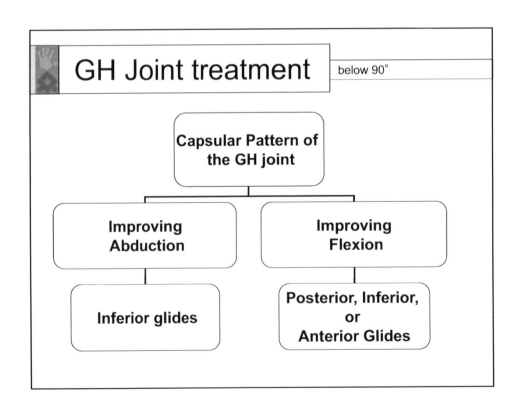

GH Joint treatment   below 90°

Capsular Pattern of the GH joint

- Improving Abduction
  - Inferior glides
- Improving Flexion
  - Posterior, Inferior, or Anterior Glides

GH Joint treatment

Addressing the inferior capsule…

The patient's scapula is stabilized to isolate motion at the GH joint

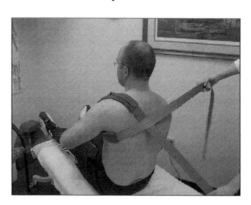

Stabilizing the Scapula….

… the belt!

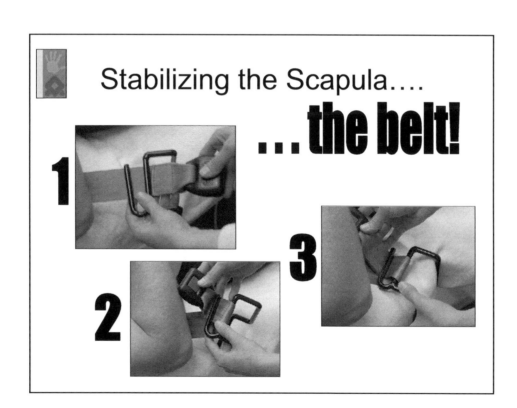

Clamp Tip

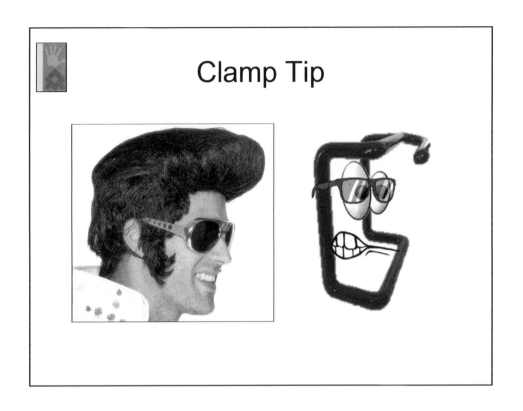

GH Joint treatment

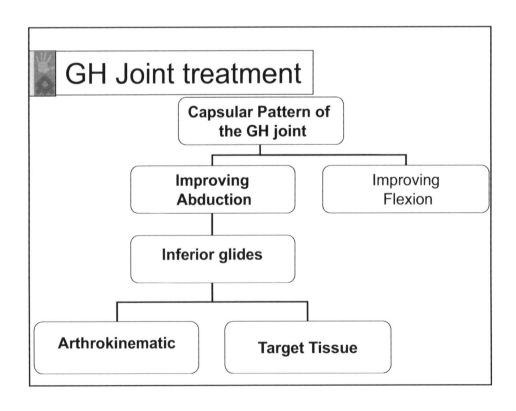

GH Joint treatment

Addressing the superior-anterior capsule…

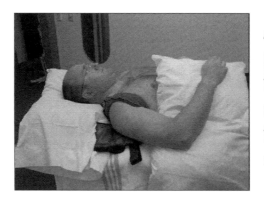

A cuff weight placed beneath the patient's scapula can further prevent scapular motion

---

GH Joint treatment

Addressing the superior-anterior capsule…

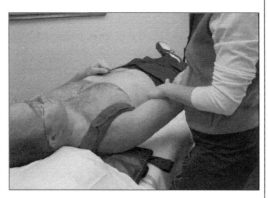

Indications:
- for large limitations
- this technique provides a stretch to the Coraco-humeral ligament (CHL)!

GH Joint treatment | Inferior glide to increase abduction

Emphasis on the inferior-anterior capsule...

Arthrokinematic method:

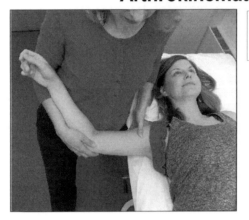

Pre-position the GH joint into:

- abduction

- extension

- ER

 GH Joint treatment | Inferior glide to increase abduction

Emphasis on the inferior-anterior capsule...

Arthrokinematic method:

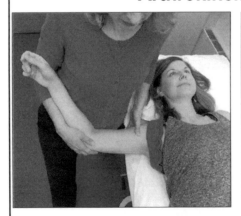

Direction of the glide:

- **Inferior, slightly lateral, slightly posterior**

- **this is an angular motion (swing the humerus): curved glide (Gr. III)**

GH Joint treatment

Inferior glide to increase abduction

Emphasis on the inferior-anterior capsule…
Arthrokinematic method:

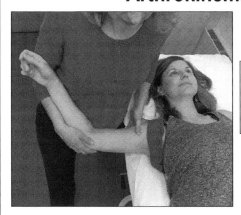

This is performed with:
• rhythmic movements
(Gr. III)

GH Joint treatment

Inferior glide to increase abduction

Emphasis on the inferior-anterior capsule…
Target Tissue Method:

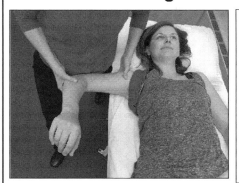

- **Translate, verses swing the humerus**

- **Great technique for patients who have impingement with arthrokinematic method!**

GH Joint treatment

Inferior glide to increase abduction

Emphasis on the inferior-anterior capsule…

Target Tissue Method:

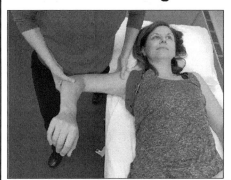

Pre-position the GH joint into:

- Abduction
- Extension
- Internal Rotation

GH Joint treatment

Inferior glide to increase abduction

Emphasis on the inferior-anterior capsule…

Target Tissue Method:

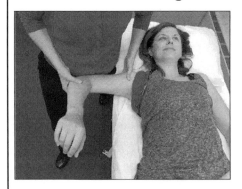

- **translate the humerus in an inferior, slightly lateral, slightly posterior direction**

GH Joint treatment

Inferior glide to increase abduction

Emphasis on the inferior-anterior capsule…

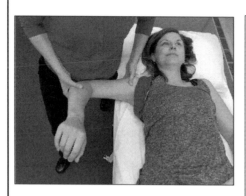

Target Tissue Method:

This can be performed with either:

- **static holds (Gr. IV) (40 seconds x 6 reps) or**

- **rhythmic movements (Gr. III)**

Neuro-muscular re-ed

Neuro-muscular re-education: to ↑ abduction

Once the mobilization is complete, remove the belt and perform:

- **PROM into abduction**

- **AAROM**

- **isometric Ω: agonist, antagonist, agonist**

- **Maintain the glide!**

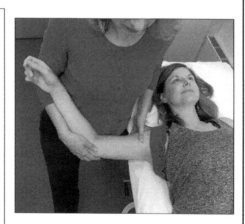

Home Program Ideas

To maintain GH abduction ROM

Inferior Capsule Stretch

- **Keep the scapula stabilized!**

- **Patient gently leans away to promote a stretch on the inferior portion of the capsule**

Home Program Ideas

To maintain GH abduction ROM

Anterior-Inferior Capsule Stretch

- **Increase the stretch on the anterior-inferior portion of the capsule by bringing the shoulder into ER**

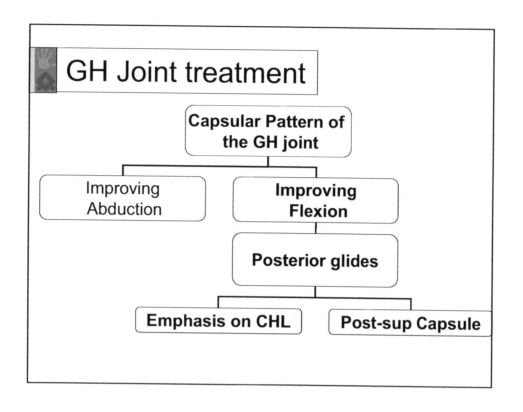

GH Joint treatment

Capsular Pattern of the GH joint

Improving Abduction

Improving Flexion

Posterior glides

Emphasis on CHL

Post-sup Capsule

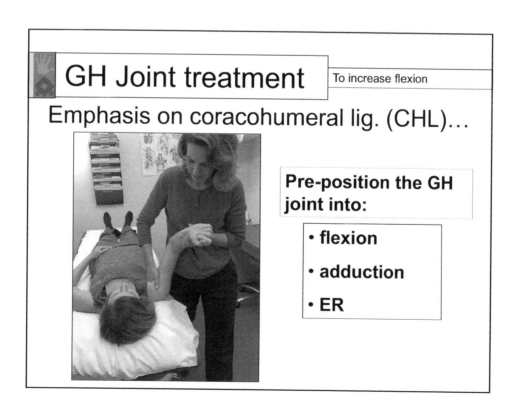

GH Joint treatment To increase flexion

Emphasis on coracohumeral lig. (CHL)…

Pre-position the GH joint into:

- **flexion**
- **adduction**
- **ER**

GH Joint treatment

Posterior glide to increase flexion

Emphasis on the CHL…

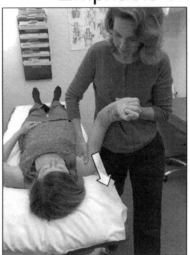

Target Tissue method

Direction of the glide:

- **Posterior, slightly superior, slightly lateral**

- **this is a translation (not an angular motion)**

GH Joint treatment

Posterior glide to increase flexion

Emphasis on CHL…

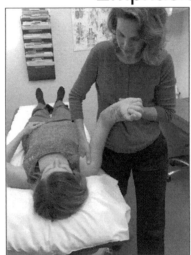

Target Tissue method

This can be performed with either:
- **static holds (40 seconds x 6 reps)**
  or
- **rhythmic movements**

GH Joint treatment

To increase flexion

Emphasis on the posterior-superior capsule

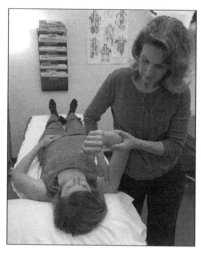

Pre-position the GH joint into:

- **flexion**
- **adduction**
- **slight IR**

GH Joint treatment

To increase flexion

Emphasis on the posterior-superior capsule

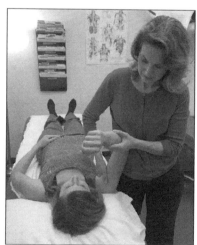

Target Tissue method

Direction of the glide:

- **Posterior, slightly superior, slightly lateral**
- **this is a translation**

GH Joint treatment To increase flexion

Emphasis on the posterior-superior capsule

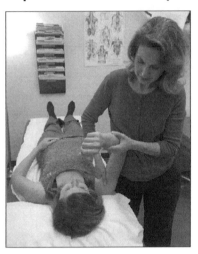

Target Tissue method

This can be performed with either:
- static holds
  (40 seconds x 6 reps)
  or
- rhythmic movements

GH Joint treatment

Neuro-muscular re-education: to ↑ flexion

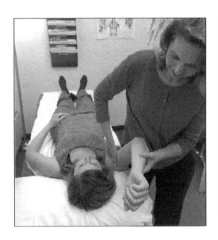

Once the mobilization is complete, perform:

- PROM into flexion

- AAROM

- isometric Ω: agonist, antagonist, agonist

- Maintain the glide!

Home Program Ideas

To maintain GH flexion ROM

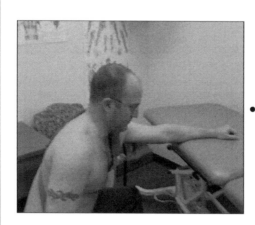

Self-Stretching technique

- The scapula is stabilized with a belt or strap to prevent elevation

Home Program Ideas

To maintain GH flexion ROM

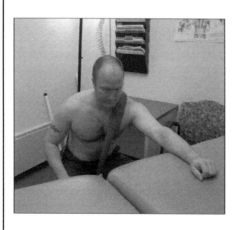

Self-stretching technique

- Patient gently leans back to promote a stretch throughout entire the capsule

Home Program Ideas

To maintain GH flexion & abduction ROM

Self-Stretching technique

- This can also be performed on a countertop!

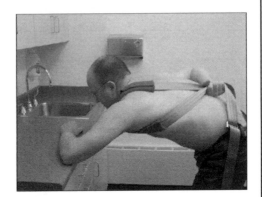

Home Program Ideas

To maintain GH joint motion

Pulleys

- **This can be used to address limitations below shoulder level**

- **Use a strap to prevent the scapula from compensating!**

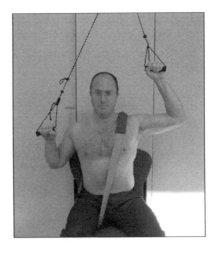

The "evidence"

Mobilization with treating ER limitations

Subjects in the ant. mobilization group had a mean improvement in external rotation ROM of 3.0°, whereas subjects in the post. mobilization group had a mean improvement of 31.3°.

Posterior mobilization showed a significant increase of ER of the shoulder. This treatment also reduces pain and improves function compared to a conventional PT treatment.

Gutiérrez Espinoza HJ, Pavez F, Guajardo C, Acosta M. Glenohumeral posterior mobilization versus conventional physiotherapy for primary adhesive capsulitis: a randomized clinical trial. Medwave 2015 Sep;15(8):e6267.

Johnson AJ, Godges JJ, Zimmerman GJ, Ounanian LL. The effect of anterior versus posterior glide joint mobilization on external rotation range of motion in patients with shoulder adhesive capsulitis. J Orthop Sports Phys Ther. 2007 Mar;37(3):88-99.

End-range GH Treatment

Orientation of the glenoid

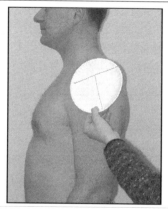

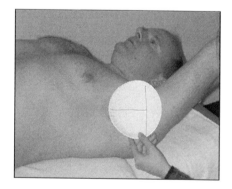

With arm at side

At end-range

The "evidence"

End-range mobilization techniques more effective with treatment of frozen shoulder, versus mid-range techniques

Yang J, Chang C, Chen S, Wang S, Lin J. Mobilization techniques in subjects with frozen shoulder syndrome: randomized multiple-treatment trial. Physical Therapy. 2007; 87: 10, 307-315.

End-range GH Joint testing

- **Anterior**: toward patient's chin

- **Inferior**: perpendicular to a line from the patient's chin to the posterior acromion and perpendicular to the scapular spine

- **Posterior**: toward the posterior acromion

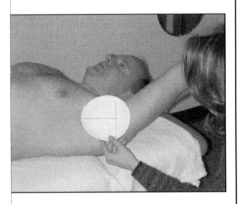

End-range GH Joint testing

Anterior

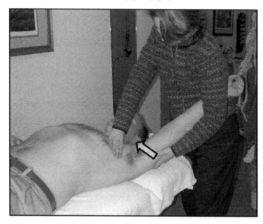

Stabilizing hand: stabilizes the scapula via placing pressure on the coracoid process

Mobilizing hand: pulls the humeral head toward the patient's chin

End-range GH Joint testing

Inferior

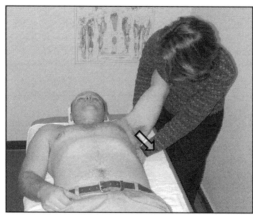

Stabilizing hand: stabilizes the scapula along the lateral border

End-range GH Joint testing

Inferior

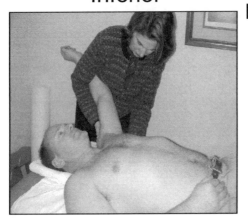

Mobilizing hand: perpendicular to a line connecting patient's chin to the posterior acromion and perpendicular to the spine of the scapula

End-range GH Joint testing

Posterior

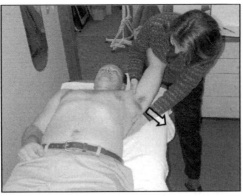

Stabilizing hand: stabilizes the scapula along the lateral border

Mobilizing hand: away from the patient's chin toward the posterior acromion

End-range GH Joint treatment

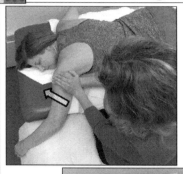

Anterior Glide

Mobilizing hand:

glides the humeral head toward the patient's chin, using opposite hand to assist (if needed)

Progression:

pre-position the shoulder in further elevation

- static holds (40 sec x 6 reps) or
- rhythmic movements

End-range GH Joint treatment

Anterior Glide: neuromuscular re-ed

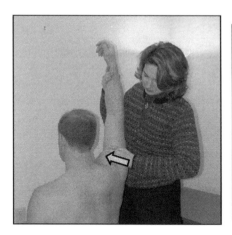

- P/AA/AROM into shoulder elevation
- Therapist assists with directing the humeral head in an anterior direction (toward the patient's chin)
- Isometric at end-range: agonist-antagonist-agonist

153

End-range GH Joint treatment

Superior Scapular glide
(Inferior glide)

Mobilizing hand:

glides the lateral aspect of the scapula in a superior direction (thereby stretching the inferior capsule)

Stabilizing hand:

stabilizes the humeral head

Progression:

pre-position the shoulder in further elevation

• curved glide, so must use rhythmic movements (Gr. III)

End-range GH Joint treatment

Inferior Glide: neuromuscular re-ed

- P/AA/AROM into shoulder elevation
- Therapist assists with directing the humeral head in an inferior direction (perpendicular to a line from the patient's chin to the posterior acromion and perpendicular to the spine of the scapula)
- Isometric at end-range: agonist-antagonist-agonist

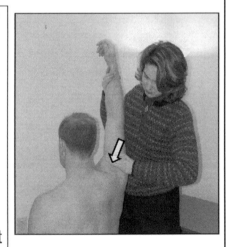

End-range GH Joint treatment

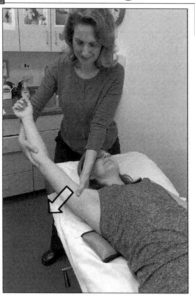

Posterior Glide

Mobilizing hand:

- glides the humeral head away from the patient's chin, toward the posterior acromion

Progression:

- pre-position the shoulder in further elevation

- static holds (40 sec x 6 reps)
  or
- rhythmic movements

End-range GH Joint treatment

Posterior Glide: Neuro-muscular Re-ed

- P/AA/AROM into shoulder elevation
- Therapist assists with directing the humeral head in a posterior direction, toward the posterior acromion
- Isometric at end-range: agonist-antagonist-agonist

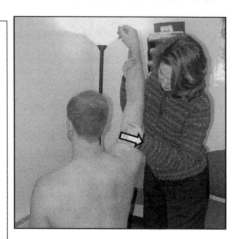

End-range GH Joint treatment

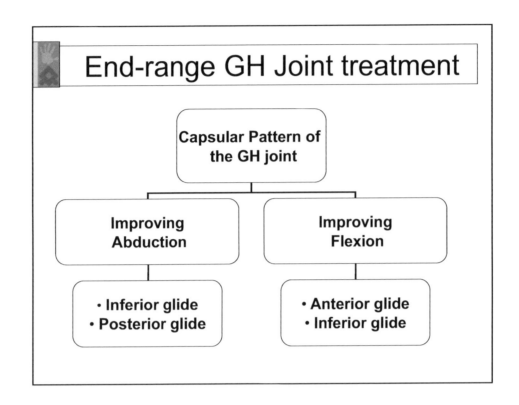

Capsular Pattern of the GH joint

Improving Abduction

- Inferior glide
- Posterior glide

Improving Flexion

- Anterior glide
- Inferior glide

Home Program Ideas

To maintain end-range shoulder motion

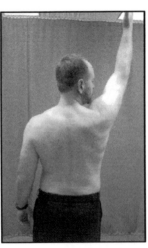

- Emphasis placed on the last 20-30° of elevation
- Strengthening in this range will promote carry-over of joint mobilization techniques!

Secondary Adhesive Capsulitis

Rotator Cuff & Scapular Stabilizer Strengthening

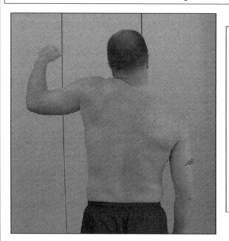

Due to the tendency of patient's with shoulder stiffness to compensate with the upper trapezius (UT), try to select exercises that minimize the UT and maximize the targeted muscle groups

Secondary Adhesive Capsulitis

Rotator Cuff Strengthening

- RCT involving 42 patients with secondary adhesive capsulitis
- One group received TENS and joint mobilization, the other TENS, joint mobilization, and rotator cuff (RC) strengthening
- 12 sessions for 4 weeks
- *Results:* Statistically significant changes were seen in all outcome measures in the RC strengthening group
- *Conclusion:* the addition of a structured RC strengthening program to TENS and joint mobilization resulted in reduction in pain and improvement in ROM and function

Rawat P, Eapen C, Seema KP. Effect of rotator cuff strengthening as an adjunct to standard care in subjects with adhesive capsulitis: a randomized controlled trial. J Hand Ther. 2017; 235-341.

Secondary Adhesive Capsulitis

Rotator Cuff Strengthening

- For patients with secondary adhesive capsulitis due to rotator cuff injury, emphasis should be given to rotator cuff strengthening

Rawat P, Eapen C, Seema KP. Effect of rotator cuff strengthening as an adjunct to standard care in subjects with adhesive capsulitis: a randomized controlled trial. J Hand Ther. 2017; 235-341.

Secondary Adhesive Capsulitis

Scapular Stabilizer Strengthening

"Strengthening of scapular stabilizers should also be introduced as soon as adequate ROM is obtained in patient with adhesive capsulitis as scapular stabilizers help to maintain the scapulohumeral rhythm that is found to be distorted in adhesive capsulitis"

Rawat P, Eapen C, Seema KP. Effect of rotator cuff strengthening as an adjunct to standard care in subjects with adhesive capsulitis: a randomized controlled trial. J Hand Ther. 2017; 235-341.

Secondary Adhesive Capsulitis

If no progress is made within

3-5 therapy visits…

Strong consideration for an
intra-articular steroid injection

This can help bring a the patient into a less-
irritable stage.

Favorable outcomes with intra-articular
injections used in combination with therapy!

Adhesive Capsulitis

Soft Tissue Treatment

Tendinitis/Tendinopathy

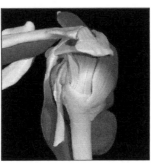

Interactive Shoulder-Primal Picture 2000

Soft Tissue Treatment Tendinitis/Tendinopathy

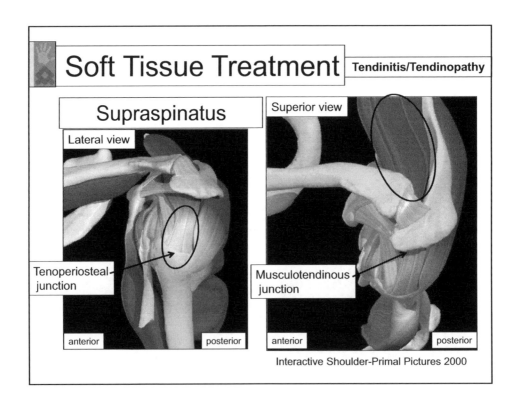

Supraspinatus

Lateral view

Superior view

Tenoperiosteal junction

Musculotendinous junction

anterior   posterior

anterior   posterior

Interactive Shoulder-Primal Pictures 2000

Soft Tissue Treatment

Tendinitis/Tendinopathy

TFM to Supraspinatus

- The patient places the forearm of the affected side behind the back, sitting in a reclined position (shoulder in IR, extension, and slight abduction)

- *If the patient is unable to place the hand in the back, the supraspinatus cannot be reached.*

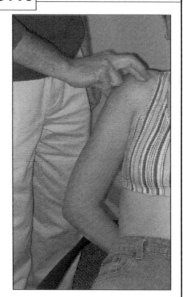

Soft Tissue Treatment

Tendinitis/Tendinopathy

TFM to Supraspinatus

With the arm internally rotated, the **greater tubercle** is now occupying the space of the lesser tubercle (when in neutral rotation). It lies inferior to the anterior "V" notch and lateral to a line adjacent to the lateral coracoid margin.

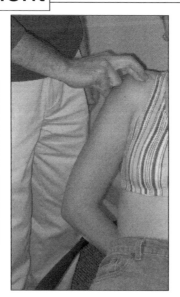

Soft Tissue Treatment

Tendinitis/Tendinopathy

TFM to Supraspinatus

Approximately 1 cm inferior to the anterior margin of the clavicle, a shelf or plateau can be palpated. The medial margin can be identified by palpating along the bony plateau medially until falling off into the intertubercular sulcus (bicipital groove). Find the anterior border of the shelf by palpating anteriorly and until falling off the shelf inferiorly.

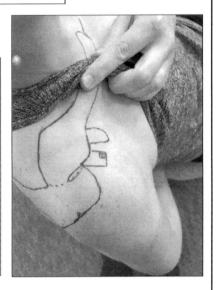

Soft Tissue Treatment

Tendinitis/Tendinopathy

TFM to Supraspinatus

The **supraspinatus insertion** is found in a 1cm by 1cm square along the anteromedial aspect of the plateau.
This is important for soft tissue treatments to differentiate between the deep and superficial fibers of the supraspinatus (differentiates between external and internal impingement)

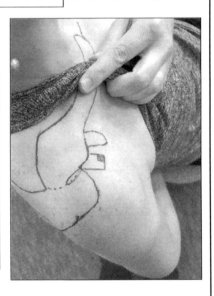

Soft Tissue Treatment

TFM to Supraspinatus

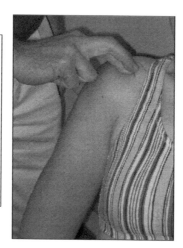

- For the *superficial fibers*, thumb placed laterally on deltoid, pressure is oriented caudal on tendon insertion
- For the *deep fibers*, thumb placed posteriorly on scapula, pressure is oriented caudal-posterior on tendon insertion

Soft Tissue Treatment

TFM to Supraspinatus

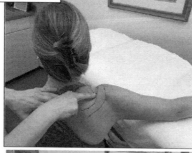

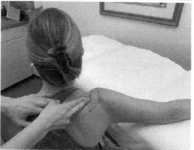

Musculotendinous junction:

-Patient's arm is supported at 90° of ABD

-The musculotendinous junction can be reached at the level of the ACJ posterior "V" notch.

-Friction is performed with the middle finger reinforced by the index in a lateral rotation motion oriented in an anterior-posterior direction.

Soft Tissue Treatment Tendinitis/Tendinopathy

Stretching to Supraspinatus

- Stabilize the scapula along the lateral border
- With the shoulder at 80° flexion and maximal ER, provide a stretch into horizontal adduction
- Acute: static stretch; subacute or chronic: rhythmic stretching

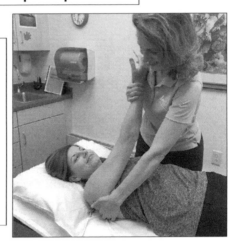

Soft Tissue Treatment Tendinitis/Tendinopathy

Infraspinatus

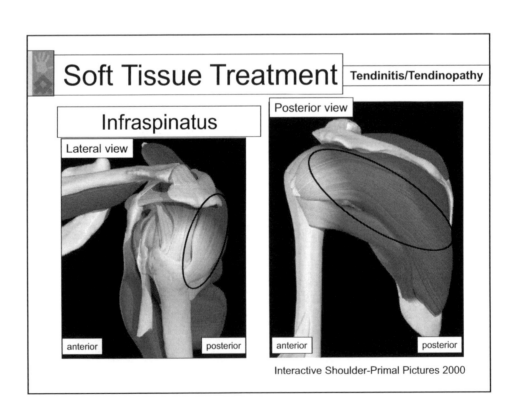

Posterior view

Lateral view

anterior   posterior

anterior   posterior

Interactive Shoulder-Primal Pictures 2000

Soft Tissue Treatment

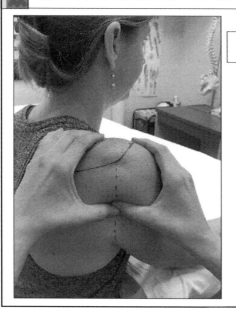

TFM to Infraspinatus

-The patient is positioned with elbows on table (with 45-60° of shoulder flexion). The shoulder is then brought into ER with the patient shifting weight over on that shoulder (providing shoulder adduction)

Soft Tissue Treatment

TFM to Infraspinatus

-Draw a helper's line from the posterior angle of the acromion inferiorly to the axilla.
-Mark an "X" on this helper's line about 2cm inferior to the posterior angle.
-Draw a medial to lateral line 1cm above this "X" and 1 cm below this "X". The space between these two lines represents the general location of the *musculotendinous junction (MTJ) of the infraspinatus.*

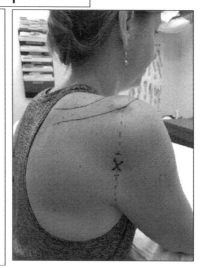

Soft Tissue Treatment

TFM to Infraspinatus

-Transverse friction can be performed to the *musculotendinous junction (MTJ) of the infraspinatus* by providing pressure from an inferior to superior direction across the tendon

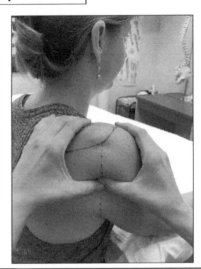

Soft Tissue Treatment

TFM to Infraspinatus

-Palpate laterally in line with the spine of the scapula until a bony ridge is reached. This bony ridge is the posterior-superior aspect of the greater tubercle, and represents the *tendinous insertion of the infraspinatus* on the greater tubercle.

-Transverse friction can be performed in an antero-medial direction on the posterior facet of the greater tuberosity

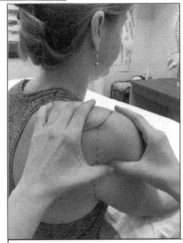

Palpation during resisted shoulder ER will confirm the location.

Soft Tissue Treatment

Tendinitis/Tendinopathy

TFM to Infraspinatus

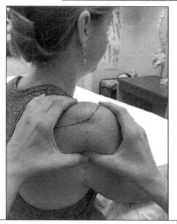

...at the
musculotendinous junction

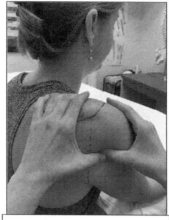

...at the
tendinous insertion

Soft Tissue Treatment

Tendinitis/Tendinopathy

Stretching to Infraspinatus

- Stabilize the scapula along the lateral border
- With the shoulder at 120° flexion in sub-maximal ER, provide a stretch into horizontal adduction
- Acute: static stretch; subacute or chronic: rhythmic stretching

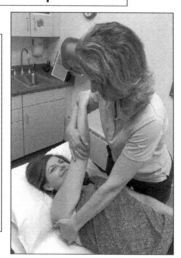

Soft Tissue Treatment | Tendinitis/Tendinopathy

Stretching to Supra & Infraspinatus

- Stabilize the scapula along the lateral border
- With the shoulder at 80-90° flexion, while exerting axial pressure through the humerus, provide a stretch into horizontal adduction
- Slight IR can be added to increase the stretch

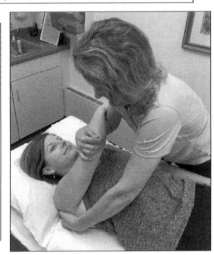

Soft Tissue Treatment | Tendinitis/Tendinopathy

Self stretch for Supra & Infraspinatus

- Stabilize the scapula along a wall to facilitate scapular retraction
- With the shoulder at 80-90° flexion and maximal ER, pull shoulder into horizontal adduction
- Acute stages: static stretch
- Subacute and chronic stages: slow rhythmic stretching

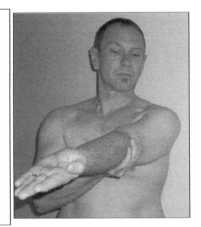

Soft Tissue Treatment

Eccentric Loading Program

Supraspinatus

Eccentric training

painful eccentric training program

3 x 15 reps, 2 times/day

7 days/week, for 12 weeks

5/9 excellent results at 12 and 52 weeks

Jonsson P, Wahlstrom P, Ohberg L, Alfredson H. Eccentric training in chronic painful impingement syndrome of the shoulder: results of a pilot study. *Knee Surg Sports TraumatolArthrosc.* 2006 Jan;14(1):76-81.

Chansky HA, Iannotti JP. The vascularity of the rotator cuff. *Clin Sports Med.* 1991; 10(4):807-22.

Impingement Management

Subscapularis:

Transverse Friction Massage (TFM)

Stretching

Microlymph Drainage
↑'d fibroblastic activity
↓'d pain
Collagen reorganization

169

Soft Tissue Treatment
Tendinitis/Tendinopathy

Subscapularis

| Anterior view |

Interactive Shoulder-Primal Pictures 2000

Soft Tissue Treatment
Tendinitis/Tendinopathy

Subscapularis

Patient Position: Sitting with the arm resting at the side
Place the middle finger over the pear shaped **lesser tubercle**. Divide the lesser tubercle into superior and inferior halves. This denotes two separate insertion sites of the **subscapularis tendon**. The *superior half* of the subscapularis tendon is most often involved with impingement during elevation in flexion.

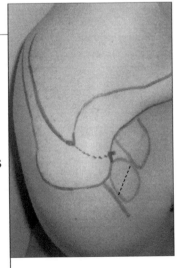

Soft Tissue Treatment

Please note that the tendon fibers run medial to lateral and continue laterally over to the medial border of the greater tubercle, forming the transverse humeral ligament that assists in restraining long head of biceps (LHB) along with the coracohumeral ligament.

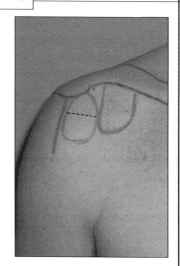

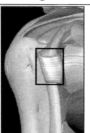

Soft Tissue Treatment

TFM to Subscapularis

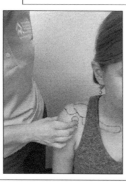  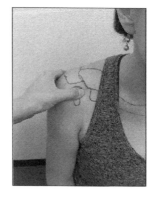

- With the patient's arm at the side, apply pressure in a posterior direction. Can use your index & middle fingers or thumb.
- Perform the TFM in a inferior to superior direction.

Soft Tissue Treatment Tendinitis/Tendinopathy

Stretching to Subscapularis

- Patient positioned in supine or in a reclined position.
- Stabilize the patient's scapula. Grasp the patient's elbow on the medial side so the patient's and therapist's forearm are parallel. The distal forearm, wrist, & hand are supported between the therapist's trunk & elbow.
- Start with the shoulder in 30° - 60° abduction with maximal ER.
- Slowly bring the patient's arm into extension and further ER.

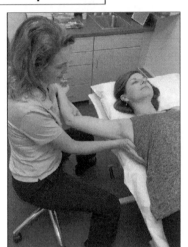

Impingement Management

Long Head of Biceps:

Transverse Friction Massage (TFM)

Stretching

Self-Stretch

| Microlymph Drainage |
| ↑'d fibroblastic activity |
| ↓'d pain |
| Collagen reorganization |

Soft Tissue Treatment

Tendinitis/Tendinopathy

Biceps-Long head

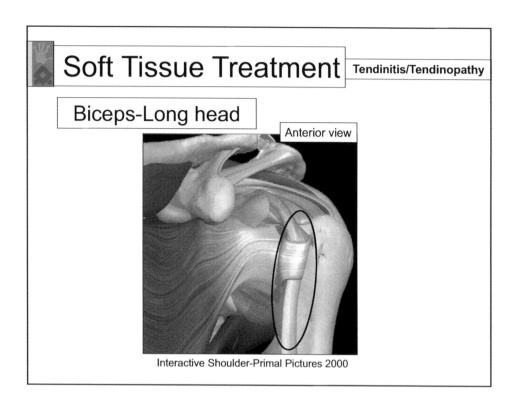

Anterior view

Interactive Shoulder-Primal Pictures 2000

Soft Tissue Treatment

TENOSYNOVITIS

TFM for biceps tenosynovitis

- The therapist grasps the patient's forearm and places the thumb (or index & middle fingers) in the bicipital groove.
- While exerting pressure, the patient's shoulder is brought from slight ER to slight IR. The therapist then relaxes the thumb and brings the forearm back to the starting position.

Soft Tissue Treatment

Stretching to LH of Biceps

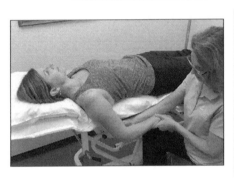 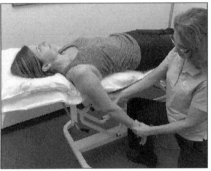

- Patient positioned in either supine or in a reclined position.
- Extend the patient's shoulder, pronates the patient's forearm, and finally extends the elbow to place maximal stretch on the long head of the biceps.

Soft Tissue Treatment

Self stretch for LH of Biceps

- The patient stabilizes the scapula by using a towel or pillow case
- Using a tabletop or counter, the patient places the forearm in pronation, elbow ext, and shoulder extension
- Acute stages: static stretch
- Subacute and chronic stages: slow rhythmic stretching

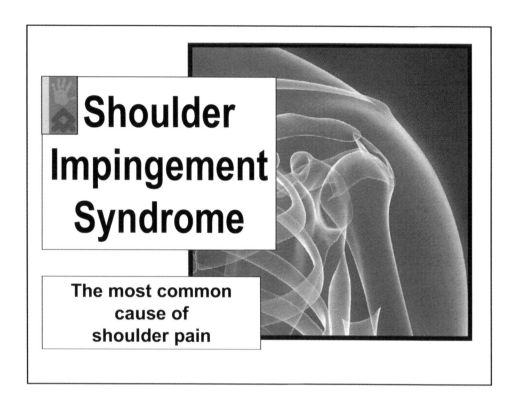

Shoulder Impingement Syndrome

The most common cause of shoulder pain

Impingement

Subacromial impingement syndrome (SIS) is a common cause of shoulder pain. Possible etiologies include a spectrum ranging from subcromial bursitis and rotator cuff tendinopathy to partial and full thickness rotator cuff tears.

Harrison AK, Flatow EL. Subacromial impingement syndrome. J Am Acad Orthop Surg. 2011;19:701-708.

Impingement

It has become evident that "Impingement Syndrome" is not likely an isolated condition that can be easily diagnosed with clinical tests or most successfully treated surgically. Rather, it is likely a *complexity of conditions involving a combination of intrinsic and extrinsic factors.*

Braman JP, Zhao KD, Lawrence RL, Harrison AK, Ludewig PM. Shoulder impingement revisited: evolution of diagnostic understanding in orthopedic surgery and physical therapy. Med Biol Eng Comput. 2014 Mar;52(3):211-219.

 ## Impingement

Disparity in understanding have developed while continuing to use the same terminology of "shoulder impingement syndrome".

These differing perspectives of therapists and surgeons appear to be causing increasing difficulties in communication with regard to both patient care and scientific investigation of the condition, its origins, and appropriate interventions.

Braman JP, Zhao KD, Lawrence RL, Harrison AK, Ludewig PM. Shoulder impingement revisited: evolution of diagnostic understanding in orthopedic surgery and physical therapy. Med Biol Eng Comput. 2014 Mar;52(3):211-219.

Impingement

Classifying patients with "impingement" based on the underlying etiology would be more effective in describing the condition.

Braman JP, Zhao KD, Lawrence RL, Harrison AK, Ludewig PM. Shoulder impingement revisited: evolution of diagnostic understanding in orthopedic surgery and physical therapy. Med Biol Eng Comput. 2014 Mar;52(3):211-219.

 # Impingement

Impingement is multifactoral

- **Anatomical**
- **Biomechanical**
- **Trauma**
- **Degeneration**
- **Vascular Δ's**

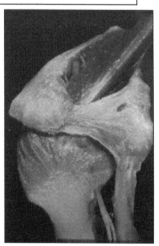

Analysis of shoulder Impingement

Etiology	Location	Pattern
Intrinsic Extrinsic -Outlet -Non-outlet	Internal (Non-outlet) -Posterosuperior -Anterosuperior External -Subacromial (Outlet) -Subcoracoid (Non-outlet)	Primary Secondary

Analysis of shoulder Impingement

Etiology

Intrinsic:
Partial to full thickness tendon tears occur as a result of the degenerative process that occurs over time with overuse, tension overload, or trauma of the tendons.

Extrinsic:
Inflammation and degeneration of the tendon as a result of mechanical compression by structures external to the tendon.

Umer M, Qadir I, Azam M. Subacromial impingement syndrome. Orthopedic Reviews 2012; 4:e18.

Intrinsic Impingement

Intrinsic impingement theorizes that partial or full thickness tendon tears occur as a result of the degenerative process that occurs over time with overuse, tension overload, or trauma of the tendons.

Umer M, Qadir I, Azam M. Subacromial impingement syndrome. Orthopedic Reviews 2012; 4:e18.

Factors
1. Muscle Fatigue
- overloaded weak muscles
- eccentric tension load
- associated with proximal humeral migration
2. Shoulder Overuse
- soft tissue inflammation
- repetitive microtrauma
- athletes / manual laborers
3. Degenerative Tendinopathy
- 1° intrinsic degeneration of RC
- ? hypovascularity
- increasing incidence with age

Extrinsic Impingement

Inflammation and degeneration of the tendon occur as a result of mechanical compression by structures external to the tendon.

Umer M, Qadir I, Azam M. Subacromial impingement syndrome. Orthopedic Reviews 2012; 4:e18.

Analysis of shoulder Impingement

Etiology	Location	Pattern
Intrinsic **Extrinsic** -Outlet -Non-outlet	**Internal** (Non-outlet) -Posterosuperior -Anterosuperior **External** -Subacromial (Outlet) -Subcoracoid (Non-outlet)	**Primary** **Secondary**

Analysis of shoulder Impingement

Location

Internal: (Non-outlet)
Compression on the articular side of the RC tendons.
- -Posterosuperior
- -Anterosuperior

External:
Compression on the bursal side of the RC tendons.
- -Subacromial **(Outlet)**
- -Subcoracoid **(Non-outlet)**

Analysis of shoulder Impingement

Location

Internal Impingement	External Impingement
• under 40 years of age • more active population • deep rotator cuff lesion (articular side)	• over 40 years of age • referred pain over the deltoid region • superficial rotator cuff lesions (bursal side-beneath the acromion)

Internal Impingement: **Posterosuperior**

- First discussed by Walch et al. in 1992 as a cause of pain in overhead throwing athletes with extreme abduction and external rotation of the arm.

- Repetitive and excessive impingement between the humeral head and posterosuperior glenoid with impingement upon the interposed rotator cuff and posterosuperior glenoid labrum.

Internal Impingement: **Posterosuperior**

www.pixabay.com

Clinical Presentation

- posterior shoulder pain
- occurs with throwing and overhead activities
- may be associated with subtle shoulder instability

Davidson et al. Rotator cuff and posterior-superior glenoid labrum injury associated with increased glenohumeral motion: A new site of impingement. J Shoulder Elbow Surg 1995; 4:384-90.

Tramontana A, Moneteleone G, Tiloca A, et al. Internal impingement in overhead athletes: an ultrasound imaging proposal. Ultrasonography. 2018;Jul;37(3):275-276.

Internal Impingement: **Anterosuperior**

- Described by Gerber & Sebesta in 2000 as a clinical entity responsible for unexplained shoulder pain.

- Impingement between the insertion of the subscapularis tendon and biceps pulley (SGHL, CHL, superior subscapularis) with the anterior glenoid occurring in flexion, adduction and internal rotation.

Internal Impingement: **Anterosuperior**

Clinical Presentation

- anterior shoulder pain
- occurs in follow-through phase of activities

Maria Kirilenko forehand follow through
Tennis.topbuzz.com

Internal Impingement: **Anterosuperior**

Pulley lesion
- **pattern 1: isolated SGHL lesion**
- **pattern 2: SGHL , partial articular-side supraspinatus tendon tear**
- **pattern 3: SGHL, deep surface of subscapularis tendon**
- **pattern 4: SGHL, partial articular-side supraspinatus & subscap tendon tears**

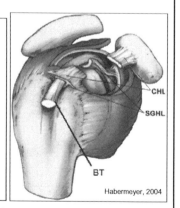

Habermeyer, 2004

Barber FA, Field LD, Ryu RKN. Biceps tendon and superior labrum injuries: Decision making. J Bone and Joint Surg Am. 2007:89:1844-55.

Habermeyer P, Magosch P, Pritsch M, Scheibel M, Lichtenberg S. Anterosuperior impingement of the shoulder as a result of pulley lesions: a prospective arthroscopic study. *J Shoulder Elbow Surg.* 2004; 13: 5-12.

Internal Impingement: **Anterosuperior**

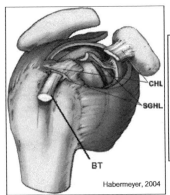

Habermeyer, 2004

Prevalence of pulley lesions:
-evaluated 1007 shoulder
arthroscopies; 72 patients
presented with pulley lesion as the
main pathologic finding (7.1%)

Barber FA, Field LD, Ryu RKN. Biceps tendon and superior labrum injuries: Decision making. J Bone and Joint Surg Am. 2007:89:1844-55.

Baumann B, Genning K, Bohm D, Rolf O, Gohlke F. Arthroscopic prevelance of pulley lesions in 1007 consecutive patients. *J Shoulder Elbow Surg.* 2008; 17: 14-20.

 Internal Impingement: **Anterosuperior**

Associated Findings:

Anterosuperior humeral head translation (pulley lesion leads to instability of the Long Head of Biceps (LHB), and LHB subluxation/dislocation decreases anterior stability)

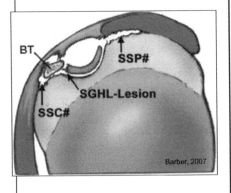

Barber, 2007

Barber FA, Field LD, Ryu RKN. Biceps tendon and superior labrum injuries: Decision making. J Bone and Joint Surg Am. 2007:89:1844-55.

Internal Impingement: **Anterosuperior**

Is there an association between SLAP Lesions and Biceps Pulley Lesions?

- prospectively analyzed 3,395 shoulder arthroscopies performed by 2 surgeons between 2004-2008
- The presence of a SLAP lesion & pulley lesion was significantly rare
- A history of falling on the abducted & ER'd arm was typical in patients with SLAP lesions
- A history of falling on the arm with IR was often noted in patients with pulley lesions.

Patzer T, Kircher J, Lichtenberg S, et al. Is there an association between SLAP and biceps pulley lesions? Arthroscopy: J of Arthroscopic & Related Surg. 2011:27(5):611-618

External Impingement: **Subacromial**

- First described by Charles Neer in 1852 to mean an anatomic narrowing between the head of the humerus and the acromion.
- Bursitis and subacromial inflammation leading to intrasubstance tendon microtears, tendinosis and ultimately gross tears.
- The exact pathogenesis of rotator cuff disease remains controversial.
- Bursal sided tears more common.

External Impingement: **Subacromial**

Stages of impingement according to Neer:

Stage 1: edema and hemorrhage of the bursa and cuff is typical in persons under twenty-five years old.

Stage 2: involves irreversible changes, such as fibrosis and tendinitis of the rotator cuff, and typically occurs in patients who are twenty-five to forty years old.

Stage 3: marked by partial or complete tears of the rotator cuff and usually is seen in patients over forty years of age.

 External Impingement: **Subacromial**

Clinical Presentation

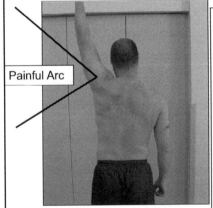

Painful Arc

- referred pain to the deltoid, but can occur distally to the elbow
- most significant diagnostic feature: painful arc of motion

(usually between 80-130°)

Flatow et al. Excursion of the rotator cuff under the acromion. Am J Sports Med. 1994; 22,6:779-788.

External Impingement: **Subacromial**

A more global view ...

- Many diagnoses associated with subacromial pain include rotator cuff pathology, shoulder instability, scapular dysfunction, biceps pathology, superior labrum anterior to posterior (SLAP) lesions, and chronic stiffness of the posterior capsule are the most common

Cools AM, Cambier D, Witvrouw EE. Screening the athlete's shoulder for impingement symptoms: a clinical reasoning algorithm for early detection of shoulder pathology. Br J Sports Med. 2008:42:628-635.

External Impingement: **Subacromial**

FACTORS ATTRIBUTED TO EXTERNAL IMPINGEMENT:

- Scapular downward rotation and anterior tilt
- Kyphotic thoracic posture
- Insufficient humeral head control from weakness or pain
- Swelling of the rotator cuff and bursal soft tissues
- Downsloping shape of the acromion
- Subacromial spurring or osteophyte formation

Bleichert S, Renaud G, MacDermid J, et al. Rehabilitation of symptomatic atraumatic degenerative rotator cuff tears: a clinical commentary on assessment and management. J Hand Ther. 2017;30:125-135.

External Impingement: **Subacromial**

Role of acromial morphology

Outlet view

Type 1: Flat 20% of normal pop.	**Type 2**: Curved 40% of normal pop.	**Type 3**: Hooked 40% of normal pop.; 80% of RC tears

Bigliani / Assess on Supraspinatous Outlet View / Scapula Lateral
http://www.boneschool.com/upper-limb/shoulder/rotator-cuff/impingement/impingement

---

External Impingement: **Subacromial**

Outlet Impingement

Possibility of 5 Structures that could be affected…

- Subacromial Bursa
- Supraspinatus (Superficial)
- Infraspinatus (Superficial)
- Subscapularis (Proximal)
- Long head of the biceps (Proximal)

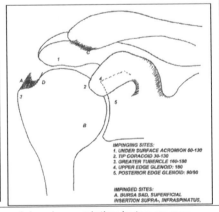

IMPINGING SITES:
1. UNDER SURFACE ACROMION 60-130
2. TIP CORACOID 30-130
3. GREATER TUBERCLE 160-180
4. UPPER EDGE GLENOID: 180
5. POSTERIOR EDGE GLENOID: 90/90

IMPINGED SITES:
A. BURSA SAD, SUPERFICIAL
INSERTION SUPRA-, INFRASPINATUS,

Panni et al. Histologic analysis of the coracoacromial arch: correlation between age-related changes and rotator cuff tears. Arthroscopy. 1996; 12: 531-540.

External Impingement: **Subcoracoid**

Clinical Presentation

- anterior shoulder pain
- most significant diagnostic feature: painful arc of motion (usually between 80-130°)

Garofalo R, et al. Subcoracoid impingement syndrome: a painful shoulder condition related to different pathologic factors. Musculoskelet Surg. 2011; 95: S25-S29.

Gerber C, Terrier F, Ganz R. The role of the coracoid process in the chronic impingement syndrome, *J Bone Joint Surg* 1985, 67B, 703-8.

External Impingement: **Subcoracoid**

Non-outlet Impingement

Potential structures involved:

Subscapularis

Long Head Biceps (LHB) Tendon

LHB Tenosynovium

Loose Bodies

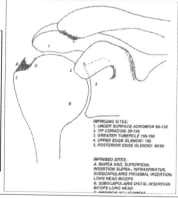

Gerber C, Terrier F, Ganz R. The role of the coracoid process in the chronic impingement syndrome, *J Bone Joint Surg* 1985, 67B, 703-8.

Analysis of shoulder Impingement

Etiology	Location	Pattern
Intrinsic	Internal (Non-outlet) -Posterosuperior -Anterosuperior	Primary
Extrinsic -Outlet -Non-outlet	External -Subacromial (Outlet) -Subcoracoid (Non-outlet)	Secondary

Analysis of shoulder Impingement

Pattern

Primary:
Direct result of compression of the rotator cuff tendons between the humeral head and the overlying anterior third of the acromion, coracoacromial lig., coracoid, or AC joint.

Secondary:
Impingement or compressive symptoms may result from underlying instability of the GH joint. May be associated with attenuation of static stabilizers of the GH joint. May also be associated with dynamic instability of the RC and scapular stabilizers.

21.2 Current concepts of orthopaedic physical therapy, 3rd ed.

Primary Impingement

Types of primary impingement:
-Subacromial
-Subcoracoid

Can occur as a result of:
-Reduction of the subacromial space: shape of acromion
-Space occupying structure such as subacromial or ACJ bone spurs
-scapular kinematics, humeral kinematics

Bleichert S, et al. Rehabilitation of symptomatic atraumatic degenerative rotator cuff tears: a clinical commentary on assessment and management. J Hand Ther. 2017;30:125-135.

Secondary Impingement

Results from underlying instability of the GH joint or scapula.

GHJ Instability

Possible causes:
-Labral injury
-Laxity or injury of the static stabilizers (ligaments, labrum)
-Weakness of the dynamic stabilizers (RC cuff musculature)
-Decreased proprioception and neuromuscular control of the GHJ.

Secondary Impingement

Os Acromiale

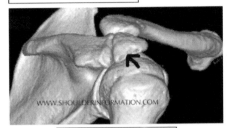

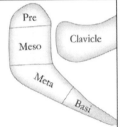

- results from failure of an anterior acromial ossification center to fuse to the acromial process;
- ossification centers appear at age 15 and should fuse by age 22-25;

- mesoacromion most common
- hypermobile unfused epiphysis
- tilts anteriorly
- 1-15% normal population
- increased incidence with impingement

Secondary Impingement

Other possible causes

- Tuberosity fracture nonunion/malunion
- Calcific tendonitis
- Iatrogenic

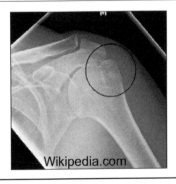

Wikipedia.com

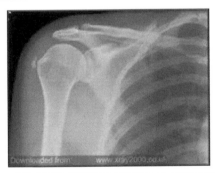

Impingement-Contributing Factors

Scapulothoracic Motion:

The scapula functions as a "bridge" between the shoulder complex and the cervical spine and plays a very important role in providing both mobility and stability to the neck/shoulder region.

Cools AMJ, Struyf F, De Mey K, et al. Rehabilitation of scapular dyskinesis: from the office worker to the elite overhead athlete. Br J Sports Med. 2014 Apr;48(8):692-697.

Impingement-Contributing Factors

Alterations in Scapulothoracic Motion:

Shoulder impingement patients are particularly affected by scapular dyskinesis

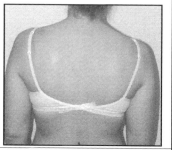

Kibler WB, Ludewig PM, McClure PW, et al. Clinical implications of scapular dyskinesis in shoulder injury: the 2013 consensus statement from the "scapular summit". Br J Sports Med. 2013;47:877-885.

Kibler WB, Uhl TL, Maddux WQ, Brooks PV, Zeller B, McMullen J. Qualitative clinical evaluation of scapular dysfunction: A reliability study. J Shoulder Elbow Surg 2002; 11:550-6.

Impingement-Contributing Factors

Scapulothoracic Motion:

NORMAL SCAPULAR MOTION
with humeral elevation:

- Upward rotation

- Posterior tilt

- Either internal or external rotation

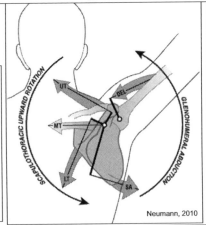

Neumann, 2010

Neumann D. Kinesiology of the musculoskeletal system: foundations for rehabilitation. 2nd ed. St. Louis: Mosby 2010.

Ludwig PM, Phadke V, Braman JP, et al. Motion of the shoulder during multiplanar humeral elevation. J Bone Joint Surg Am. 2009;91:378-389.

 # Impingement-Contributing Factors

- Subacromial pain is viewed as a "dynamic condition" (movement-related) versus a "static" anatomical phenomenon

Castelein B, Cagnie B, Cools A. Scapular muscle dysfunction associated with subacromial pain syndrome. J Hand Ther. 2017;30:136-146.

Impingement-Contributing Factors

Alterations in Scapulothoracic Motion:

The most frequent findings:

- **Reduced upward rotation**

- **Reduced posterior tilting**

- **Increased internal rotation**

Ludwig PM, Reynolds JF. The association of scapular kinematics and glenohumeral joint pathologies. J Orthop Sports Phys Ther. 2009;39:90-104.

Castelein B, Cagnie F, Cools A. Scapular muscle dysfunction associated with subacromial pain. J Hand Ther. 2017;30:136-146.

Impingement-Contributing Factors

Alterations in Scapulothoracic Motion:

"It is unclear if scapular alterations are compensatory (results from injury) or contributory (predisposes the subject to injury) to shoulder pathology."

Castelein B, Cagnie F, Cools A. Scapular muscle dysfunction associated with subacromial pain. J Hand Ther. 2017;30:136-146.

Impingement-Contributing Factors

Muscular contributions:

- **The trapezius (upper, middle, and lower trap) and the serratus anterior work together as a "force couple" which is necessary for optimal scapular movement**

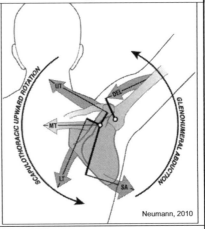

Neumann, 2010

Neumann D. Kinesiology of the musculoskeletal system: foundations for rehabilitation. 2nd ed. St. Louis: Mosby 2010.

Castelein B, Cagnie B, Cools A. Scapular muscle dysfunction associated with subacromial pain syndrome. J Hand Ther. 2017;30:136-146.

 # Impingement-Contributing Factors

Muscle Performance problems related to subacromial pain:

| **Strength deficits** | **Muscle Activation Alterations** |

Castelein B, Cagnie F, Cools A. Scapular muscle dysfunction associated with subacromial pain. J Hand Ther. 2017;30:136-146.

Impingement-Contributing Factors

Strength deficits

- Compared the isokinetic muscle performance of the scapular muscles (protraction and retraction, at low & high velocity) between overhead athletes with subacromial pain and uninjured overhead athletes
- Those with subacromial pain showed decreased force output/body weight at both velocities in the protractor muscles compared to the uninjured side & the control

Cools AM, et al. Isokinetic scapular muscle performance in overhead athletes with and without shoulder impingement symptoms. J Athl Train. 2005;40:104-110.

 # Impingement-Contributing Factors

Strength deficits

- On both sides of the subjects with subacromial pain, the patient group had significantly lower protraction/retraction ratios than the control group, measured at low velocity
- These results confirm that patients with subacromial pain show abnormal muscle strength performance at the scapulothoracic joint

Cools AM, et al. Isokinetic scapular muscle performance in overhead athletes with and without shoulder impingement symptoms. J Athl Train. 2005;40:104-110.

Impingement-Contributing Factors

Muscle Activation Alterations

- Systematic review summarizing the differences in scapulothoracic muscle EMG activity in patients with subacromial pain compared to healthy subjects
- 3 of the 6 articles found <u>increased upper trap (UT) activity</u>
- 3 of 5 articles showed <u>decreased lower trap (LT) and serratus anterior (SA) activity</u>

Struyf F, Cagnie B, Cools A. Scapulothoracic muscle activity and recruitment timing in patients with shoulder impingement symptoms and glenohumeral joint instability. J Electromyogr Kinesiol. 2014;24:277-284.

Impingement-Contributing Factors

Muscle Activation Alterations

- Scapulothoracic muscle activity was compared between patients with subacromial pain and healthy controls during arm elevation tasks
- Results: during all arm elevation tasks, the **pect minor** was significantly more active in the subacromial impingement group compared to the healthy controls

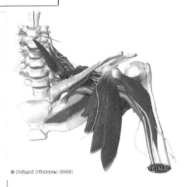

Castelein B, Cagnie F, Parlevliet T, et al. Scapulothoracic muscle activity during elevation tasks measured with surface and fine wire EMG: a comparative study between patients with subacromial impingement syndrome and healthy controls. Man Ther. 2016;23:33-39.

Impingement-Contributing Factors

Muscle Activation Alterations

SUMMARY

- increased upper trap (UT) activity
- increased pect minor activity
- decreased lower trap (LT) and serratus anterior (SA) activity

Other findings:

- Shorter pect minor
- Higher prevalence of trigger points in the levator scap

Castelein B, Cagnie F, Cools A. Scapular muscle dysfunction associated with subacromial pain. J Hand Ther. 2017;30:136-146.

Impingement-Contributing Factors

Relationship between posterior shoulder tightness & impingement

Ticker JB, Beim GM, Warner JJ. Recognition and treatment of refractory posterior capsular contracture of the shoulder. *Arthroscopy* 2000; 16:27-34.

Bach H, Goldberg B. Posterior capsular contracture of the shoulder. J of Amer Academy of Orthopaedic Surg. 2006; 14 (5): 265-277.

Kibler WB, Sciascia A, Thomas SJ. Glenohumeral internal rotation deficit: pathogenesis and response to acute throwing.Sports Med Arthrosc.2012;20:34–38.

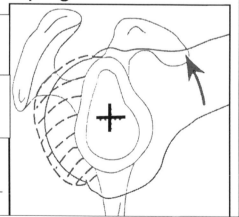

Downar JM, Sauers EL. Clinical measures of shoulder mobility in the professional baseball player. J Athl Train. 2005;40:23-29.

Impingement-Contributing Factors

Relationship between posterior shoulder tightness & impingement

Ticker JB, Beim GM, Warner JJ. Recognition and treatment of refractory posterior capsular contracture of the shoulder. *Arthroscopy* 2000; 16:27-34.

Bach H, Goldberg B. Posterior capsular contracture of the shoulder. J of Amer Academy of Orthopaedic Surg. 2006; 14 (5): 265-277.

Kibler WB, Sciascia A, Thomas SJ. Glenohumeral internal rotation deficit: pathogenesis and response to acute throwing.Sports Med Arthrosc.2012;20:34–38.

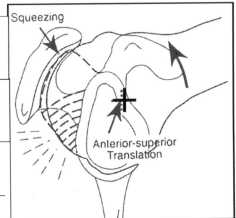

Squeezing

Anterior-superior Translation

Downar JM, Sauers EL. Clinical measures of shoulder mobility in the professional baseball player. J Athl Train. 2005;40:23-29.

Impingement-Contributing Factors

GIRD (Glenohumeral Internal Rotation Deficit)

- An adaptive process in which the throwing shoulder experiences a loss of internal rotation
- *Definition*: loss of IR with combined with loss of total rotational motion
- Associated with posterior-superior labral tears, partial articular-sided rotator cuff tears, and SLAP lesions
- *Mainstay of treatment*: posterior capsule stretching and strengthening to improve scapular mechanics

Rose M & Noonan T. Glenohumeral internal rotation deficit in throwing athletes: current perspectives. Journal of Sports Medicine. 2018;69-78.

Impingement-Contributing Factors

Posterior Shoulder & Diabolo Effect

-found that peak contact pressure beneath the subacromial arch significantly increased with posterioinferior capsule tightness during the follow-through phase of throwing

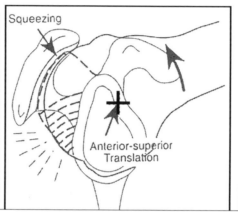

Squeezing

Anterior-superior
Translation

Muraki, et al. Effect of posteroinferior capsule tightness on contact pressure and area beneath the coracoacromial arch during pitching motion. Am J Sports Med. 2010; 38:600-607.

 # Impingement-Contributing Factors

Testing for posterior shoulder tightness

Posterior-Superior:	Posterior-Inferior:
• Can limit ability to reach behind back • Tested in a standing position	• Can limit ability to IR shoulder in an abducted position (example: don/doffing shirts or coats) • Tested in standing or supine

Impingement-Contributing Factors

Testing the Posterior-Superior Shoulder

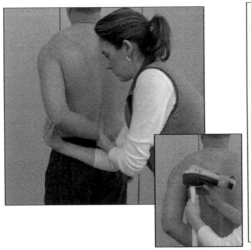

- Patient stands with arms relaxed
- Therapist brings arm behind back (achieving full shoulder adduction), then gently pulls forearm off patient's low back into further IR

Impingement-Contributing Factors

Testing the Posterior-Superior Shoulder

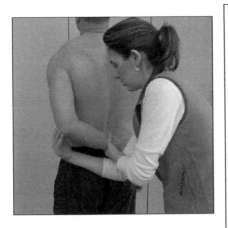

- If patient's arm cannot be brought behind back, no need to continue the test
- Monitor scapular position with testing: if scapula moves significantly, also an indication of capsular tightness

Impingement-Contributing Factors

For Posterior-Inferior Shoulder Tightness

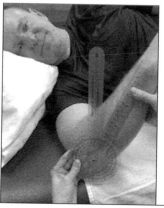

- Patient is in sidelying (scaption plane) with the shoulder in abduction
- While maintaining scapular stabilization, passive internal rotation is assessed

Lunden JB, Muffenbier M, Giveans MR, et al. Reliability of shoulder internal rotation passive range of motion measurements in the supine versus sidelying position. JOSPT. 2010; 40(9): 589-594.

Impingement-Contributing Factors

For Posterior-Inferior Shoulder Tightness

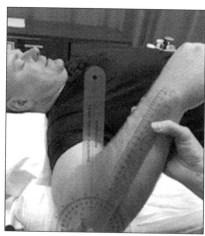

- Alternate position: patient in supine (if unable to tolerate sidelying due to shoulder pain

Impingement-Contributing Factors

Posterior Shoulder & Ant Scapular Tilt

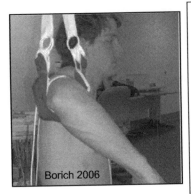

Borich 2006

- the IR deficit group had a significantly greater scapular anterior tilt (9.2°)
- Conclusion: these findings demonstrate a significant relationship between GHJ IR deficit & abnormal scapular positioning, particularly increased anterior tilt

Borich, et al. Scapular angular positioning at end range internal rotation in cases of glenohumeral internal rotation deficit. J Orthop Sports Phys Ther. 2006; 36(12): 926-934.

Impingement-Contributing Factors

Thoracic Spine Restrictions

Conclusion:
The mobility of the thoracic spine should receive more attention in the diagnosis and therapy of patients
with shoulder outlet impingement syndrome.

Theisen et al. Co-occurrence of outlet impingement syndrome of the shoulder and restricted range of motion in the thoracic spine - a prospective study with ultrasound-based motion analysis. BMC Musculoskeletal Disorders 2010, 11:135

Clinical Examination   EXTRA TESTS

What if there is no painful arc?

> patient is over 40
> presents with C5 referred pain
> pain provocation with resisted ER

We need other tests!

 Extra tests for impingement

- In the absence of a capsular pattern, it is very likely that the problem is an impingement.
- If there are no positive clinical signs from the basic evaluation, i.e. painful arc, painful passive elevation, then perform extra tests:
  - Hawkins-Kennedy
  - Subcoracoid impingement test

Extra tests for impingement

Hawkins-Kennedy test: for external impingement

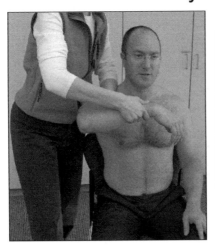

This test only needs to be performed if you do not have a

Painful Arc or
(+) Passive Elevation Test in the Basic Clinical Exam!

Extra tests for impingement

Hawkins-Kennedy test: for external impingement

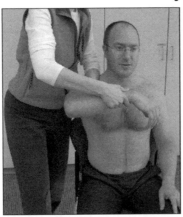

- Patient's scapula is stabilized by the therapist's forearm placed on the superior aspect of shoulder girdle
- The patients shoulder is brought passively into 90° of flex with IR

Gismerivik SO, Drogset JO, Granviken, et al. Physical examination tests of the shoulder: a systematic review and meta-analysis of diagnostic test performance. BMC Musculoskeletal Disord. 2017;18(1):41-50.

Extra tests for impingement

Hawkins-Kennedy test: for external impingement

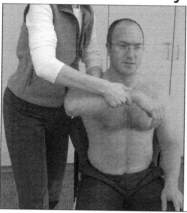

- Over-pressure is exerted into IR
- (+) test: reproduces bursal pain or patient's vague C5 pain

Sensitivity: 87-92%; Specificity: 25-44%

Gismerivik SO, Drogset JO, Granviken, et al. Physical examination tests of the shoulder: a systematic review and meta-analysis of diagnostic test performance. BMC Musculoskeletal Disord. 2017;18(1):41-50.

Extra tests for impingement

Hawkins-Kennedy test: for internal impingement?

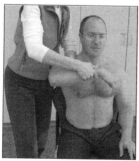

- Authors found this test narrows the distance between the insertions of the subscap and supraspinatus and anterosuperior labrum, which leads to impingement mechanism (i.e. anterosuperior internal impingement)
- Need to focus on the location of the patient's pain:
  - If more lateral deltoid, consider external impingement
  - If more anterosuperior, consider internal

Leschinger T, Wallraff C, Muller D, et al. Internal impingement of the shoulder: a risk of false positive test outcomes in external impingment tests? BioMed Research International. 2017;2017:2941238.

Extra tests for impingement

Subcoracoid impingement test

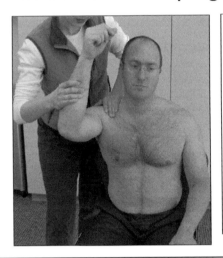

- Indications: for patients with anterior shoulder pain
- Patient's scapula is stabilized via the superior aspect of shoulder girdle
- The shoulder is passively brought into flexion, then adduction

Extra tests for impingement

Subcoracoid impingement test

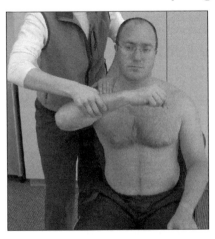

- Patients arm is then passively brought into IR
- (+) test: anterior shoulder pain is provoked with internal rotation

Extra tests for impingement

Modified Relocation Test for Posterior Internal Impingement

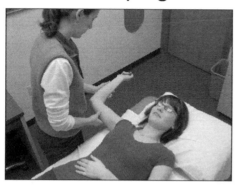

- Indications: patients with pain at end-range shoulder elevation
- The patient's shoulder is passively abducted to 90°, then externally rotated to end-range

Extra tests for impingement

Modified Relocation Test

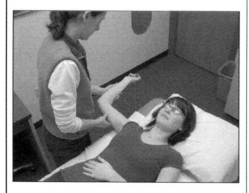

Is pain produced? Where?

- Anterior pain: indicative of an anterior-inferior instability
- Posterior pain: indicative of an internal impingement

Extra tests for impingement

Modified Relocation test

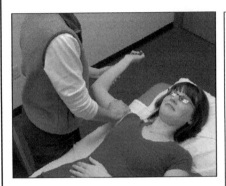

- Push the humeral head in a posterior direction (to relocate it)
- If the patient's anterior pain goes away with posterior relocation, this is a (+) test.
- The patient's posterior pain may not change with relocation.

Exam findings

Tendinopathy versus Tenosynovitis

Tendinopathy

- resisted test must be painful

Tenosynovitis

- stretch test must be painful

Exam findings

Lesions of the Biceps

- Painful arc or painful external impingement test
- **Tendinopathy**: Resisted test must be most painful
- **Tenosynovitis**: Stretch test must be most painful

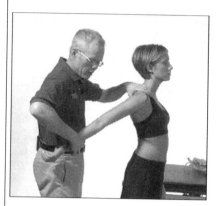

Extra tests

Biceps Stretch Test

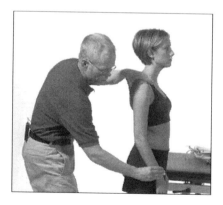

- Purpose: to provoke pain from a biceps tenosynovitis
- Stabilize the patient's scapula via the superior aspect of shoulder girdle
- Grasp the distal forearm in a neutral position

Extra tests

Biceps Stretch Test

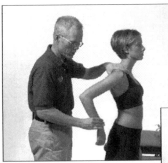

- Raise the humerus with the elbow in flexion, following the posterior-lateral orientation of the glenoid

- While maintaining extension of the shoulder, pronate the forearm

---

Extra tests

Biceps Stretch Test

- While maintaining forearm pronation, extend the elbow
- This places maximal stretch on the biceps tendon sheath (it should be felt in the biceps belly)
- (+) test: reproduction of anterior shoulder/biceps pain

Exam findings

External Impingement

- Painful arc: 80 - 130° (flexion or abduction)
- Supraspinatus: moderate pain with Ω Abduction; mild pain with Ω ER
  or severe pain with Ω Abd @ 30°
- Infraspinatus: moderate pain with Ω ER
- Long Head of Biceps (Proximal): moderate pain with Ω Elbow Flexion
- Bursa: (+) Bursal Pull Test

Neer CS. Impingement lesions. Clin Orthop 1983; 173:70.

Exam findings

External Impingement

Potential structures involved:

- Subacromial Bursa
- Supraspinatus (Superficial)
- Infraspinatus (Superficial)
- Subscapularis (Proximal)
- Long head of the biceps (Proximal)

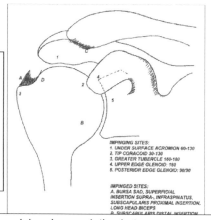

IMPINGING SITES:
1. UNDER SURFACE ACROMION 60-130
2. TIP CORACOID 30-130
3. GREATER TUBERCLE 160-180
4. UPPER EDGE GLENOID: 180
5. POSTERIOR EDGE GLENOID: 90/90

IMPINGED SITES:
A. BURSA SAD, SUPERFICIAL INSERTION SUPRA-, INFRASPINATUS, SUBSCAPULARIS PROXIMAL INSERTION, LONG HEAD BICEPS
B. SUBSCAPULARIS DISTAL INSERTION

Panni et al. Histologic analysis of the coracoacromial arch: correlation between age-related changes and rotator cuff tears. Arthroscopy. 1996; 12: 531-540.

Exam findings

Rotator Cuff Tendinopathy

- Painful arc or painful external impingement test
- Resisted test MUST be painful

Exam findings

Subacromial Bursitis

- Painful arc or painful external impingement test
- One or more resisted tests can be painful
- One or more passive tests can be painful
- Bursal pull test **must** be positive

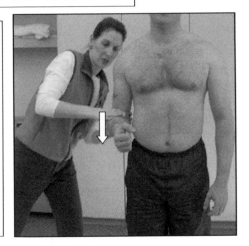

Exam findings

Subcoracoid Impingement

- Painful arc: 80 - 130° (flexion or abduction)
- Subcoracoid Impingement Test is the **most significant test**
- Subscapularis: mild pain with Ω IR; Possible (+) Lift Off Sign
- LHB Tendon: mild pain with Ω Elbow Flex

Ferrick MR. Coracoid impingement. A case report and review of the literature. Am J Sports Med 2000; 28:117-9.

Guckel C, Nidecker A. MR arthrographic findings in tenosynovitis of the long bicipital tendon of the shoulder. *Skeletal Radiol.* 1998;27:7-12.

Exam findings

Subcoracoid Impingement

Potential structures involved:

- **Subscapularis**
- **Long Head of Biceps (LHB) Tendon**
- **LHB Tenosynovium**
- **Loose Bodies**

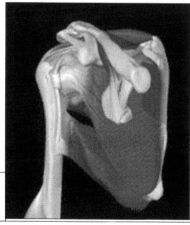

Barber FA, Field LD, Ryu RKN. Biceps tendon and superior labrum injuries: Decision making. J Bone and Joint Surg Am. 2007:89:1844-55.

Gerber C, Terrier F, Ganz R. The role of the coracoid process in the chronic impingement syndrome, *J Bone Joint Surg* 1985, 67B, 703-8.

Exam findings

Internal Impingement

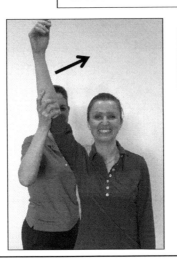

- May have pain with end-range elevation
- Passive Elevation test: pain with medial overpressure
- Posterior pain with Relocation test

Impingement Management

3 COMPONENTS to address with REHABILITATION

GHJ

- Bursal involvement?
- Posterior capsule tightness?
- Generalized hypermobility, especially at end-range?

SCAPULA

- Resting position
- Scapular stabilizer strength & control

SOFT TISSUE

- Tendinopathy

Impingement Management

If Bursa is Involved:

    Bursal Massage

    Injection

If Tendons are Involved:

    Transverse Friction

    Rhythmic Stretching

> Microlymph Drainage
> ↑'d fibroblastic activity
> ↓'d pain
> Collagen reorganization

Impingement Management   BURSITIS

Subacromial Bursal Massage

- Old concept: from Hippocrates!
  if you move without causing pain, you are healing
- Purpose: to move the 2 bursal layers in relation to each other to promote healing
- Provides temporary pain relief for decreasing inflammation & swelling
- Prevents the formation of adhesions within the bursa

Impingement Management

Subacromial Bursal Massage

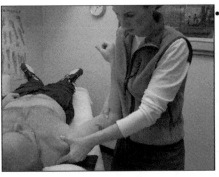

- Purpose: to move the 2 bursal layers in relation to each other to promote healing

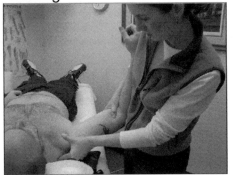

- Can manually stabilize the scapula or use a belt to optimize space between the acromion and humeral head

---

Impingement Management

Subacromial Bursal Massage

- A cuff weight can provide inferior pull for bursal massage with pendulum exercise
- Great for patient's HEP!

Caution: avoid if patient presents with tendinopathy!

Impingement Management

Bursal Injection

- 3-5 mL Corticosteroid (10 mg/mL)
- 2-3 mL local anesthetic

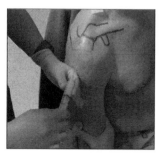

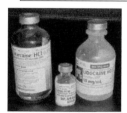

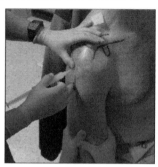

Impingement Management: GHJ

If tightness is present at the Posterior Shoulder:

Joint specific treatment (JST)

Indications:

Impingement

Anterior Laxity

Anterior pain with supraspinatus stretch

Impingement Management: GHJ

Indications for Testing and Subsequently Treating a Tight Posterior Shoulder Through Posterior glide Mobilization

1) **Impingement**

A tight posterior capsule will lever the humeral head upward during arm elevation, resulting in an impingement syndrome *or* causing recurrent problems in patients already treated for an impingement syndrome. When an athlete has a tight posterior capsule, leading to impingement problems, one often sees a winging of the scapula during throwing motions.

2) **Anterior Laxity**

A chronic anterior laxity in which the humeral head is "de-centered" (mal-aligned) anteriorly can eventually lead to a tight posterior capsule. A "vicious circle" then develops in which the tight posterior capsule (which may even have been there first) prevents the humeral head from re-aligning, leading to an increased movement of the head forward thus increasing the laxity.

3) **Stretching**

In stretching the supraspinatus or infraspinatus muscles, the patient sometimes complains of pain anteriorly (even though the scapula is held in retraction). This is often due to a limited internal rotation/ tight posterior capsule (whereby the humeral head has rolled too far forward). First mobilize the capsule with posterior gliding and a preposition in horizontal adduction, then try the stretch.

Impingement Management: GHJ

Posterior Shoulder Joint Specific Treatment

Techniques: Post-Superior

Post-Inferior

Self-Stretch

Bing MB, Deyle GD. Comparison of supervised exercise with and without manual physical therapy for patients with shoulder impingement syndrome. JOSPT. 2000; 30: 126-137.

Impingement Management: GHJ

Mobilizing the Posterior-Superior shoulder

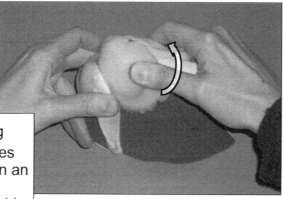

- Patient in side lying
- Therapist's mobilizes the humeral head in an anterior direction parallel to the glenoid

Impingement Management: GHJ

Mobilizing the Posterior-Superior shoulder

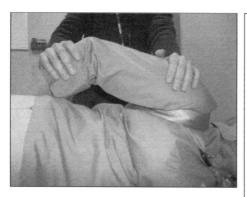

- Patient is side lying

- Scapula is stabilized with the mobilization belt over the coracoid process

- Arm is prepositioned in maximum available IR @ 0-20 degrees of ABD

Impingement Management: GHJ

Mobilizing the Posterior-Superior shoulder

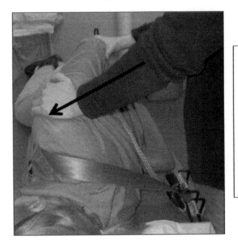

Direction of the glide:

Parallel to a line between the posterior angle of the acromion and the coracoid process.

Impingement Management: GHJ

Mobilizing the Posterior-Superior shoulder

This can be performed with either:
- static holds (40 seconds x 6 repetitions)

  or
- rhythmic movements

With repeated mobilizations, the patient's arm can be prepositioned farther in IR, increasing tension in the posterior-superior portion of the GHJ capsule.

Impingement Management: GHJ

Mobilizing the Posterior-Superior shoulder
(curved glide)

- Patient lies in supine
- Therapist's mobilizing hand performs a posterior glide directed in a posterior-superior-lateral direction
- Therapist's other hand provides an IR oscillation at the distal humerus

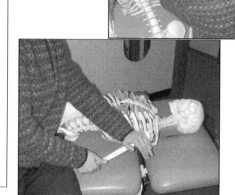

Impingement Management: GHJ

Mobilizing the Posterior-Superior shoulder
(curved glide)

- Begin with patient's hand resting on abdomen (with the GH joint capsule in a looser position)
- With repeated mobilizations, the patient's hand can be placed behind the back
- Placing increased tension on the posterior-superior portion of the GH joint capsule

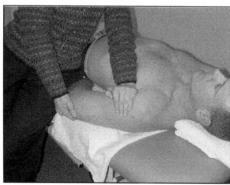

Impingement Management: GHJ

Mobilizing the Posterior-Superior shoulder
(curved glide)

- The patient should feel a "mild stretch" in the top-back portion of the shoulder

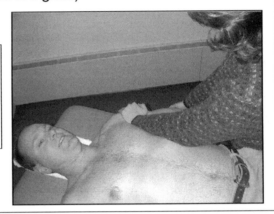

Patient should <u>not</u> feel any "stretch" in the anterior capsule!

Impingement Management: GHJ

Neuro-muscular re-education

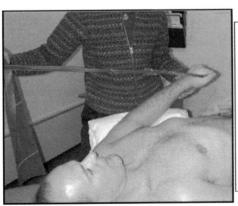

- After the mobilization is complete, follow-up with gentle resistance (either with manual resistance or bands): IR at 20-30° of abduction
- Monitor for scapular substitution

GHJ: home program ideas

For Posterior-Superior Shoulder Tightness

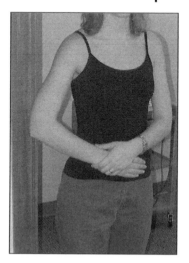

Doorframe Stretch

- Patient maintains scapular retraction to keep the scapula stabilized!
- Patient is advised to keep hand on abdomen if *mod/severe* capsular tightness is present

GHJ: home program ideas

For Posterior-Superior Shoulder Tightness

Doorframe Stretch

- If *mild* post-superior capsular tightness present: the hand and forearm are placed behind patient's back
- Emphasize the need to maintain scapula in a retracted position (to avoid scapular compensation)

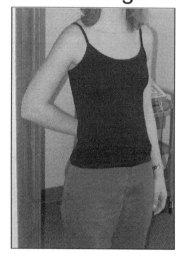

GHJ: home program ideas

For Posterior-Superior Shoulder Tightness

Alternate stretch: standing against wall

- Stand at a 30° angle to wall (this stabilizes the scapula)
- If *mild* post-superior capsular tightness present: the hand is placed behind patient's back
- Using the opposite hand directly (or with a towel), pull the elbow forward

---

GHJ: home program ideas

For Posterior-Superior Shoulder Tightness

Passing a weighted ball behind back

- Be sure patient is maintaining scapular stabilization (avoiding anterior tilting!)

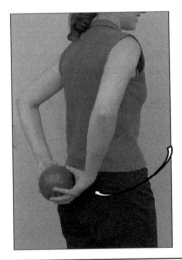

Impingement Management: GHJ

Mobilizing the Posterior-Inferior Shoulder

- Therapist places the proximal hand (either in a pronated or supinated position) in the axilla to perform posterior glide of the humeral head
- The other hand supports the patient's shoulder in flexion and horizontal adduction

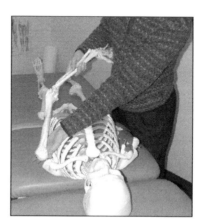

Impingement Management: GHJ

Mobilizing the Posterior-Inferior Shoulder

- Proximal hand provides glide in a posterior-superior-lateral direction, while the distal hand gently pulls the patient's arm into horizontal adduction

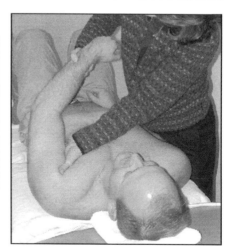

Impingement Management: GHJ

Mobilizing the Posterior-Inferior Shoulder

- Rhythmic oscillations
- The patient's shoulder capsule can be further stretched by pre-positioning the patient's shoulder into more flexion

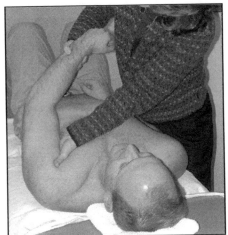

Impingement Management: GHJ

Mobilizing the Posterior-Inferior Shoulder

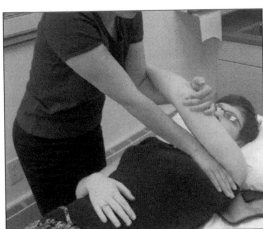

Alternate method!

Impingement Management: GHJ

Neuromuscular Re-education

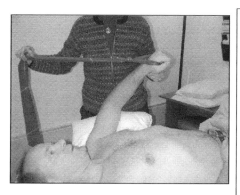

- After the mobilization is complete, follow-up with gentle resistance (either with manual resistance or bands): Internal Rotation at 60-90° of abduction
- Monitor for scapular substitution

GHJ: home program ideas

For Posterior-Inferior Shoulder Tightness

Sleeper Stretch: traditional version

- Patient lies in a semi-sidelying position to stabilize the scapula
- The shoulder is abducted, then internally-rotated
- The forearm is maintained in this position, while the patient slightly rolls onto the involved side

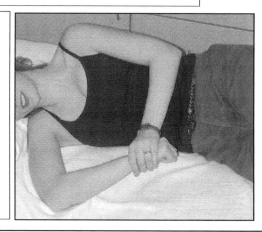

GHJ: home program ideas

For Posterior-Inferior Shoulder Tightness

Traditional Sleeper Stretch

- Patient should feel a stretch in the post-inferior portion of the shoulder capsule
- PAIN-FREE!

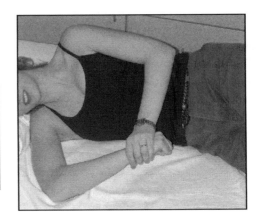

GHJ: home program ideas

For Posterior-Inferior Shoulder Tightness

Modified Sleeper Stretch

- Patient lays 20-30° from frontal plane to stabilize the scapula
- Towel is placed under patient's elbow to further increase the stretch on the posterior capsule

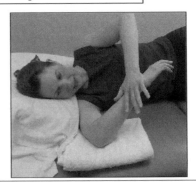

Wilk KE, Hooks TR, Macrina LC. The modified sleeper stretch and modified cross-body stretch to increase shoulder internal rotation range of motion in the overhead throwing athlete. JOSPT. 2013; 43(12): 891-894.

GHJ: home program ideas

For Posterior Shoulder Tightness

Sleeper Stretch

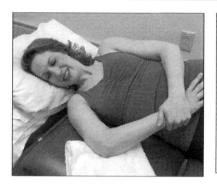

Optimal position:
Cavader study found that performing this stretch at 30 degrees of elevation in scapular plane will stretch both the posterior-superior & posterior-inferior aspects of the capsule

Izumi T, Aoki M, Takayuki M, et al. Stretching positions for the posterior capsule of the glenohumeral Joint. Am J Sports Med. 2008 36: 2014-2022.

GHJ: home program ideas

For Posterior-Inferior Shoulder Tightness

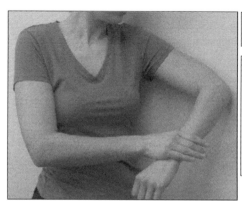

Sleeper Stretch

- This stretch can also be performed against a wall in standing, which is helpful for patients to perform during the day

GHJ: home program ideas

For Posterior-Inferior Shoulder Tightness

Sleeper Stretch

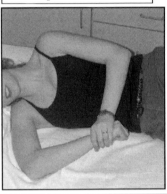

Cross-Body Stretch

McClure P, Balaicuis J, Heiland D. A randomized controlled comparison of stretching procedures for posterior shoulder tightness. JOSPT. 2007; 37 (3): 108-114.

GHJ: home program ideas

For Posterior-Inferior Shoulder Tightness

- Compared cross body stretching with and without scapular stabilization
- Results: scapular stabilization during cross body stretching was more beneficial

Joung HN, Yi CH, Jeon HS, et al. Effects of 4-week self cross body stretching with scapular stabilization on shoulder motions and horizontal adduction adductor strength in subjects with limited shoulder horizontal adduction. J Sports Med Phys Fitness. 2018; 37 (3): 108-114.

Impingement Management

Causal Management

> Post-Capsule JST
>
> End-Range JST ⟵ **covered the GHJ in adhesive capsulitis section!**
>
> Strengthening
>
>> Adductors
>>
>> Periscapular stabilizers
>>
>> Rotator Cuff

Graichen H, Hinterwimmer S, von Eisenhart-Rothe R, et al. Effect of abducting and adducting muscle activity on glenohumeral translation, scapular kinematics and subacromial space width in vivo. *J Biomech*. 2005 Apr;38(4):755-60.

Clisby EF et al. Relative contributions of the infraspinatus and deltoid during external rotation in patients with symptomatic subacromial impingement. J Shoulder Elbow Surg 2008;17:87S-92S.

Impingement Management

The elevation chain

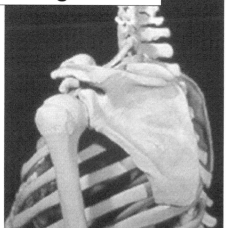

- GHJ—posterior capsule & end-range elevation
- ACJ
- SCJ
- Scapulo-Thoracic "joint"
- Cervico-Thoracic "junction"
- Ribs (especially 1st rib!)

Fung M, Kato S, Barrance PJ, et al. Scapular and clavicular kinematics during humeral elevation: A study with cadavers. J Shoulder Elb Surg. 2001, 10:278-285.

Jobe CM, Iannotti JP. Limits imposed on glenohumeral motion by joint geometry. J Shoulder Elbow Surg. 1995; 4:281-285.

Elevation Chain

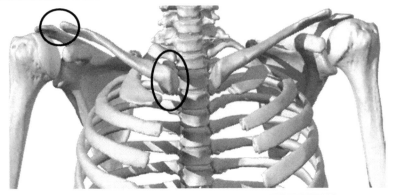

- Sternoclavicular joint (SCJ)
- Acromioclavicular joint (ACJ)

SCJ arthrokinematics

- Saddle joint: medial end of clavicle articulates with biconcave disc
- Concave-on-convex with scapular protraction and retraction
- Convex-on-concave with scapular elevation and depression

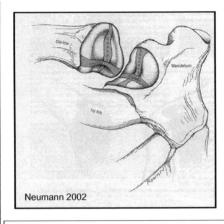

Neumann 2002

Neumann D. Kinesiology of the musculoskeletal system: foundations for physical rehabilitation. St. Louis: Mosby 2002.

SCJ arthrokinematics

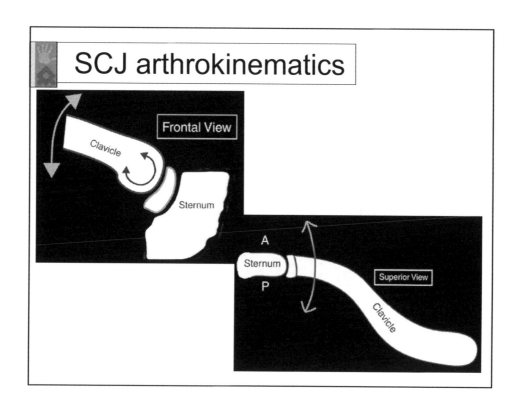

SCJ arthrokinematics

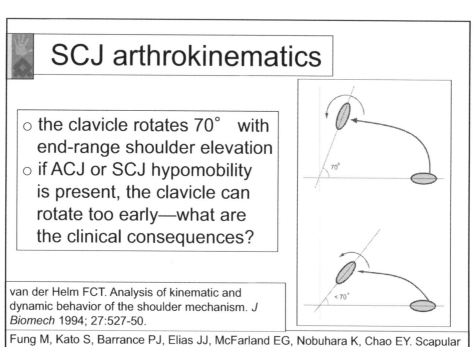

- o the clavicle rotates 70° with end-range shoulder elevation
- o if ACJ or SCJ hypomobility is present, the clavicle can rotate too early—what are the clinical consequences?

van der Helm FCT. Analysis of kinematic and dynamic behavior of the shoulder mechanism. *J Biomech* 1994; 27:527-50.

Fung M, Kato S, Barrance PJ, Elias JJ, McFarland EG, Nobuhara K, Chao EY. Scapular and clavicular kinematics during humeral elevation: A study with cadavers. J Shoulder Elb Surg, 2001, 10:278-85.

SCJ testing

CRANIAL & CAUDAL GLIDE

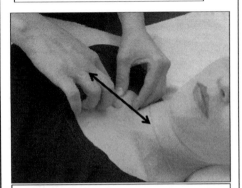

Patient's head may be rotated to contralateral side and side bended forward to place the sternocleidomastoid on slack.

- Place the SCM on slack (ipsilateral side-bending with contralateral rotation)
- Grasp the medial aspect of the clavicle as you palpate the SCJ with your opposite index finger
- Caudal glide: direction is mostly caudal, slightly lateral and ventral
- Cranial glide: cranial, slightly medial and dorsal
- Assess excursion and end-feel

Joint specific treatment

MANIPULATION in maximal loose-packed position

Manipulation Techniques: **Absolute Contraindications**

- Capsular pattern with no known cause
- Unexplainable pain during the night
- Use of anticoagulants
- Symptoms are elicited or worsen during the treatment
- If your state practice act does not allow it

Joint specific treatment

MANIPULATION in maximal loose-packed position

Manipulation Techniques: **Precautions**

- Osteoporosis
- Pregnancy
- Use of birth control pills
- General hypermobility
- Negative functional examination
- History of abuse (consider psycho-social)

SCJ treatment

TRACTION MANIPULATION in maximal loose-packed position

Goal: to improve elevation

- Place a rolled towel just medial to the scapular border, to allow the scapula to retract freely

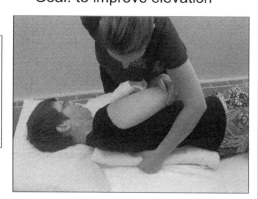

SCJ treatment

TRACTION MANIPULATION in maximal loose-packed position

Goal: to improve elevation

- Place a towel over the patient's sternum
- Using your forearm, place pressure on the sternum to provide stabilization

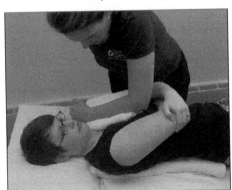

SCJ treatment

TRACTION MANIPULATION in maximal loose-packed position

Goal: to improve elevation

- Place your hand on the distal aspect of the patient's clavicle
- As the patient exhales, retract the scapula to the end of available range
- At end range of retraction, perform the traction in line with the clavicle

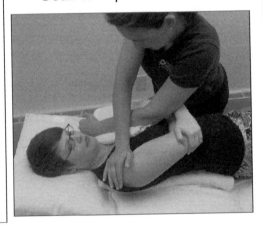

SCJ neuromuscular re-ed

- Place your hand on the medial aspect of the clavicle as close to the SCJ line as possible
- As you move the patient's arm into elevation, guide the medial clavicle in a caudal, slightly ventral and lateral direction
- Re-test mobility

Goal: to improve elevation

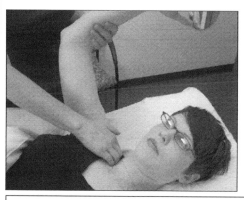

Direction of glide does not change

SCJ neuromuscular re-ed

Goal: to improve elevation

At end-range elevation
- Passive
- Active-assisted
- Isometric: agonist, antagonist, agonist
- Maintain the glide!

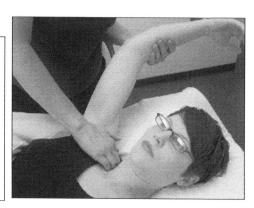

239

ACJ arthrokinematics

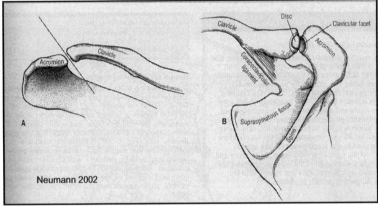

Neumann 2002

Convex distal end of the clavicle articulates with a concave acromion

Neumann D. Kinesiology of the musculoskeletal system: foundations for physical rehabilitation. St. Louis: Mosby 2002.

ACJ arthrokinematics

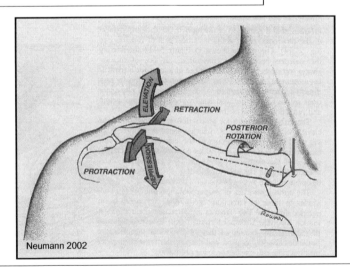

Neumann 2002

Neumann D. Kinesiology of the musculoskeletal system: foundations for physical rehabilitation. St. Louis: Mosby 2002.

ACJ arthrokinematics

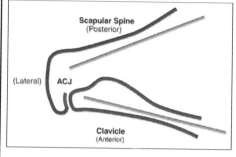

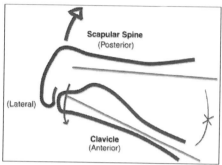

Superior view

With shoulder elevation, the distal end of the clavicle rolls in a posterior direction and slides in an ventral direction

ACJ testing

CRANIAL GLIDE of the acromion in relation to the clavicle

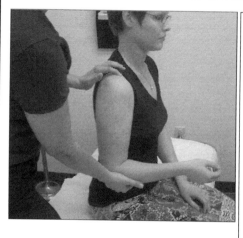

- While palpating the ACJ, push the humerus superiorly
- Test cranial and caudal glide
- Assess excursion and end-feel
- Important for hypermobility

ACJ testing

ANTERIOR GLIDE of the clavicle in relation to the acromion

- Stabilizing hand: thumb on coracoid process and fingers around the posterior aspect of the acromion
- Mobilizing hand: gently grasps the lateral aspect of the clavicle and follow the ACJ orientation

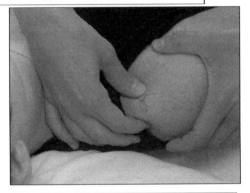

- The ACJ is best tested in supine, in order to take the stretch off the trapezius
- Slightly sidebend the patient to the side you're testing

ACJ testing

ANTERIOR GLIDE of the clavicle in relation to the acromion

- Test anterior glide
- Assess excursion and end-feel
- Important for hypo- & hypermobility

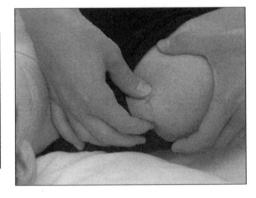

ACJ treatment

JOINT MOBILIZATION:
Anterior "curved" glide

Therapist stabilizes the lateral border of the scapula with his/her ipsilateral forearm while holding the upper extremity proximal to the patient's elbow and providing passive abduction.

The contralateral thumb (or heel of hand) provides gentle anterior medial glide to the distal clavicle.

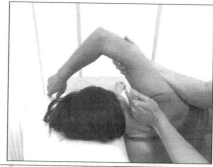

This technique is performed rhythmically with passive shoulder abduction.

ACJ treatment

TRACTION MANIPULATION in maximal loose-packed position

Goal: to improve elevation

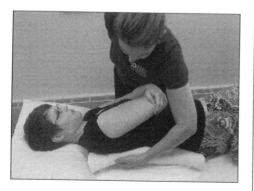

- Place a rolled towel along the medial scapular border
- Place your hand on top of the towel and roll the patient into supine, insuring the radial border of your hand meets the medial border of the patient's scapula

ACJ treatment

TRACTION MANIPULATION in maximal loose-packed position

Goal: to improve elevation

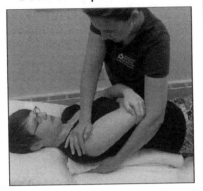

- Place your hand on the patient's coracoid process, anterior humerus, and acromion
- As the patient exhales, externally rotate the scapula through its available range
- At end range of scapular ER, perform the traction in line with the clavicle
- Re-test mobility

ACJ neuromuscular re-ed

Goal: to improve elevation

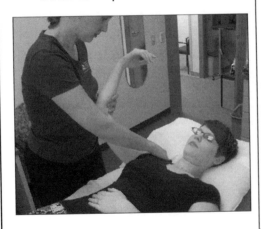

- Place your hand on the cranial aspect of the clavicle as close to the ACJ line as possible
- As you move the patient's arm into elevation, guide the distal aspect of the clavicle in a ventral direction <u>in relation to the acromion</u>

ACJ neuromuscular re-ed

Goal: to improve elevation

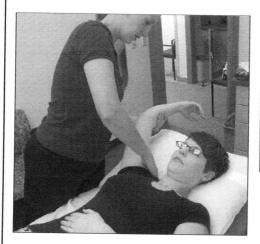

At end-range elevation
- Passive
- Active-assisted
- Isometric: agonist, antagonist, agonist

Elevation Chain

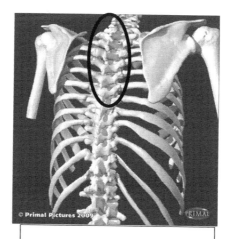

Thoracic Spine

thoracic spine treatment

Exercise
Orthopedic Manual Therapy
Thoracic manipulation

Haik, M, Alburquerque-Sendin F, Silva s. Scapular kinematics pre- and post- thoracic manipulation in individuals with and without shoulder impingement symptoms: a randomized controlled study. JOSPT. 2014; 44(7); 475-497.

Boyles RE et al. The short-term effects of thoracic spine thrust manipulation on patients with shoulder impingement syndrome. *Man Ther.* 2009, Aug;14(4):375-80.

Senbursa G et al. Comparison of conservative treatment with and without manual physical therapy for patients with shoulder impingement syndrome: a prospective, randomized clinical trial. Knee Surg Sports Traumatol Arthrosc. 2007;15:915-21.

Lombardi I et al. Progressive resistance training in patients with shoulder impingement syndrome: a randomized controlled trial. *Arthritis & Rheumatism.* 2008;59(5):615-22.

Cools AM et al. Internal impingement in the tennis player: rehabilitation guidelines. *Br J Sports Med.* 2008;42:165-71.

thoracic spine treatment

Upper Thoracic Gapping Manipulation

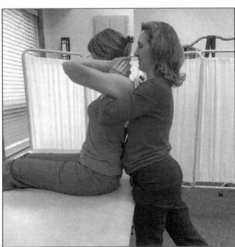

thoracic spine treatment

Thrust Techniques: Contraindications

1. Malignancy
2. Infection
3. Compromised pulmonary system (e.g., COPD)
4. Evidence of Prolapse with Dural test findings
5. Severe neurological - cord signs (bowel/bladder dysfunction, sexual dysfunction, pathological reflexes, discoordination, etc.)
6. Acute strains or sprains
7. Unhealed fracture
8. Prolonged use of corticosteroids
9. Osteoporosis
10. Claustrophobia
11. Capsular pattern with no known cause
12. Unexplainable pain during the night
13. Use of anticoagulants
14. Symptoms are elicited or worsen during the treatment

thoracic spine treatment

Thrust Techniques: Precautions

1. Pregnancy
1. Use of birth control pills
2. General hypermobility
3. Anomalies and fusion of the vertebrae
4. Negative clinical examination
5. Anxiety

thoracic spine treatment

This Lab: Extra Considerations

1. Practice within the boundaries of your license
2. Let your colleague know if you have any underlying conditions.
3. Give your colleagues good feedback about their techniques.
4. Be cautious and be gentle!

thoracic spine treatment

Upper Thoracic Gapping Manipulation

Starting Position

- Place a folded towel between the therapist's sternum and the patient's upper t-spine
- Grasp patient's thumbs and bring arms overhead (if patient can tolerate without shoulder pain)

- Therapist's legs are in a stride position with knees slightly bent
- Patient relaxes back into therapist in a slumped position, so the therapist's sternum is vertical

Upper Thoracic Gapping Manipulation

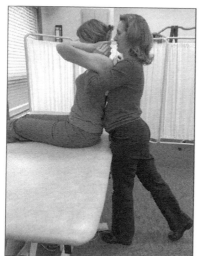

Ending Position

- Therapist asks patient to take a deep breath
- As the patient exhales, therapist retracts the patient's scapula performs the manipulation by extending the knees and bringing the sternum in a cranial-ventral direction
- After thrust, as patient to take another deep breath and gently bring patient back to sitting

thoracic spine treatment

CTJ: **neuromuscular re-education**

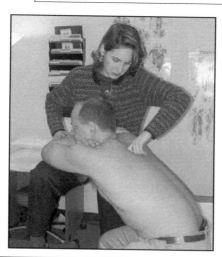

- **Improving dorsal-ventral segmental motion**
- Therapist facilitates ventral glide of thoracic segments (perpendicular to local curvature) during thoracic extension.

thoracic spine treatment

CTJ: **neuromuscular re-education**

This is performed in an oscillatory fashion, starting from T1 to T6

Move down one level each time the patient's trunk is passively brought into extension

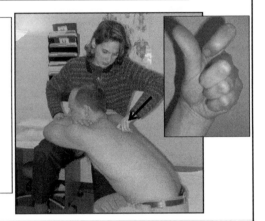

Crosbie J, Kilbreath SL, Hollman L, York S. Scapulohumeral rhythm and associated spinal movements. Clinical Biomechanics. 2008; 23: 184–192.

thoracic spine treatment

Video: Jenkner technique

Glenohumeral Instability

Instability: interrelationships

What is the relationship with instability and impingement?

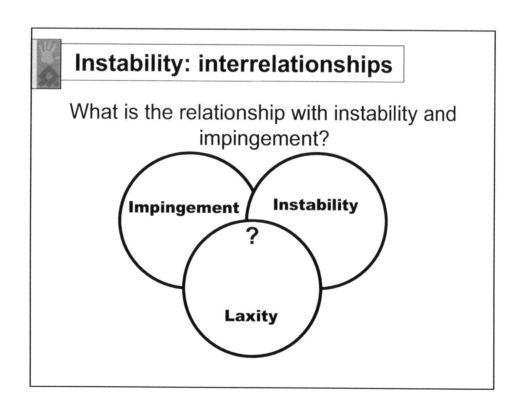

Instability: interrelationships

Laxity of GHJ

Refers to an asymptomatic hypermobile joint with the ability to maintain centering of the humeral head in the glenoid fossa.

Instability of GHJ

Pathological condition where the centering of the humeral head is lost and results in pain, discomfort, paresthesia, apprehension, &/or fatigue.

Beasley L, Faryniarz DA, Hannafin JA. Multidirectional instability of the shoulder in the female athlete. Clin Sports Med. 2000;19(2):331-349.

Guerrero P, Busconi B, Deangelis N, et al. Congenital instability of the shoulder joint: assessment and treatment options. JOSPT. 2009;39(2):124-134.

Stability Consequences

What happens arthrokinematically?
....the instantaneous axis of rotation moves outside of the joint

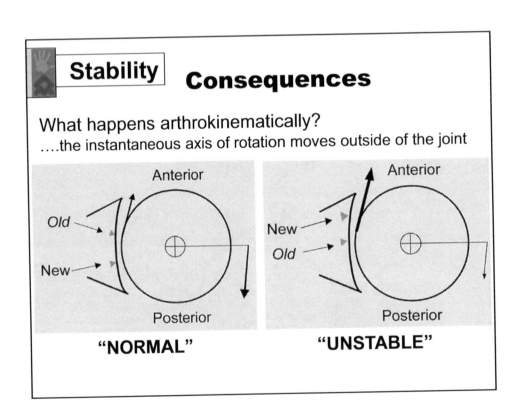

"NORMAL"   "UNSTABLE"

Instability: etiologies

"Etiology is a particularly important consideration as the presence or the absence of trauma can assist in treatment selection"

Lewis A, Kitamura T, Bayley JIL. The classification of shoulder instability: new light through old windows!. Curr Orthop. 2004;18(2):97-108.

Warby SA, Watson L, Ford JJ, et al. Multidirectional instability of the glenohumeral joint: etiology, classification, assessment, and management. J Hand Ther. 2017;30: 175-181.

Instability: etiologies

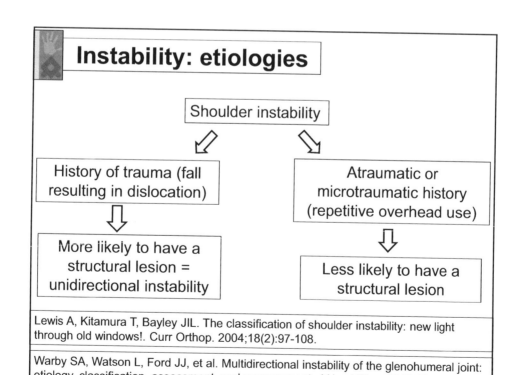

Lewis A, Kitamura T, Bayley JIL. The classification of shoulder instability: new light through old windows!. Curr Orthop. 2004;18(2):97-108.

Warby SA, Watson L, Ford JJ, et al. Multidirectional instability of the glenohumeral joint: etiology, classification, assessment, and management. J Hand Ther. 2017;30: 175-181.

Instability: etiologies

Shoulder instability

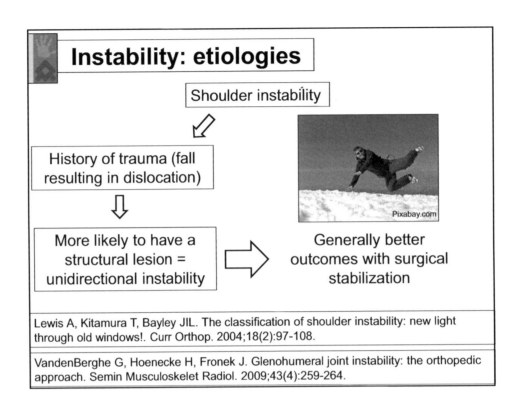

History of trauma (fall resulting in dislocation)

⬇

More likely to have a structural lesion = unidirectional instability

➡ Generally better outcomes with surgical stabilization

Pixabay.com

Lewis A, Kitamura T, Bayley JIL. The classification of shoulder instability: new light through old windows!. Curr Orthop. 2004;18(2):97-108.

VandenBerghe G, Hoenecke H, Fronek J. Glenohumeral joint instability: the orthopedic approach. Semin Musculoskelet Radiol. 2009;43(4):259-264.

Instability: traumatic etiologies

- **Capsular lesion**
  - Venting
- **Labral lesion**
  - Superior Labrum
    - **SLAP**
    - @ Biceps insertion
  - Anterior-Inferior Labrum
    - **Bankart lesion** (labral/bony @ glenoid)
    - Often accompanied by Hill-Sachs lesion*

    (damage to posterior humeral head)

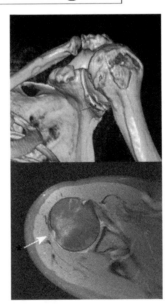

Instability: traumatic etiologies

- **Muscular: Tears**
  - **Partial versus complete**
    - Supraspinatus
    - Infraspinatus
    - Subscapularis
    - Long head of biceps

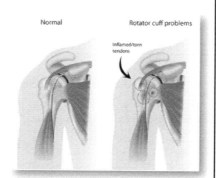

Nakagaki et al 1996; Murray et al 2002; Sakurai et al 1998; Neer 1990; Levine & Flatow 2000; Matomedi et al 2002; Wirth et al, 1997

Instability: traumatic etiologies

- **Nerve**
  - Long Thoracic
    - Serratus anterior
  - Suprascapular
    - Supraspinatus
    - Infraspinatus

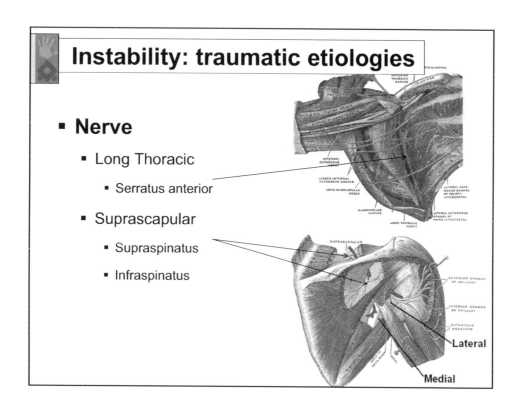

Instability: etiologies

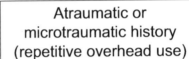

Shoulder instability

- More likely to have signs of poor motor control, scapular dyskinesis, and multiple directions of instability.
- Generally have better outcomes with rehabilitation

Atraumatic or microtraumatic history (repetitive overhead use)

⇩

Less likely to have a structural lesion

Lewis A, Kitamura T, Bayley JIL. The classification of shoulder instability: new light through old windows!. Curr Orthop. 2004;18(2):97-108.

Warby SA, Pizzari T, Ford JJ, et al. Exercise-based management versus surgery for multidirectional instability of the glenohumeral joint: a systematic review. Br J Sports Med. 2016;50:1115-1123.

Instability: nontraumatic etiologies

The etiology of MDI is multifactorial

- Congenital
- Acquired
- Post-traumatic
- Neuromuscular factors

…can contribute to the pathology to differing degrees

Warby SA, Watson L, Ford JJ, et al. Multidirectional instability of the glenohumeral joint: etiology, classification, assessment, and management. J Hand Ther. 2017;30: 175-181.

Guerrero P, Busconi B, Deangelis N, et al. Congenital instability of the shoulder joint: assessment and treatment options. JOSPT. 2009;39(2):124-134.

Instability: nontraumatic etiologies

CONGENITAL FACTORS:
- Hypoplastic glenoids
- Increased retroversion
- Decreased ant-post diameter of humeral head

Reduces the bony constraint of the humeral head and can predispose to all directions of instability

Warby SA, Watson L, Ford JJ, et al. Multidirectional instability of the glenohumeral joint: etiology, classification, assessment, and management. J Hand Ther. 2017;30: 175-181.

Kikuchi K, Itoi E, Yamamoto N, et al. Scapular inclination and glenohumeral instability: a cadaveric study. J Orthop Sci. 2008;13(1):72-77.

Guerrero P, Busconi B, Deangelis N, et al. Congenital instability of the shoulder joint: assessment and treatment options. JOSPT. 2009;39(2):124-134.

Instability: etiologies

"When subgrouping patients with multidirectional instability (MDI), it is important to distinguish those who present with microtrauma and intact capsules from those who have sustained significant trauma and are more likely to have a structural lesion"

Lewis A, Kitamura T, Bayley JIL. The classification of shoulder instability: new light through old windows!. Curr Orthop. 2004;18(2):97-108.

Instability: nontraumatic etiologies

MDI as a continuum

⬅️ ➡️

CONNECTIVE TISSUE DISORDERS:
- Marfan's syndrome
- Ehlers-Danlos syndrome
- Less-severe generalized joint laxity

AQUIRED INSTABILITY:
- Result of repetitive overuse on a background of muscle imbalance

Warby SA, Watson L, Ford JJ, et al. Multidirectional instability of the glenohumeral joint: etiology, classification, assessment, and management. J Hand Ther. 2017;30: 175-181.

Instability: classification

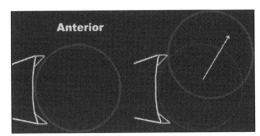

Labral Perching

Hawkins Classification

- Type I: ↑'d motion; no "Perching"
- Type II: Labral Perching
- Type III: "Over the Hill"; Luxation/dislocation

Hawkins RJ, Mohtadi NGH. Clinical evaluation of shoulder instability. Clin J Sport Medicine. 1991; 1: 39-64.

Instability: imaging

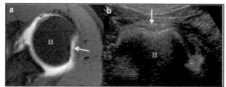

Simao, 2012

Axial T1 MRA   posterior transverse US image

Purpose: determine the diagnostic accuracy in patients with recurrent anterior instability by comparing ultrasound (US) and MR arthrography (MRA) with findings at surgery.

US: sensitivity: 20-100%; specificity: 25-90%
MRA: sensitivity: 80-100%; specificity: 50-100%

Conclusion: US is capable of demonstrating bone and soft tissue lesion related to chronic instability of the shoulder in the presence of intra-articular fluid.

Simao MN, Noguera-Barbosa MH, Muglia VF, et al. Anterior shoulder instability: correlation between magnetic resonance arthrography, ultrasound arthrography and intraoperative findings. Ultrasound in Med. & Biol. 2012; 38: 551-560.

Clinical Exam: Who?

Who?
What?
When?
Where?
Why?
To what extent?

Younger Population
    Macrotraumatic
    Overuse

Middle to Older Age Population
    Macrotraumatic

Athletic Population
    Impact Sports: macrotraumatic
    Swimmers: capsular lesions
    Volleyball / tennis: suprascapular n.

Lifting Population

Clinical Exam: What?

Pain
        Sharp with sudden, novel movements
        Dull aching @ rest, after sharp pain
"Dead Arm"
        Few Seconds to several minutes
        Follows sharp pain
Painful Click & Apprehension if labrum
Overuse in tendons: impingement

Possibly asymptomatic now, problematic later

Yamaguchi K, et al. Natural history of rotator cuff tears: a longitudinal analysis of asymptomatic tears detected sonographically. J Shoulder Elbow Surg. 2001;10: 199-203.

Miniachi A. Magnetic resonance imaging evaluation of the rotator cuff tendons in the asymptomatic shoulder. Amer J Sports Med. 1995; 2: 142-145.

Silliman JF, Hawkins RJ. Classification and physical diagnosis of instability of the shoulder. Clinical Orthoped & Related Research. 1993; 291: 7-19.

Clinical Exam: When?

Subluxation during...

Throwing
    Dead arm during cocking: anterior instability
    Dead arm during follow through: posterior

Reaching
Sudden, novel, or unexpected movements

Clinical Exam: When?

HISTORY

Anterior Instability
- Associated with overhead movements, especially with ER, such as swimming or throwing a ball

Posterior Instability
- Associated with flexion and IR activities, such as push-ups, pushing open a heavy door, volleyball, football, tennis

Bahu MJ, Trentacosta N, Vorys GC, et al. Multidirectional instability: evaluation and treatment options. Clin Sports Med. 2008;27(4):671-689.

Beasley L, Faryniarz DA, Hannafin JA. Multidirectional instability of the shoulder in the female athlete. Clin Sports Med. 2000;19(2):331-349.

Dhir J, Willis M, Watson L, et al. Evidence-based review of clinical diagnostic tests and predictive clinical tests that evaluate response to conservative rehabilitation for posterior glenohumeral instability: a systematic review. Sports Health. 2018;10(2):141-145.

Clinical Exam: instability tests

PROM: (2) Possibilities

     ↑'d angular motions

     ↓'d angular motions in NCP (due to incongruity)

End-Feel during PROM:
    Typically Softer
    Directional according to hypermobility

Clinical Exam: anterior GHJ

Anterior

LAXITY TESTS
- Anterior Drawer (static, neutral position)
- Load & Shift test
  - maximal loose packed position (MLPP)
  - 90° abduction with maximal ER

INSTABILITY TESTS
- RELOCATION TEST
- REVERSE RELOCATION TEST

Laxity Tests: anterior

Anterior Drawer

Aka: Fukuda test

- from the neutral position with patient's arm at side
- stabilize the scapula at the superior aspect of the shoulder
- grasp proximal humerus and shift it straight anterior
- assess excursion & end-feel

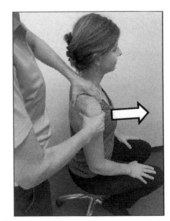

*Can be performed in supine or sitting position, Itoi et al, 2001

Bahk M, Keyurapan E, Tasaki A, et al. Laxity testing of the shoulder: a review. Am J Sports Med.2007;35(1):131-144.

Warby SA, Watson L, Ford JJ, et al. Multidirectional instability of the glenohumeral joint: etiology, classification, assessment, and management. J Hand Ther. 2017;30: 175-181.

Clinical tests: anterior

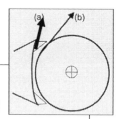

Laxity tests (Load & Shift)

— McHaffey & Smith (1999); Halder (2001)

– From the loose packed position (MLPP)

– "Prepositioned" in 0 degrees (Itoi 2001)

– @ 45* & 90 degrees

(*for labrum; Turkel et al, 1981)

Mahaffey BL, Smith PA. Shoulder instability in young athletes. Am Fam Physician. 1999 May 15;59(10):2773-82, 2787.

Halder AM, Halder CG, Zhao KD, et al. Dynamic inferior stabilizers of the shoulder joint. Clin Biomechan. 2001; 16: 138-143.

Itoi E, Sashi R, Minagawa H, et al. Position of immobilization after dislocation of the glenohumeral joint. 2001; 83-A; 661-667.

Turkel SJ, Panio MW, Marshall JL, et al. Stabilizing mechanisms preventing anterior dislocation of the glenohumeral joint. J Bone Joint Surg Am. 1981; 63: 1208-1217

Laxity Tests: anterior

Load & Shift from MLPP

(supine or sitting position)

- from MLPP: 50° abd in scaption plane
- stabilize the scapula at the superior aspect of the shoulder
- grasp proximal humerus, load the joint and shift it anteriorly
- assess excursion & end-feel
- compare to uninvolved side

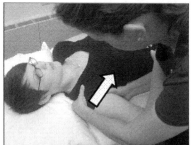

Laxity Tests: anterior

Load & Shift at 90° Abd with maximal ER

- pre-position at 90° Abd with maximal ER
- stabilize the scapula anteriorly at the coracoid process
- grasp the proximal humerus, load the joint and shift it anteriorly
- assess excursion & end-feel
- compare to uninvolved side

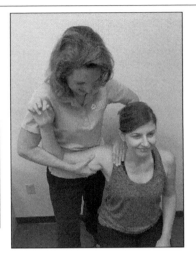

Instability Tests: anterior

Relocation Test

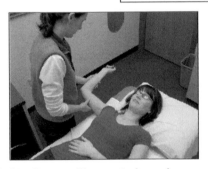

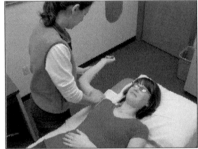

1. Starting position: anterior pain

2. Relocation: no pain with posterior glide to relocate

- Since the GHJ joint is now centered, the ROM will improve, thereby causing pain from the irritated anterior capsule at the end of the new range

Instability Tests: anterior

Reverse Relocation Test

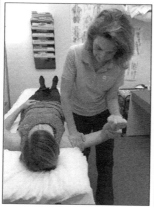 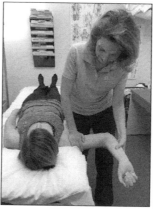 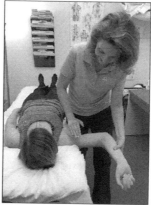

1. Starting position

2. Throwing motion with relocation: no pain

3. Release of relocation: pain

Clinical Exam: posterior GHJ

HISTORY

Posterior

Can be associated with…
- **a single traumatic onset (such as a tackle in football)**
- **Repetitive overuse and microtrauma**
- **Soft tissue disorders**

Provencher MT, King S, Solomon DJ, et al. Recurrent posterior shoulder instability: diagnosis and treatment. Oper Tech Sports Med. 2005;13:196-205.

Clinical Exam: posterior GHJ

Posterior

LAXITY TESTS
-Posterior Drawer (static, neutral position)
-Load & Shift test
-maximal loose packed position (MLPP)
-90° flexion, IR, horizontal add

Note: With the posterior laxity tests: static from the MLPP and static from the neutral position are the same as the anterior laxity tests from the above mentioned positions, only the direction of translation is different.

Laxity Tests: posterior

Posterior Drawer

- from the neutral position with patient's arm at side
- stabilize the scapula at the superior aspect of the shoulder
- grasp proximal humerus and shift it posterior and lateral
- assess excursion & end-feel

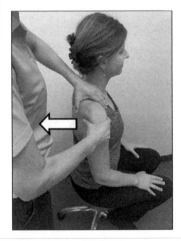

Bahk M, Keyurapan E, Tasaki A, et al. Laxity testing of the shoulder: a review. Am J Sports Med.2007;35(1):131-144.

Warby SA, Watson L, Ford JJ, et al. Multidirectional instability of the glenohumeral joint: etiology, classification, assessment, and management. J Hand Ther. 2017;30: 175-181.

Laxity Tests: posterior

Load & Shift from MLPP

(supine or sitting position)

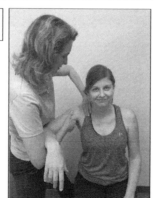

- from MLPP: 50° abd in scaption plane
- stabilize the scapula at the superior aspect of the shoulder
- grasp proximal humerus, load the joint and shift it posterior & lateral
- assess excursion & end-feel
- compare to uninvolved side

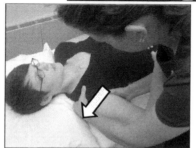

Laxity Tests: posterior

Load & Shift at 90° Flex with IR

- pre-position at 90° Flex with IR
- stabilize the scapula superiorly & along posterior acromion
- grasp the proximal humerus, load the joint and shift it posterior & laterally
- assess excursion & end-feel
- compare to uninvolved side

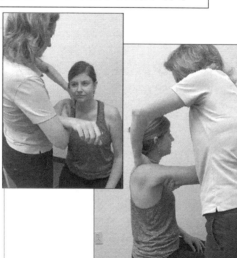

Clinical Exam: inferior GHJ

Inferior

Part of Multidirectional Instability

Failure accompanies failures in different directions*

LAXITY TESTS
Sulcus Test
-in 0° of abduction
-in neutral position
-in externally rotated position
-in internally rotated position
-in 90° of abduction (neutral)

*Yoldas EA, Translation of the glenohumeral joint in patients with multidirectional and posterior instability: awake examination versus examination under anesthesia. J Shoulder Elbow Surg 2001; 10:416-20.

Clinical tests: inferior

- Laxity tests
  - "Prepositioned" in 0 degrees with
    - neutral rotation
    - external rotation
    - internal rotation

Inferior Laxity Tests

Sulcus Test

- tests the superior capsule
- from a neutral position with patient's arm at side
- palpate the subacromial space
- grasp proximal humerus and pull inferiorly
- assess excursion & end-feel
- repeat in IR, then in ER

neutral

IR

ER

Inferior Laxity Tests

Sulcus Test

- a (+) Sulcus sign with pre-positioned shoulder ER suggests more involvement of the rotator cuff interval

ER

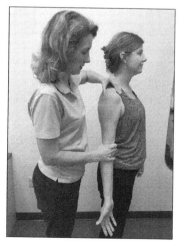

Bahk M, Keyurapan E, Tasaki A, et al. Laxity testing of the shoulder: a review. Am J Sports Med. 2007;35(1):131-144.

Inferior Laxity Tests

- Laxity tests
  - Prepositioned in 90° of abduction
    - neutral rotation

  - a (+) test suggests more involvement of the inferior capsule

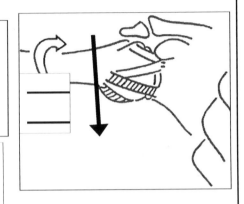

Jia X, Ji JH, Petersen SA, Freehill MT, McFarland EG. An analysis of shoulder laxity in patients undergoing shoulder surgery. J Bone Joint Surg Am. 2009;91(9):2144-50.

Bahk M, Keyurapan E, Tasaki A, et al. Laxity testing of the shoulder: a review. Am J Sports Med. 2007;35(1):131-144.

Inferior Laxity Tests

Laxity Test in 90° abduction

- tests the inferior capsule
- with patient's shoulder in 90° abduction (neutral rotation)
- push proximal humerus in an inferior direction
- assess excursion & end-feel

Jia X, Ji JH, Petersen SA, Freehill MT, McFarland EG. An analysis of shoulder laxity in patients undergoing shoulder surgery. J Bone Joint Surg Am. 2009;91(9):2144-50.

Labrum & Stability

FUNCTION OF THE GLENOID LABRUM:

- $\uparrow$'d depth of fossa: $\downarrow$'d translation
- $\uparrow$'d surface area contact
- Attachment for Ligaments
- Supports negative pressure

Levine WN, Flatow EL. The pathophysiology of shoulder instability. Am J Sports Med 2000; 28:911-17.

Labral Lesions

- **Labral tests**

    If there is no improvement in conservative treatment, the patient should be referred back to the specialist. With every instability, the labrum is usually torn, but the question is, "Is this clinically significant?"

    Labrum is clinically significant when:
    - There is a typical history for labral lesions: complaints of painful click in the history. Patient complains of locking or pseudo-luxation.
    - Positive provocation tests

Analysis of shoulder Instability

Labral Lesions	Classification
Bankart SLAP	• **TUBS** • **AMI** • **AMBRII**

Instability: labral lesions

- Anterior-Inferior Labral Lesions
  - **Bankart Lesions**
    - Detachment of Inferior GH Ligament from anterior glenoid and labrum
    - most common lesion

Levine WN, Flatow EL. The pathophysiology of shoulder instability. Am J Sports Med 2000; 28:911-17.

Instability: labral lesions

Bankart lesions

<u>2° to macrotrauma</u>
- Type 1: 0.5 cm Capsular Avulsion
- Type 2: 1.0 cm Labrum
- Type 3: 1.5 cm Labrum, Glenoid Neck
- Type 4: 1.0 cm Type 3

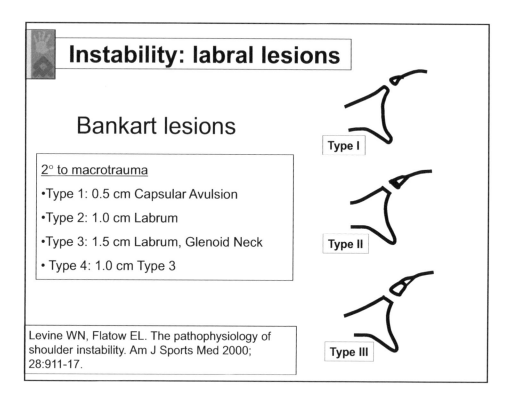

Type I

Type II

Type III

Levine WN, Flatow EL. The pathophysiology of shoulder instability. Am J Sports Med 2000; 28:911-17.

Instability: labral lesions

- SLAP
  - Superior Labrum, Anterior to Posterior
    - Possible combination: SLAP & Ant / Inf Labral tear
  - Induced by forceful, eccentric loading of biceps
    - FOOSH
    - Traction
    - Shear while throwing

LaBan, et al. Slip of the lip—tears of the superior glenoid labrum-anterior to posterior (SLAP) syndrome. A report of four cases. Am J Sports Med 1995; 74:448-52.

Levine WN, Flatow EL. The pathophysiology of shoulder instability. Am J Sports Med 2000; 28:911-17.

Instability: labral lesions

- SLAP
    - Predisposed by high tensile tolerance of proximal tendon.
    - Greatest strain during late cocking, followed by eccentric activity of the biceps with follow through

McGough, et al. Mechanical properties of long head of biceps tendon. Knee Surg, Sports Traum, Arthr 1996; 3:226-229.

Pradhan et al. Superior labral strain during the throwing motion - A cadaveric study. Am J Sports Med 2001; 29:488-492.

Instability: labral lesions

- SLAP
    - Lesions are seldom isolated
    - Pain is most common clinical feature. Popping or catching, especially in full flexion or abduction
    - Plethora of tests

Huijbregts. SLAP lesions: Structure, function, and physical therapy diagnosis and treatment. J Manip Man Ther. 2001; 9,1:71-83.

Instability: labral lesions

SLAP Classification

Type I: fraying and degeneration

Type II: a detachment of the biceps and superior labrum from the glenoid.

Type III: a clean bucket-handle tear

Type IV: an extension of the bucket handle into the biceps tendon substance

Huijbregts. SLAP lesions: Structure, function, and physical therapy diagnosis and treatment. J Manip Man Ther. 2001; 9,1:71-83.

Synder SJ, Banas MP, Karzel RP. An analysis of 140 injuries to the superior glenoid labrum. J Shoulder Elbow Surg. 1995; 4: 243-248.

Instability: labral lesions

SLAP Classification

Type V a superior extension of a Bankart lesion with a biceps separation from glenoid,

Type VI a flap tear of the labrum.

Type VII extends caudally into the middle glenohumeral ligament

Huijbregts. SLAP lesions: Structure, function, and physical therapy diagnosis and treatment. J Manip Man Ther. 2001; 9,1:71-83.

Synder SJ, Banas MP, Karzel RP. An analysis of 140 injuries to the superior glenoid labrum. J Shoulder Elbow Surg. 1995; 4: 243-248.

Instability: labrum tests

What are the best tests to evaluate a SLAP lesion?

Results:
- the most sensitive for identifying type II SLAP tears were the active compression, Hawkins, Speed, Neer, and Jobe relocation tests

Conclusion:
- the authors' results contradict the current literature regarding provocative testing for both stable and unstable SLAP lesions
- There is no single maneuver that can accurately diagnose SLAP lesions; arthroscopy remains the standard to diagnoses these lesions

Parentis MA, Glousman RE, Mohr KS, et al. An evaluation of the provocative tests for superior labral anterior to posterior lesions. Am J Sports Med. 2006;34(2):265-268.

Instability: labrum tests

Modified Crank Test

- Performed in pain-free end-range elevation: usually about 150° to 160° . Joint is loaded and the shoulder is moved into IR and ER.
- Pain with click or crepitation = positive for superior labrum.
- With posterior, superior, and anterior emphasis
- More often SLAP, less often Bankart

Liu SH, Henry MH, Nuccion SL. A prospective evaluation of a new physical examination in predicting glenoid labral tears. *Am J Sports Med.* 1996;24(6):721-5.

Instability: labrum tests

Modified Crank Test (in sitting)

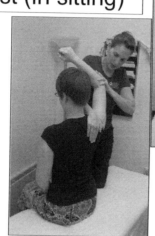

- Performed in painfree end-range elevation – usually about 150° to 160°. Joint is loaded and the shoulder is moved into IR and ER.

- Pain with click or crepitation = positive for superior labrum.

- With posterior, superior, and anterior emphasis

Liu SH, Henry MH, Nuccion SL. A prospective evaluation of a new physical examination in predicting glenoid labral tears. *Am J Sports Med.* 1996;24(6):721-5.

Instability: labrum tests

Modified Crank Test (in supine)

- Patient in supine

- The joint is loaded, and beginning at 90° small IR and ER movements are made, moving upward into end-range elevation

- This is then repeated with the arm more in flexion and then again more in abduction

- with posterior, superior, & anterior emphasis

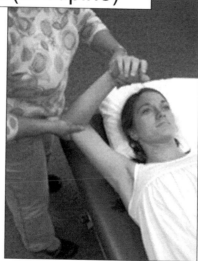

Instability: labrum tests

Active Compression (O'Brien) Test

- (+) with 90° flex, slight horizontal adduction (10-15°) & full IR
- (-) with 90° flex, slight horizontal adduction (10-15°) & full ER
- Downward Pressure at proximal forearm

  <u>Look for Pain</u> (patient's symptoms)
  -C4 (ACJ) or
  -Deep C5 (labrum) in IR

O'Brien SJ, Pagnani MJ, Fealy S, McGlynn SR, Wilson JB. The active compression test: a new and effective test for diagnosing labral tears and acromioclavicular joint abnormality. *Am J Sports Med.* 1998;26(5):610-3.

Instability: labrum tests

Modified Clunk Test

- Patient is in **sidelying** with shoulder at 90° abduction without rotation. The joint is axially loaded and the examiner makes a scooping movement inferiorly. The idea is to capture the bucket handle tear with the humerus.
- More often SLAP, less often Bankart
- Look for
  - Click
  - Pain (possibly -)
  - Positive with click or clunk, not necessarily with pain

Modified Clunk Test

Load and Scoop:
Inferior

Load and Scoop:
Posterior-Inferior

Load and Scoop:
Anterior –Inferior

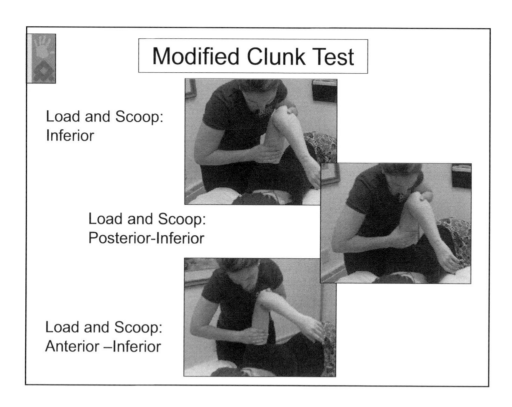

Instability: labrum tests

Biceps Load Test I

- For evaluating SLAP lesions in patients with recurrent anterior dislocations
- In the **supine** position, the arm is abducted to 90 deg and ER to its maximal point (apprehension), with the elbow at 90° flexion with forearm in supination. The patient is asked to flex the elbow against resistance.
- (+) for SLAP lesion if the active flexion of the elbow against resistance increases the discomfort of the apprehension test or if there is no change in the symptoms of apprehension
- (-) if pain or apprehension symptoms improve

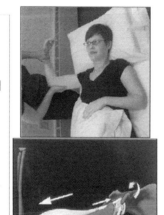

Kim SH, Ha KI, Han KY. Biceps load test: a clinical test for superior labrum anterior and posterior lesions in shoulders with recurrent anterior dislocations. Am J Sports Med. 1999;27(3):300-3.

Instability: labrum tests

Biceps Load Test II

- For evaluating SLAP lesions
- In the supine position, the arm is elevated to 120 degrees and externally rotated to its maximal point, with the elbow in the 90 deg flexion and the forearm in the supinated position. The patient is asked to flex the elbow while resisting the elbow flexion by the examiner.
- (+): if the patient complains of their pain during the resisted elbow flexion.
- (-): if pain is not elicited or if the pre-existing pain during the elevation and external rotation of the arm is unchanged or diminished by the resisted elbow flexion

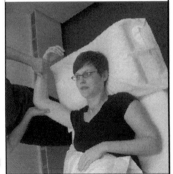

Kim SH, Ha KI, Ahn JH, Kim SH, Choi HJ. Biceps load test II: A clinical test for SLAP lesions of the shoulder. Arthroscopy. 2001 Feb;17(2):160-4.

Instability: labrum tests

Crank (Liu)

Sensitivity	Specificity	(+) Predictive	(-) Predictive
91.0%	93.0%	94%	90%

Biceps Load (Kim)

Sensitivity	Specificity	(+) Predictive	(-) Predictive
90.9%	96.9%	83.0%	98.0%

Instability: labrum tests

Active Compression for SLAP (O' Brien)

Sensitivity	Specificity	(+) Predictive	(-) Predictive
100.0%	98.5%	94.6%	100.0%

Active Compression for ACJ (O' Brien)

Sensitivity	Specificity	(+) Predictive	(-) Predictive
100%	96.6%	88.7%	100.0%

Analysis of shoulder Instability

Labral Lesions	Classification
Bankart	• **TUBS**
SLAP	• **AMI**
	• **AMBRII**

Instability: TUBS

- Traumatic

- Unidirectional

- Bankart

- Surgery

Recurrent anterior instability of the shoulder is a complex disorder which mainly affects the younger population, and generally requires surgical intervention to restore joint stability.

Sofu H, Gursu S, Kockara N, et al. Recurrent anterior shoulder instability: review of the literature and current concepts. World J Clin Cases. 2014; 2(11): 676-682.

Instability: AMI

- A-traumatic

- Multidirectional

- Instability

- Pts report feeling unstable in an elevated position; avoids overhead positions
- Multidirectional instability findings
- Characterized by elongated capsulo-ligamentous structures

Noted posterior positioning of humeral head @ 135° elevation when compared to controls

Schlemmer B, Dosch JC, Gicquel P, Boutemy P, Wolfram R, Kempf JF, Sick Hhiroaki I et al. Three-dimensional relationship of the glenohumeral joint in the elevated position in shoulder with multidirectional instability. J Shoulder Elbow Surg 2002; 11:510-515.

Instability: AMBRII

- A-traumatic
- Multidirectional
- Bilateral
- Rehabilitation
- Inferior capsule
- rotator cuff Interval

Instability: treatment

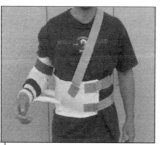

Management of dislocation

- Temporary Immobilization
- Traditional: IR, at patient's side
- Reported ↑'d glenohumeral coaptation & ↓'d aphysiological translation when the glenohumeral joint is immobilized in external rotation (mean = 35°)

Itoi E, Sashi R, Minagawa H, Shimizu T, Wakabayashi I, Sato K. Position of immobilization after dislocation of the glenohumeral joint. J Bone Joint Surg. 2001; 83-A:661-7.

Instability: treatment

Management of dislocation

- Reviewed 7 of 896 studies involving 663 patients with a primary anterior shoulder dislocation: 338 in the ER group and 325 in the IR group
- Conclusion: Immobilization in ER did not reduce the recurrence rates for patients after primary anterior shoulder dislocation nor improve the quality of life compared with immobilization in IR

Lin A, Xue X, Chen Y, et al. The external rotation immobilisation does not reduce recurrence rates or improve quality of life after primary anterior dislocation: a systematic review and meta-analysis. Injury. 2014; 45:1842-1847.

Anterior Instability: management

- Avoid
  - ER
  - Horizontal Abd
  - Extension
  - End ROM Abd

Anterior Instability: management

- Stretching to Posterior Capsule
- Strengthening: WB .... NWB Supine .... NWB upright
- Scapular plane.... Sagittal Plane .... Frontal Plane
- Emphasize endurance & proprioception
- Avoid over exertion
- Train each group only 2-3 times / week

Anterior Instability: management

- 1. Weight bearing (friction)
  - in the plane of the scapula ("in abduction")
  - in the plane of the glenoid ("in flexion")
    - Scapular stabilizers
      - serratus
      - lower trap
      - rhomboids
    - Glenohumeral muscles
      - subscapularis
      - infraspinatus/teres minor
  - (the support can be stable/unstable)

Anterior Instability: management

- 2. Nonweight-bearing
  - supine, sidelying
  - sitting
  - standing
    - Scapular stabilizers
      - rhomboids
    - Glenohumeral muscles
      - subscapularis
      - infraspinatus/teres minor

- Proprioceptive

Anterior Instability: management

Early on...

Avoid:

- ER
- Horizontal Abd
- Extension
- End ROM Abd
- Open Chain Ex (due to anterior shift)

Emphasize:

- Exercise with retracted scapula
- Scapular plane, before sagittal plane, before frontal plane exercises (e.g. anterior instability)

Instability: treatment for MDI

Watson MDI program

- Based around retraining and maintaining good scapular and humeral head motor control before any rotator cuff and deltoid strengthening
- Progresses exercises into functional ranges
- Program is divided into 6 stages

Watson L, Warby SA, Balster S, et al. Treatment of multidirectional instability with an exercise program: part 1. Shoulder Elbow. 2016;8(4):271-278.

Watson L, Warby SA, Balster S, et al. Treatment of multidirectional instability with an exercise program: part 2. Shoulder Elbow. 2016;9(1):46-53.

Scapular Rehabilitation

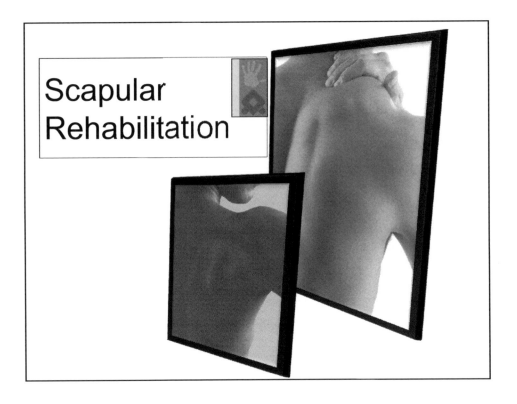

Scapulothoracic "joint"

The scapula functions as a "bridge" between the shoulder complex and the cervical spine and plays a very important role in providing both mobility and stability to the neck/shoulder region.

Cools AMJ, Struyf F, De Mey K, et al. Rehabilitation of scapular dyskinesis: from the office worker to the elite overhead athlete. Br J Sports Med. 2014 Apr;48(8):692-697.

288

Scapular Rehabilitation

It is not clear whether the observed dyskinesis is a cause, an effect or a compensation for rotator cuff pathology.

Kibler WB, Ludewig PM, McClure PW, et al. Clinical implications of scapular dyskinesis in shoulder injury: the 2013 consensus statement from the "scapular summit". Br J Sports Med. 2013;47:877-885.

Scapular Rehabilitation

There is compelling evidence in the literature indicating exercise and patient education decreases pain and improves function at short- and long-term follow-ups for patients with impingement syndrome

Uhl T, Smith-Forbes EV, Nitz, AJ. Factors influecing final outcomes in patients with shoulder pain: a retrospective review. J Hand Ther. 2017;30:200-207.

Hanratty CE, McVeigh JG, Kerr DP, et al. The effectiveness of physiotherapy exercises in subacromial impingement syndrome: a systematic review and meta-analysis. Semin Arthritis Rheum. 2012;42:297-316.

Scapular Assessment

GOAL: Identify abnormal scapular motion (dyskinesis), determine any relationship between altered motion and symptoms and identify the underlying causative factors of the movement dysfunction.

Possible contributors to the development of scapular dyskinesis:
- Deficits in strength or motor control of scapular-stabilizing muscles (serratus anterior, middle and lower trapezius),
- Postural abnormalities,
- Impaired flexibility.

Kibler WB, Ludewig PM, McClure PW, et al. Clinical implications of scapular dyskinesis in shoulder injury: the 2013 consensus statement from the "scapular summit". Br J Sports Med. 2013;47:877-885.

Scapular Rehabilitation

Scapular Rehabilitation Algorithm

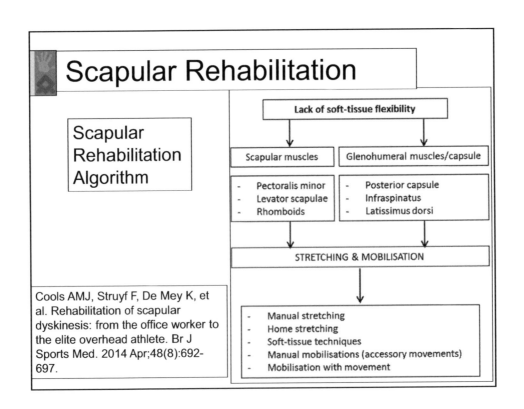

Cools AMJ, Struyf F, De Mey K, et al. Rehabilitation of scapular dyskinesis: from the office worker to the elite overhead athlete. Br J Sports Med. 2014 Apr;48(8):692-697.

Scapular Rehabilitation

Scapular Rehabilitation Algorithm

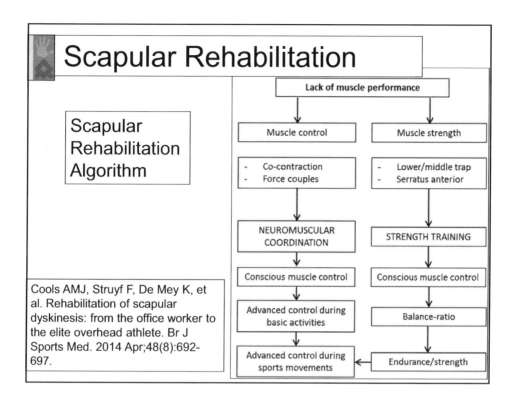

Cools AMJ, Struyf F, De Mey K, et al. Rehabilitation of scapular dyskinesis: from the office worker to the elite overhead athlete. Br J Sports Med. 2014 Apr;48(8):692-697.

Scapular Rehabilitation

First Stage: Conscious muscle control

- Improve proprioception
- Normalize scapular resting position

A study has shown higher surface EMG-activity in the targeted muscles (Middle trapezius MT, and Lower trapezius LT) during dynamic shoulder exercises when conscious correction of the scapula position was performed prior to the exercise.

Cools AMJ, Struyf F, De Mey K, et al. Rehabilitation of scapular dyskinesis: from the office worker to the elite overhead athlete. Br J Sports Med. 2014 Apr;48(8):692-697.

Scapular Rehabilitation

First Stage: Conscious muscle control

Active posterior tilt of the scapula

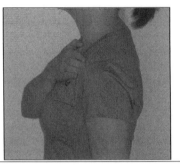 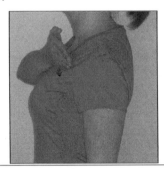

Note: It is important to incorporate scapular orientation with spinal posture correction.

Scapular Rehabilitation

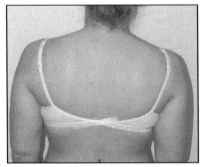 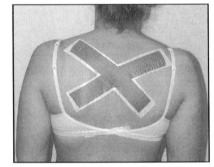

Taping the scapula into extension, posterior tilt and retraction gives **proprioceptive feedback** to the patient and improves trunk posture and shoulder ROM.

Cools AMJ, Struyf F, De Mey K, et al. Rehabilitation of scapular dyskinesis: from the office worker to the elite overhead athlete. Br J Sports Med. 2014 Apr;48(8):692-697.

Taping techniques

to improve scapular retraction

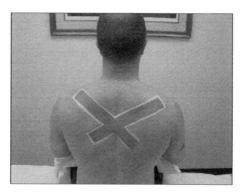

 ## Taping techniques

to improve scapular retraction

- Instruct patient to sit upright with arms supported on pillows
- perform active scapular retraction

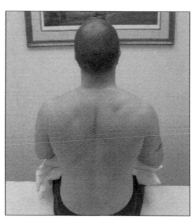

Taping techniques

to improve scapular retraction

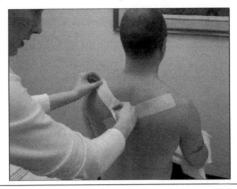

- Place white tape from medial aspect of acromion diagonally across to the inferior angle of opposite scapula

Taping techniques

to improve scapular retraction

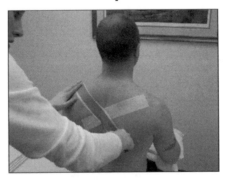

- The stabilization tape is then applied over the white tape (without excessive tension)

Taping techniques

to improve scapular retraction

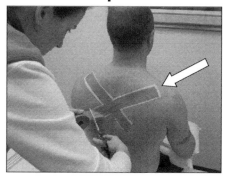

- Sometimes a small piece of white tape may be needed to anchor the tape at the superior aspect of the shoulder

Taping techniques

to improve scapular upward rotation

The patient's arms are passively brought overhead, promoting upward scapular rotation

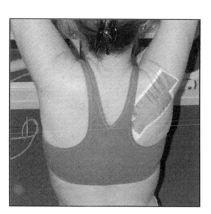

Taping techniques

to improve scapular upward rotation

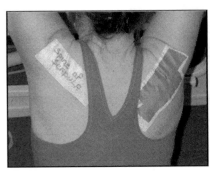
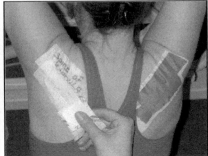

Place tape along the spine of the scapula

Taping techniques

to improve scapular upward rotation

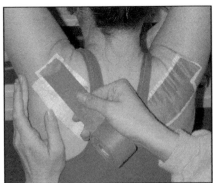
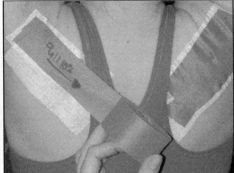

Pull tape approximately 10%, allowing the
white Hypafix/Coverall to slightly wrinkle

Taping techniques

to improve scapular upward rotation

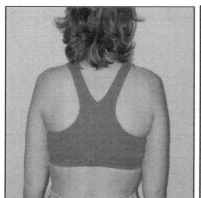 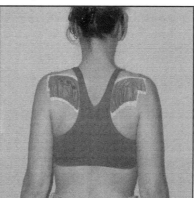

With arms relaxed at side, the scapula now present in an upwardly rotated position

Scapular Rehabilitation

Second Stage: Muscle control and strength for daily activities

- Improve muscle control and co-contraction
- Muscle strength

The shoulder girdle should be trained in both open-chain and closed-chain activities

Cools AMJ, Struyf F, De Mey K, et al. Rehabilitation of scapular dyskinesis: from the office worker to the elite overhead athlete. Br J Sports Med. 2014 Apr;48(8):692-697.

Scapular Rehabilitation

Open-chain exercises

Activate the key scapular-stabilizing muscles without putting high demands on the shoulder joint

Closed-chain exercises

"For strength deficit and muscle imbalances selective activation is an important component"

Improve dynamic GH stability through stimulation of the intra-articular and periarticular proprioceptors and enhance co-contraction of the rotator cuff.

Cools AMJ, Struyf F, De Mey K, et al. Rehabilitation of scapular dyskinesis: from the office worker to the elite overhead athlete. Br J Sports Med. 2014 Apr;48(8):692-697.

Scapular Rehabilitation

Closed-chain exercises | Isometric Low Row

Low Row: ask patient to retract and depress the scapula while pushing hand into table

Primarily targets the **lower trap** and **serratus anterior** and emphasizes scapular ER and posterior tilt

Kibler BW et al. Electromyographic analysis of specific exercises for scapular control in early phases of shoulder rehabilitation. *Am J Sports Med.* 2008;36:1789-98.

Scapular Rehabilitation

Open-chain exercises | Lawnmower Exercise

Lawnmower activated both upper and lower trap and serratus anterior equally

Kibler BW et al. Electromyographic analysis of specific exercises for scapular control in early phases of shoulder rehabilitation. *Am J Sports Med*. 2008;36:1789-98.

Scapular Rehabilitation

Open-chain exercises | Robbers Exercise

Robbers activated both upper and lower trap and serratus anterior equally

Kibler BW et al. Electromyographic analysis of specific exercises for scapular control in early phases of shoulder rehabilitation. *Am J Sports Med*. 2008;36:1789-98.

Scapular Rehabilitation

Open-chain exercises

Wall slide

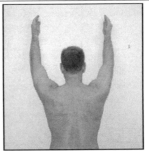 

The greatest amount of serratus anterior muscle activity occurred with an upwardly rotated and protracted scapula

Hardwick DH, et al. A comparison of serratus anterior muscle activation during a wall slide exercise and other traditional exercises. JOPST. 2006; 36: (12): 903-910.

Decker JM, et al. Serratus anterior muscle activity during selected rehabiliation exercises. Am J Sports Med. 2002; 30:374-381.

Scapular Rehabilitation

Closed-chain exercises

Push-up plus

Serratus anterior strengthening with emphasis on eccentric control

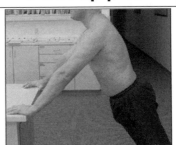

Standard push-up with a plus: produces minimal upper trap activation and maximum activation of the serratus anterior

Can start on countertop, then progress to performing on floor

Bertilli JA & Ghizoni MF. Long thoracic nerve: anatomy and functional assessment. J Bone Joint Surg. 2005; 87:993-998.

Decker MF, et al. Serratus anterior muscle activity during selected rehabilitation exercises. Am J Sports Med. 2002; 30:374-381.

Scapular Rehabilitation

Closed-chain exercises

Inferior Glide

Primarily targets the **lower trap** and **serratus anterior**, while emphasizing humeral head depression and scapular retraction

Inferior Glide: push hand into mat/table while retracting and depressing shoulder girdle

Kibler BW et al. Electromyographic analysis of specific exercises for scapular control in early phases of shoulder rehabilitation. *Am J Sports Med.* 2008;36:1789-98.

Scapular Rehabilitation

Open-chain exercises

Prone Extension

-highest maximal voluntary isometric contraction of the **middle trap** with a low upper trap (UT) to lower trap (LT) ratio

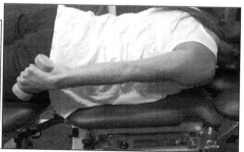

Castelein B, Cagnie B, Cools A. Scapular muscle dysfunction associated with subacromial pain syndrome. J Hand Ther. 2017;30:136-146.

Cools AM, Dewitte V, Lanszweet F, et al. Rehabilitation of scapular muscle balance: which exercises to prescribe? Am J Sports Med. 2007;35:1744-1751.

Moseley JB, Jobe FW, Pink M, et al. EMG analysis of the scapular muscles during a shoulder rehabilitation program. Am J Sports Med. 1992;20:128-134.

Scapular Rehabilitation

Open-chain exercises

Sidelying ER

-Reinold et al: highest maximal isometric voluntary contraction for infraspinatus & teres minor
-Cools et al: minimized upper trap (UT) firing with a low UT to LT ratio

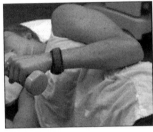

Cools AM, Dewitte V, Lanszweet F, et al. Rehabilitation of scapular muscle balance: which exercises to prescribe? Am J Sports Med. 2007;35:1744-1751.

Reinold MM, Wilk KE, Fleisig GS, et al. Electromyographic analysis of the rotator cuff and deltoid musculature during common shoulder external rotation exercises. J Orthop Sports Phys Ther. 2004;34:385-394.

Scapular Rehabilitation

Open-chain exercises

Sidelying ER

"Therapists should avoid prescribing individuals with UT/LT imbalance exercises that include ER in standing due to excessive postural activation of the upper trapezius."

Cricchio M & Frazer C. Scapulothoracic and scapulohumeral exercises: a narrative review of electromyographic studies. J Hand Ther. 2011;24:322-334.

Scapular Rehabilitation

Open-chain exercises	Sidelying forward flexion

Kibler BW et al. Electromyographic analysis of specific exercises for scapular control in early phases of shoulder rehabilitation. *Am J Sports Med.* 2008;36:1789-98.

Scapular Rehabilitation

Open-chain exercises	Horizontal Abduction with ER

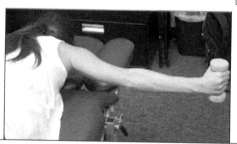

Highest maximal voluntary isometric contraction of the **supraspinatus** with a low UT to LT ratio

Castelein B, Cagnie B, Cools A. Scapular muscle dysfunction associated with subacromial pain syndrome. J Hand Ther. 2017;30:136-146.

Cricchio M & Frazer C. Scapulothoracic and scapulohumeral exercises: a narrative review of electromyographic studies. J Hand Ther. 2011;24:322-334.

Townsend H, Jobe FW, Pink M, et al. Electromyographic analysis of the glenohumeral muscles during a baseball rehabilitation program. Am J Sports Med. 1991;19:264-272.

Scapular Rehabilitation

Open-chain exercises	Horizontal Abduction with ER

- A recent study found this exercise produce a high rotator cuff synergy
- This exercise, having a low UT to LT synergy, may reduce the risk of scapular dyskinesis

Singh GK, Srivastava S, Kumar M, et al. Effects of selected rehabilitative exercises on external rotator muscles and trapezius muscles of masonry workers. Work. 2018;60(3):437-444.

Scapular Rehabilitation

Open-chain exercises	Horizontal Abduction with ER

"prone horizontal abduction at 100° with full ER produces higher levels of deltoid involvement and may not be an advantageous exercise for patients with poor dynamic shoulder stability due to superior humeral head migration with deltoid activation."

Cricchio M & Frazer C. Scapulothoracic and scapulohumeral exercises: a narrative review of electromyographic studies. J Hand Ther. 2011;24:322-334.

Scapular Rehabilitation

Open-chain exercises | T's

Activates middle trap and posterior deltoid

Scapular Rehabilitation

Third Stage: Advanced control during sports movements

Exercise advanced scapular muscle control and strength during sport-specific movements.

-Plyometrics
-Eccentric exercises
-"W" and "V" exercises
-Core exercises
(Selection of exercises based of sport demands)

Cools AMJ, Struyf F, De Mey K, et al. Rehabilitation of scapular dyskinesis: from the office worker to the elite overhead athlete. Br J Sports Med. 2014 Apr;48(8):692-697.

Scapular Rehabilitation

Eccentric scapular protraction

- **Serratus anterior recruitment with emphasis on eccentric control**

Scapular Rehabilitation

Serratus anterior isometrics

- **Serratus anterior in weight-bearing on a compliant surface**

Scapular Rehabilitation

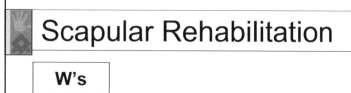

W's

Activates Rhomboids

Scapular Rehabilitation

V's

Activates Lower trapezius

Scapular Rehabilitation

Plyometrics

Drop and catch

Side to side pass with a weighted ball

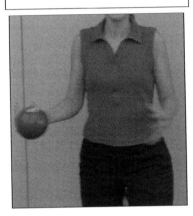

Scapular Rehabilitation

Plyometrics

dallmeyerpt.com

Body Blade

Pullsh.net

Exercise considerations

Impingement

Focus on:
- Activation of serratus anterior to improve scapular ER and upward rotation
- Inhibition of upper trapezius
- Balance of upper trapezius and lower trapezius
- Retraction

Kibler WB, Ludewig PM, McClure PW, et al. Clinical implications of scapular dyskinesis in shoulder injury: the 2013 consensus statement from the "scapular summit". Br J Sports Med. 2013;47:877-885.

Exercise considerations

Impingement

- Management:
  - Scapular stabilizer strengthening: this keeps the acromion up, as well as provides a stable base for the RTC
  - Adductor recruitment: pulls the humerus inferiorly to increase the AHI
  - Internal & External Rotators: maintains the humeral head centered on the glenoid
  - Positioning of patient progression depends on type of impingement

Exercise considerations

Impingement

- Avoid
  - ROM between 60 & 130 deg. (painful arc range)
  - End ROM positions
  - Horizontally Adducted position
  - Deltoid activity in 0-30 deg
  - Protraction
  - Excessive fatigue

Exercise considerations

Impingement

- **Active adduction, in combination with RTC recruitment**
- **This promotes an inferior pull on the humeral head!**

Exercise considerations

Impingement

- **Exercise with a retracted scapula, as this maintains more subacromial space**

  *Activation of Middle Trap during shoulder abduction increases the subacromial space

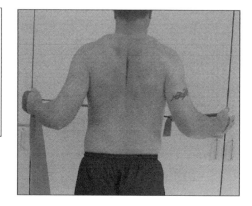

Guney-Deniz H, Harput G, Toprak U, et al. Acromiohumeral distance change relates to middle trap muscle activation during shoulder elevation with scapular retraction. J Sport Rehabil. 2018;May 29:1-21.

Exercise considerations

Rotator cuff tears

In presence of dyskinesis:
Focus on:
- Scapular stability as the first step in the rehabilitation process
- Activation of serratus anterior to improve scapular ER and upward rotation
- Activation of the lower trapezius as retractor

Kibler WB, Ludewig PM, McClure PW, et al. Clinical implications of scapular dyskinesis in shoulder injury: the 2013 consensus statement from the "scapular summit". Br J Sports Med. 2013;47:877-885.

Exercise considerations

Rotator cuff tears

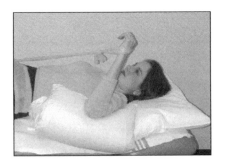 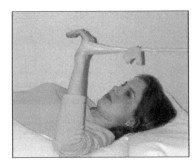

- **For a lower level patient, can begin rotator cuff strengthening in supine (with the scapula supported)**

Exercise considerations

Superior labral injuries

Internal rotation (of scapula) and anterior tilt is believed to:
- place increased tensile strain on the anterior ligament
- increase "peel back" of the biceps/labral complex
- weaken the rotator cuff co-contraction strength

Focus on:
- Activation of serratus anterior to improve ER and upward rotation
- Inhibition of upper trapezius
- Upward scapular rotation
- Retraction
- Balance of upper trapezius and lower trapezius

Kibler WB, Ludewig PM, McClure PW, et al. Clinical implications of scapular dyskinesis in shoulder injury: the 2013 consensus statement from the "scapular summit". Br J Sports Med. 2013;47:877-885.

More Rehab Suggestions

| Superior labral injuries | Zero-position internal rotation |

All photos from Cricchio & Frazer, 2011

• **higher EMG of subscapularis muscle and reduced pect major activity due to the increased shoulder abduction**

Other exercises that recruit the upper and lower subscapularis:
-push-up with a plus
-diagonal exercise

Suenaga, et al. Electromyographic analysis of internal rotation motion of the shoulder in various arm positions. J Shoulder & Elbow Surg. 2003;12:501-505.

Cricchio M & Frazer C. Scapulothoracic and scapulohumeral exercises: a narrative review of electromyographic studies. J Hand Ther. 2011;24:322-334.

Exercise considerations

Multidirectional instability

Symptoms of instability occur in the mid ranges of GH motion, where concavity/compression, GH bony alignment and muscle activation play the most important roles.

Focus on:
• Stimulation of the lower trapezius (retraction and upward rotation)
• Activation of serratus anterior

Kibler WB, Ludewig PM, McClure PW, et al. Clinical implications of scapular dyskinesis in shoulder injury: the 2013 consensus statement from the "scapular summit". Br J Sports Med. 2013;47:877-885.

Exercise considerations

Multidirectional instability

- Management
  - WB …. NWB Supine …. NWB upright
  - Retracted Scapula
  - Scap plane…. Frontal Plane …. Sagittal Plane
  - Rotator Cuff then Deltoid
  - Avoid Over exertion
  - Train each group only 2-3 x / week

Exercise considerations

Multidirectional instability

- Avoid
  - Glenohumeral ER
  - Horizontal Abd
  - Extension
  - End ROM Abd
  - Open Chain Ex (due to anterior shift)

Exercise considerations

Multidirectional instability

RTC recruitment while in a weight-bearing position

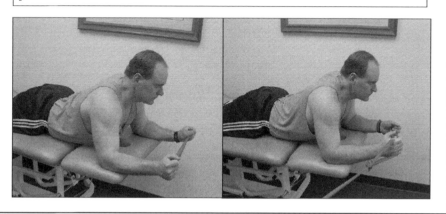

Exercise considerations

Multidirectional instability

- **Improving the dynamic control of the RTC, while in a weight-bearing position**

Thank you!!!

mirkanormand@gmail.com
aporretto-loehrke@newhands.net

Case Study #1

History

www.pixabay.com

- 54 year-old right-hand dominant female early childhood teacher fell onto her right shoulder in January of this year.
- She attended therapy, which consisted of scapular stabilizer and rotator cuff strengthening. Her symptoms improved, however, she experienced a return of symptoms after attempting to paint her walls.

Case Study #1

History

www.pixabay.com

- Pain at rest: 3/10 at the right deltoid insertion, which increases to 7/10 with attempting overhead activity or reaching behind her back.
- She is unable to reach into the back seat of her car, nor hold the top of the steering wheel due to pain. Patient is unable to sleep on her involved right shoulder.

Case Study #1

Physician referral

Evaluate and Treat: Right shoulder impingement

Case Study #1

Evaluation

- <u>AROM with elevation</u>:
  - 7/10 pain with flexion from 90-120
  - 7/10 pain with abd from 70-90 degrees
- <u>Passive GHJ testing</u>
  - ER: WNL
  - Abd: WNL
  - IR: limited by 30 degrees (unable to reach behind back)

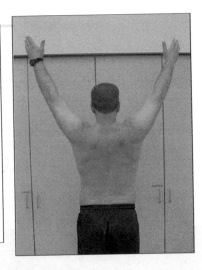

Case Study #1   Evaluation

- Resisted tests:
  - Add: 5/5 pain-free
  - Abd: 4/5 with 7/10 pain, (+) bursal pull test
  - ER: 4+/5 pain-free

- Extra tests:
  - Test for Tight Posterior Capsule: at 90 deg of abduction, IR: 35 deg on right (versus 57 on left)
  - (+) Hawkin's Kennedy Test

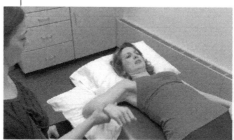

Compensation seen with anterior scapular tilting with tightness in the posteroinferior aspect of the GHJ

Case Study #1

Impairment list:

- External impingement with presence of a painful arc
- Bursal irritation
- Posterosuperior and posteroinferior GHJ capsular tightness

Case Study #1

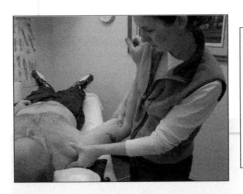

- Bursal massage
- Scapular retraining with emphasis on retraction to optimize the subacromial space

---

Case Study #1

Treatment

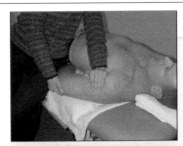

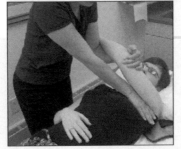

- Address posterosuperior GHJ capsular tightness to increase ability to reach behind back
- Address posteroinferior GHJ capsular tightness to prevent the diabolo effect

320

Case Study #1

Treatment

HEP:
- Codman's/pendulum with weight to address bursal irritation
- Modified sleeper stretch

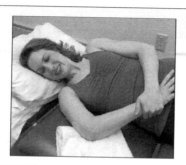

Case Study #1

Treatment

- Scapular retraction to optimize the subacromial space
- Exercises to minimize UT firing to optimize lower trap and serratus ant firing, and rotator cuff

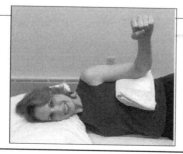

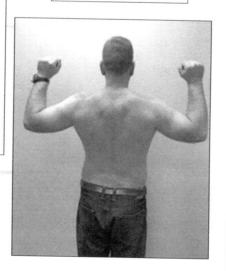

Case Study #2

38 year old male injured his right shoulder 4 months ago. He was carrying a heavy cooler full of water on his shoulder when it slipped out of his hands. He jerked his right shoulder as he caught it.

He received therapy (consisting of e-stim, ultrasound, and ROM) for 8 weeks without significant improvement.

Patient c/o pain referred proximal to elbow and "tightness" in the right side of his neck with looking over L shoulder.

Notes "there's a low level of pain in my shoulder that's always there." Quick motions irritate his shoulder and c/o difficulty with any weight-bearing or lifting.

Sleep status: able to sleep on his involved right shoulder.

Case Study #2

Physician referral

Evaluate and Treat: Right frozen shoulder

Case Study #2

Evaluation

- Resting scapular position:
  - Right scapula is depressed 2" versus the uninvolved left
- Scapulothoracic junction:
  - With pre-positioned "scolding": anterior scapula tilting present
  - Mild scapular winging present with both eccentric shoulder flexion and abduction

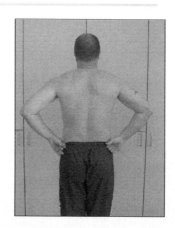

 # Case Study #2

Evaluation

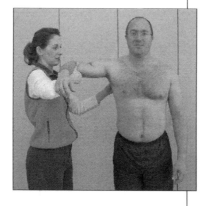

- AROM with elevation:
  - Flexion: 0-118 degrees (versus 0-156 on left) with C5 pain at end-range
  - Abduction: 0-112 degrees (versus 0-157 on left) with C5 pain at end-range
  - Scaption: 0-120 with painful arc
- Passive GHJ testing
  - ER: limited to 35 degrees (versus 51 on left)
  - Abd: mod/severely limited
  - IR: severely limited

323

Case Study #2

- Resisted tests:
  - Add: 5/5 3/10 pain
  - Abd: 4/5 with 5/10 pain at deltoid insertion, (-) bursal pull test
  - ER: 4/5 with 5/10 pain at deltoid insertion, (-) bursal pull test
  - IR: 4/5 with 5/10 pain at deltoid insertion, (-) bursal pull test

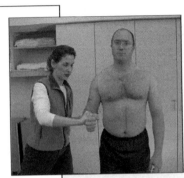

- Extra tests:
  - Test for Tight Posterior Capsule: at 90 deg of abd,
    - IR: 36 deg on right (vs 64 on left)
    - ER: 21 deg on right (vs 80 on left)

Case Study #2

Impairment list:

- Capsular pattern of limitation
- Poor resting scapular position and dynamic control

Case Study #2

Treatment

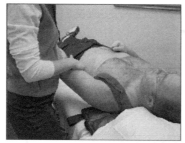

- Address GHJ capsular limitations (with belt to stabilize the scapula)
- Scapular taping to promote scapulohumeral dissociation

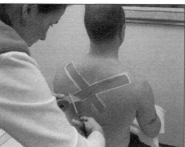

Case Study #2

Treatment

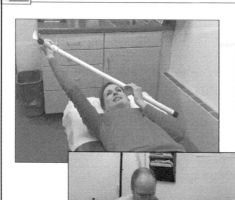

HEP:
- AAROM cane exercise (within a pain-free range)
- Capsular stretching
- Light strengthening as able

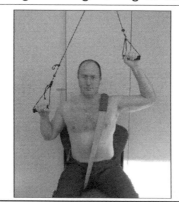

Case Study #2

Treatment

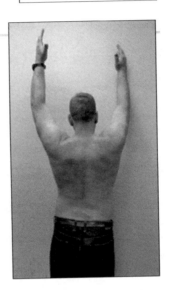

- Light strengthening as
the ROM improves
(within a pain-free range)

Case Study #3

54 year-old right-hand dominant male complains of
pain in the right posterior-lateral shoulder since inner
tubing down a river in mid-July. Since that time, he's
experienced pain with lifting, pushing and pulling, and
difficulty reaching behind his back.

www.pixabay.com

Case Study #3

Physician referral

Evaluate and Treat: Right shoulder pain

Case Study #3

Evaluation

- Resting scapular position:
  - WNL
- Scapulothoracic junction:
  - Mild winging noted with eccentric shoulder flexion and abduction
- Arm Elevation:
  - Painful arc with eccentric shoulder flexion & abduction
- Passive Elevation test:
  - with ipsilateral scapular fixation, patient c/o pain with posterior overpressure

Case Study #3

Evaluation

- Passive GHJ testing:
  - ER: WNL
  - Abd: WNL
  - IR: moderately limited

- Resisted tests:
  - Abd: 5/5
  - Add: 5/5
  - ER: 4/5 with posterolateral shoulder pain, (-) bursal pull test & pain increased
  - IR: 5/5

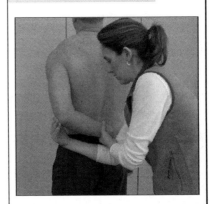

Case Study #3

Impairment list:

- External impingement
- Infraspinatus tendinopathy
- Posterosuperior GHJ capsular tightness
- Decreased dynamic scapular stabilization

Case Study #3

- TFM to the infraspinatus
- Address posterosuperior GHJ capsular tightness

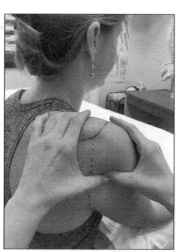

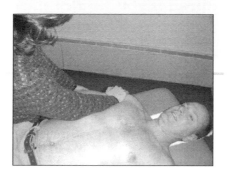

Case Study #3

Treatment

HEP:
- Rhythmic stretching into crossed adduction (to address infraspinatus tendinopathy)
- Posterosuperior GHJ capsular stretching

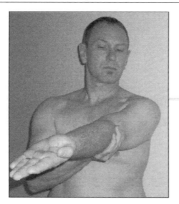

Case Study #3 | Treatment

- Focus on improving dynamic scapular control in a pain-free range

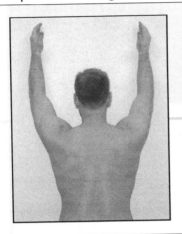
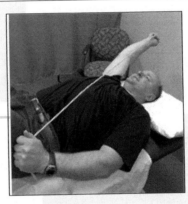

Case Study #4

34 year-old right-hand dominant male physical therapist with a history of right shoulder pain for the past 10 years.

Primary complaints:

○ Patient complains of posterosuperior shoulder pain with overhead activities. He notes "my shoulder just hurts when I try to use my arm overhead, so I just don't do it"

- Some difficulty with reaching behind his back

Case Study #4

Physician referral

Evaluate and Treat: Right shoulder pain;
history of posterior labral repair in 2007

 # Case Study #4

Evaluation

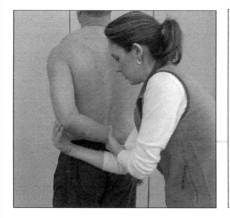

- <u>AROM with elevation:</u>
  - Flexion & Abduction:
    ROM is WNL; however,
    c/o 4/10 pain at the
    posterosuperior shoulder
    at end-range
- <u>Passive GHJ testing</u>
  - ER: WNL
  - Abd: WNL
  - IR: moderately limited

Case Study #4

- Passive Elevation test:
  - with ipsilateral scapular fixation, patient c/o pain with medial overpressure
- (+) Modified Relocation Test with posterior shoulder pain, alleviated with posterior humeral translation

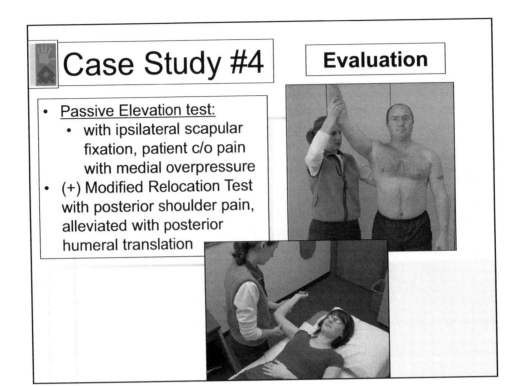

Case Study #4

Impairment list:

- Internal impingement
- Posterosuperior GHJ capsular tightness
- Decreased dynamic humeral head control at end-range elevation

Case Study #4  Treatment

- Address posterosuperior GHJ capsular tightness

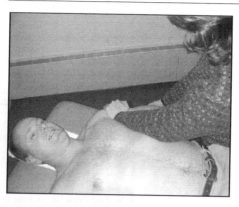

Case Study #4 Treatment

- Plyometrics

Side to side pass with a weighted ball

Drop and catch

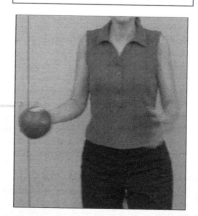

Case Study #4 | Treatment

- Plyometrics

GOAL: to improve dynamic humeral head control at end-range

dallmeyerpt.com

Body Blade

Pullsh.net

Thank you!!!

To contact us:

Ann's e-mail: aporretto@newhands.net

Mirka's e-mail: mirkanormand@gmail.com

Reference List for
A Systematic Approach to Examination, Diagnosis &
Manual Therapy of the
Shoulder

1. Alqunaee M, Galvin R, Fahey T. Diagnostic accuracy of clinical tests for subacromial impingement syndrome: a systematic review and meta-analysis. Arch Phys Med Rehabil. 2012;93:229-236.

2. Amoretti N, Grimaud A, Brocq O, et al. Shoulder distension arthrography in adhesive capsulitis. Clin Imaging. 2006; 30(4):254-256.

3. Anekstein Y, Blecher R, Smorgick Y, et al. What is the best way to apply the spurling test for cervical radiculopathy? Clin Orthop Relat Res. 2012; 470(9): 2566-72.

4. Antoniou A, Suk-Kee T, Williams GR, et al. Suprascapular Neuropathy: Variability in the Diagnosis, Treatment, and Outcome. 2001; 386: 131-138.

5. Arkkila PE, Kantola IM, Viikari JS, Ronnemaa T. Shoulder capsulitis in type I and II diabetic patients: association with diabetic complications and related diseases. *Ann Rheum Dis* 1996; 55(12):907-14.

6. Atkins E. Construct validity of Cyriax's selective tension examination: Association of end-feels with pain at the knee and shoulder; Invited commentary. JOSPT, 2000; 30:523-525.

7. Bahk M, Keyurapan E, Tasaki A, et al. Laxity testing of the shoulder: a review. Am J Sports Med. 2007;35(1):131-144.

8. Bak K, et al. Reformation of the coracoacromial ligament after open resection of arthroscopic release. J Shoulder Elbow Surg. 2000; 9: 289-293.

9. Balci N. Balci MK. Tuzuner S. Shoulder adhesive capsulitis and shoulder range of motion in type II diabetes mellitus: association with diabetic complications. Journal of Diabetes & its Complications, 1999; 13(3):135-40.

10. Barber FA, Field LD, Ryu RKN. Biceps tendon and superior labrum injuries: Decision making. J Bone and Joint Surg Am. 2007:89:1844-55.

11. Baumann B, Genning K, Bohm D, Rolf O, Gohlke F. Arthroscopic prevelance of pulley lesions in 1007 consecutive patients. *J Shoulder Elbow Surg.* 2008; 17: 14-20.

12. Beasley L, Faryniarz DA, Hannafin JA. Multidirectional instability of the shoulder in the female athlete. Clin Sports Med. 2000;19(2):331-349.

13. Bektas U, et al. Spinoglenoid septum: a new anatomic finding. J Shoulder Elbow Surg 2003;12:491-492.

14. Ben-Yishay A, Zuckerman JD, Gallagher M, Cuomo F. Pain inhibition of shoulder strength in patients with impingement syndrome. Orthopedics.1994;17:685-688.

15. Bertilli JA & Ghizoni MF. Long thoracic nerve: anatomy and functional assessment. J Bone Joint Surg. 2005; 87:993-998.

16. Bleichert S, Renaud G, MacDermid J, et al. Rehabilitation of symptomatic atraumatic degenerative rotator cuff tears: a clinical commentary on assessment and management. J Hand Ther. 2017;30:125-135.

17. Blevins FT. Rotator cuff pathology in athletes. Sports Med. 1997; 24: 205-220.

18. Bigliani et al. The relationship of acromial architecture to rotator cuff disease. Clin Sports Med. 1991; 10:823-838.

19. Bigliani et al. Current concepts review: Subacromial impingement syndrome. J Bone Joint Surg. 1997; 79A: 1854-1866.

20. Bing MB, Deyle GD. Comparison of supervised exercise with and without manual physical therapy for patients with shoulder impingement syndrome. JOSPT. 2000; 30: 126-137.

21. Borsa PA, Sauers EL, Herling DE. Patterns of glenohumeral joint laxity and stiffness in healthy men and women. Med Sci Sports Ex. 2000; 32:1685-1690.

22. Boyles RE et al. The short-term effects of thoracic spine thrust manipulation on patients with shoulder impingement syndrome. *Man Ther.* 2009, Aug;14(4):375-80.

23. Braman JP, Zhao KD, Lawrence RL, Harrison AK, Ludewig PM. Shoulder impingement revisited: evolution of diagnostic understanding in

orthopedic surgery and physical therapy. Med Biol Eng Comput. 2014 Mar;52(3):211-219.

24. Bunker TD. The pathology of frozen shoulder. J Bone Joint Surg.1995;77B:677-683.

25. Bynum CK. Tasto J. Arthroscopic treatment of synovial disorders in the shoulder, elbow, and ankle. *Am J Knee Surg.* 2002; 15(1):57-59.

26. Calligan N et al. Effectivelness of hydroplasty and therapeutic exercise for treatment of frozen shoulder. J Hand Ther. 2003;16:219-224.

27. Castelein B, Cagnie F, Cools A. Scapular muscle dysfunction associated with subacromial pain. J Hand Ther. 2017;30:136-146.

28. Castelein B, Cagnie F, Parlevliet T, et al. Scapulothoracic muscle activity during elevation tasks measured with surface and fine wire EMG: a comparative study between patients with subacromial impingement syndrome and healthy controls. Man Ther. 2016;23:33-39.

29. Chansky HA, Iannotti JP. The vascularity of the rotator cuff. *Clin Sports Med.* 1991; 10(4):807-22.

30. Churchill RS et al. Glenoid size, inclination & version. An anatomic study. J Sh Elbow Surg 2001; 10:327-32.

31. Clewey D, Flynn TW, Koppenhaver S. Trigger point dry needling as an adjunct treatment for a patient with adhesive capsulitis of the shoulder. J Orthop Sports Phys Ther. 2014;44(2):92-101.

32. Clinical Instructor of Orthopaedics and Plastic Surgery, Harvard Medical School in Boston. Conservative open acromioplasty. J Bone Joint Surg. 1995;77B:933-936.

33. Clisby EF et al. Relative contributions of the infraspinatus and deltoid during external rotation in patients with symptomatic subacromial impingement. J Shoulder Elbow Surg 2008;17:87S-92S.

34. Cochrane Collaboration. Arthrographic distension for adhesive capsulitis (frozen shoulder) (Review) 2009.

35. Cole BJ et al. The anatomy and histology of the rotator interval capsule of the shoulder. Clin Orthop Rel Res 2001;390:129-137.

36. Cools AM et al. Internal impingement in the tennis player: rehabilitation guidelines. *Br J Sports Med.* 2008;42:165-71.

37. Cools AM, Cambier D, Witvrouw EE. Screening the athlete's shoulder for impingement symptoms: a clinical reasoning algorithm for early detection of shoulder pathology. Br J Sports Med. 2008:42:628-635.

38. Cools AMJ, Struyf F, De Mey K, et al. Rehabilitation of scapular dyskinesis: from the office worker to the elite overhead athlete. Br J Sports Med. 2014 Apr;48(8):692-697.

39. Cools AM, Declercq G, Cagnie B, Cambier D, Witvrouw E. Internal impingement in the tennis player: rehabilitation guidelines. Br J Sports Med. 2008 Mar;42(3):165-71.

40. Cools AM, Dewitte V, Lanszweet F, et al. Rehabilitation of scapular muscle balance: which exercises to prescribe? Am J Sports Med. 2007;35:1744-1751.

41. Cools AM, Witvrouw EE, Declercq GA, et al. Isokinetic scapular muscle performance in overhead athletes with and without shoulder impingement symptoms. J Athl Train. 2005;40:104-110.

42. Coronado RA, Simon CB, Valencia C, George SX. Experimental pain responses support peripheral and central snesitization in patients with unilateral shoulder pain. Clin J Pain. 2013 Apr 23. [Epub ahead of print]

43. Cricchio M & Frazer C. Scapulothoracic and scapulohumeral exercises: a narrative review of electromyographic studies. J Hand Ther. 2011;24:322-334.

44. Curl, LA & Warren, RF. Glenohumeral joint stability. Selective cutting studies on the static capsular restraints. Clin Orthopedics & Related Research. 1996; 330: 54-65.

45. Davidson et al. Rotator cuff and posterior-superior glenoid labrum injury associated with increased glenohumeral motion: A new site of impingement. J Shoulder Elbow Surg 1995; 4:384-90.

46. Dayanidhi S, Orlin M, Kozin S, Duff S, Karduna A. Scapular kinematics during humeral elevation in adults and children. Clin Biomech 2005; 20:600-606.

47. Debski RE et al. The collagen fibers of the anterior inferior capsulolabrum have multiaxial orientation to resist shoulder dislocation. J Shoulder Elbow Surg, 2003; 12: 247-52.

48. Decker JM, et al. Serratus anterior muscle activity during selected rehabiliation exercises. Am J Sports Med. 2002; 30:374-381.

49. Dejong BA, Dahmen R, Hogeweg JA, Marti RK. Intraarticular triamcinolone acetonide injection in patients with capsulitis of the shoulder-A comparative-study of 2 dose regimens. *Clin Rehab*. 1998; 2:211-5.

50. DeWolf AN, MD, de Bruyn R, PT. Results of injection in adhesive capsulitis. Dutch Academy of Orthopedic Medicine.

51. Diercks R, Stevens M. Gentle thawing of the frozen shoulder: A prospective study of supervised neglect verses intensive physical therapy in seventy-seven patients with frozen shoulder syndrome followed up for two years. J Shoulder Elbow Surg 2004; 13: 499-502.

52. Dobson M, et al. Traumatic anterior shoulder instability: current concepts in management. Br J Hosp Med (Lond). 2009 May;70(5):260-265.

53. Downar JM, Sauers EL. Clinical measures of shoulder mobility in the professional baseball player. J Athl Train. 2005;40:23-29.

54. Dhir J, Willis M, Watson L, et al. Evidence-based review of clinical diagnostic tests and predictive clinical tests that evaluate response to conservative rehabilization for posterior glenohumeral instability: a systematic review. Sports Health. 2018;10(2):141-145.

55. Ebadi S, Forogh B, Fallah E, et al. Does ultrasound therapy add to the effect of exercise and mobilization in frozen shoulder? A pilot randomized double-blind clinical trial. Journal of Bodywork & Movement Therapies. 2017;21:781-787.

56. Edelson JG, et al. Bony changes of the glenoid as a consequence of shoulder instability. J Shoulder Elbow Surg. 1996; 5(4): 293-298.

57. Ekelund AL, Rydell N. Combination treatment for adhesive capsulitis of the shoulder. Clin Orthop. 1992;282:105-109.

58. Eyring EJ, Murray Wr. The effect of joint position on the pressure of intraarticular effusion. J Bone Joint Surg. 1964; 46-A:1235-1241.

59. Fareed DO, Gallivan WR. Office management of frozen shoulder syndrome. Clin Orthop. 1989;242:177-183.

60. Farrell CM, Sperling JW, Cofield RH. Manipulation for frozen shoulder: long-term results. J Shoulder Elbow Surg. 2005;14(5):480-4.

61. Ferrick MR. Coracoid impingement. A case report and review of the literature. Am J Sports Med 2000; 28:117-9.

62. Ferrick MR & Marzo JM. Ganglion cyst of the shoulder associated with a glenoid labrum tear and symptomatic glenohumeral instability. A case report. Am J Sports Med. 1997; 25(5): 717-719.

63. Forthomme B, Crielaard JM, Croisier JL. Scapular Positioning in Athlete's Shoulder : Particularities, Clinical Measurements and Implications. Sports Med. 2008;38(5):369-86.

64. Garofalo R, et al. Subcoracoid impingement syndrome: a painful shoulder condition related to different pathologic factors. Musculoskelet Surg. 2011; 95: S25-S29.

65. Gelberman RH, ed. Operative nerve repair and reconstruction. Philadelphia: J.B. Lippincott Co;1991

66. Gerber C, Galantay R, Hersche O. The pattern of pain produced by irritation of the acromioclavicular ioint and the subacromial space. J Shoulder Elbow Surg. 1998; 7: 352-355.

67. Glousman R, et al. Dynamic electromyographic analysis of the throwing shoulder with glenohumeral instability. J Bone Joint Surg Am. 1988; 70: 220-226.

68. Gill T, Zarins B. Open repairs for the treatment of anterior shoulder instability. Am J Sports Med. 2003; 31,1:142-153.

69. Giombini et al. Posterosuperior glenoid rim impingement as a cause of shoulder pain in top level waterpolo players. J Sports Med Phys Fit 1997; 37:273-8.

70. Gismerivik SO, Drogset JO, Granviken, et al. Physical examination tests of the shoulder: a systematic review and meta-analysis of diagnostic test performance. BMC Musculoskeletal Disord. 2017;18(1):41-50.

71. Gokeler A, van Paridon-Edauw GH, DeClercq S, Matthijs O, Dijkstra PU. Quantitative analysis of traction in the glenohumeral joint. In vivo radiographic measurements. Manual Therapy 2003; 1-6.

72. Graichen H, Hinterwimmer S, von Eisenhart-Rothe R, et al. Effect of abducting and adducting muscle activity on glenohumeral translation, scapular kinematics and subacromial space width in vivo. J Biomech. 2005 Apr;38(4):755-60.

73. Grant JA, Schroeder N, Miller BS, Carpenter JE. Comparison of manipulation and arthroscopic capsular release for adhesive capsulitis: a systematic review. J Shoulder Elbow Surg. 2013;22:1135-1145.

74. Guerrero P, Busconi B, Deangelis N, et al. Congenital instability of the shoulder joint: assessment and treatment options. JOSPT. 2009;39(2):124-134.

75. Guckel C, Nidecker A. MR arthrographic findings in tenosynovitis of the long bicipital tendon of the shoulder. *Skeletal Radiol*. 1998;27:7-12.

76. Guler-Uysal F, Kozanoglu E. Comparison of the early response to two methods of rehabilitation in adhesive capsulitis. Swiss Med Wkly. 2004; 134: 353-358.

77. Guney-Deniz H, Harput G, Toprak U, et al. Acromiohumeral distance change relates to middle trap muscle activation during shoulder elevation with scapular retraction. J Sport Rehabil. 2018;May 29:1-21.

78. Gwilym SE, Oag HC, Tracey I, Carr AJ. Evidence that central sensitisation is present in patients with shoulder impingement syndrome and influences the outcome after surgery. J Bone Joint Surg Br. April 2011;93(4);498-502.

79. Habermeyer P, Schuller U. [Significance of the glenoid labrum for stability of the glenohumeral joint. An experimental study] *Unfallchirurg* 1990; 93:19-26.

80. Habermeyer P, Magosch P, Pritsch M, Scheibel M, Lichtenberg S. Anterosuperior impingement of the shoulder as a result of pulley lesions: a prospective arthroscopic study. *J Shoulder Elbow Surg*. 2004; 13: 5-12.

81. Haik, M, Alburquerque-Sendin F, Silva s. Scapular kinematics pre- and post- thoracic manipulation in individuals with and without shoulder impingement symptoms: a randomized controlled study. JOSPT. 2014; 44(7); 475-497.

82. Halder AM, Halder CG, Zhao KD, ODriscoll SW, Morrey BF, An KN. Dynamic inferior stabilizers of the shoulder joint. Clin Biomech 2001; 16:138-143.

83. Halder AM, Halder CG, Zhao KD, et al. Dynamic inferior stabilizers of the shoulder joint. Clin Biomechan. 2001; 16: 138-143.

84. Halder, ME Zobitz, F Schultz, KN An. Structural properties of the subscapularis tendon. J Orthop Res, 2000;18: 829-834.

85. Halder AM, Kuhl SG, Zobitz ME, Larson D, An KN. Effects of the glenoid labrum and glenohumeral abduction on stability of the shoulder joint through concavity-compression. *J Bone Joint Surg* 2001; 83-A 1062-9.

86. Halverson L, Maas R. Shoulder joint capsule distention (hydroplasty); A case series of patients with "frozen shoulders" treated in a primary care office. *J Fam Prac* 2002; 51:61-4.

87. Hamner DL, Pink MM, Jobe FW. A modification of the relocation test: arthroscopic findings associated with a positive test. J Shoulder & Elbow Surg. 2000; 9(4): 263-267.

88. Hannafin JA. Chiaia TA. Adhesive capsulitis. A treatment approach. Clin Orthop Rel Res. 2000; (372): 95-109.

89. Hardwick DH, Beebe JA, McDonnell MK, et al. A comparison of serratus anterior muscle activation during a wall slide exercise and other traditional exercises. JOPST. 2006; 36: (12): 903-910.

90. Harrison AK, Flatow EL. Subacromial impingement syndrome. J Am Acad Orthop Surg. 2011;19:701-708

91. Hato Y, Saitoh S, Murakami N, Seki H, Kobayashi H, Takaoka K. Shrinkage in the inferior pouch of the scapulohumeral joint is related to posterior pain after rotator cuff repair: Radiographic and arthrographic comparison between patients with postoperative pain and those without it. J Shld Elbow Surg. 2001, 10 (4): 333-339.

92. Hawkins RJ, Mohtadi NGH. Clinical evaluation of shoulder instability. Clin J Sport Medicine. 1991; 1: 39-64.

93. Haik, M, Alburquerque-Sendin F, Silva s. Scapular kinematics pre- and post- thoracic manipulation in individuals with and without shoulder impingement symptoms: a randomized controlled study. JOSPT. 2014; 44(7); 475-497.

94. Hanratty CE, McVeigh JG, Kerr DP, et al. The effectiveness of physiotherapy exercises in subacromial impingement syndrome: a systematic review and meta-analysis. Semin Arthritis Rheum. 2012;42:297-316.

95. Holloway GB. Schenk T. Williams GR. Ramsey ML. Iannotti JP. Arthroscopic capsular release for the treatment of refractory

postoperative or post-fracture shoulder stiffness. Journal of Bone & Joint Surgery. 83-A(11):1682-7, 2001

96. Homsi C, Bordalo-Rodrigues M, da Silva JJ, et al. Ultrasound in adhesive capsulitis of the shoulder: is assessment of the coracohumeral ligament a valuable diagnostic tool? Skeletal Radiol. 2006; 35(9): 673-678.

97. Hoskins WT, Pollard HP, McDonald AJ. Quadrilateral space syndrome: a case study and review of the literature. Brit J Sports Med. 2005; 39:E9.

98. Hsu AT, Hedman T, Chang JH, et al. Changes in abduction and rotation range of motion in response to simulated dorsal and ventral translational mobilization of the glenohumeral joint. Phys Ther. 2002 Jun;82(6):544-56.

99. Huijbregts. SLAP lesions: Structure, function, and physical therapy diagnosis and treatment. J Manip Man Ther. 2001; 9,1:71-83.

100. Hutchinson JW, Tierney GM, Parsons SL, Davis TRC. Dupuytren's disease and frozen shoulder induced by treatment with a matrix metalloproteinase inhibitor. J Bone Joint Surg. 1998;80B:907-908.

101. Ihashi K, Matsushita N, Yagi R, Handa Y. Rotational Action of the Supraspinatus Muscle on the Shoulder Joint. J Electromyography and Kinesiology. 1998;8:337-346.

102. Itoi E, Sashi R, Minagawa H, Shimizu T, Wakabayashi I, Sato K. Position of immob-ilization after dislocation of the glenohumeral joint. J Bone Joint Surg 2001; 83-A:661-667.

103. Itoi E, Watanabe W, Yamada S, Shimizu T, Wakabayashi I. Range of motion after Bankart repair - Vertical compared with horizontal capsulotomy. *Am J Sports Med* 2001; 29:441-45.

104. Izumi T, Aoki M, Takayuki M, et al. Stretching positions for the posterior capsule of the glenohumeral Joint. Am J Sports Med. 2008; 36: 2014-2022.

105. Jacobs LG, Smith MG, Khan SA, et al. Manipulation or intra-articular steroids in the management of adhesive capsulitis of the shoulder? A prospective randomized trial. J Shoulder Elbow Surg. 2009 May-Jun;18(3):348-53.

106. Jain TK and Sharma NK. The effectiveness of physiotherapeutic interventions in treatment of frozen shoulder/adhesive capsulitis: a systematic review. J Back and Musculoskeletal Rehab. 2014;27:247-273.

107. Jerosch J. 360 degrees arthroscopic capsular release in patients with adhesive capsulitis of the glenohumeral joint--indication, surgical technique, results. Knee Surgery, Sports Traumatology, Arthroscopy. 9(3):178-86, 2001

108. Jerosch J, Saad M, Greig M, Filler T. Suprascapular nerve block as a method of preemptive pain control in shoulder surgery. Knee Surg Sports Traumatol Arthrosc. 2008 Jun;16(6):602-607.

109. Jerosch J et al. Mid-term results following arthroscopic capsular release in patients with primary and secondary adhesive capsulitis. Knee Surg Sports Traumatol Arthrosc 2012.

110. Jessell TM, Kelly DD. 1991. Pain and analgesia. In: Kandel ER, Schwartz JH, Jessell TM (Eds.) Principles of Neural Science (3rd ed.) Norwalk: Appleton & Lange, pp. 385-399.

111. Jia X, Ji JH, Petersen SA, Freehill MT, McFarland EG. An analysis of shoulder laxity in patients undergoing shoulder surgery. J Bone Joint Surg Am. 2009;91(9):2144-50.

112. Jobe CM, Iannotti JP. Limits imposed on glenohumeral motion by joint geometry. J Shoulder Elbow Surg. 1995; 4:281-285.

113. Johnson AJ, Godges JJ, Zimmerman GJ, Ounanian LL. The effect of anterior versus posterior glide joint mobilization on external rotation range of motion in patients with shoulder adhesive capsulitis. J Orthop Sports Phys Ther. 2007 Mar;37(3):88-99.

114. Jones DS, Chattopadhyay C. Suprascapular nerve block for the treatment of frozen shoulder in primary care: a randomized trial. British J Gen Practice. 1999; 49: 39-41.

115. Jonsson P, Wahlstrom P, Ohberg L, Alfredson H. Eccentric training in chronic painful impingement syndrome of the shoulder: results of a pilot study. Knee Surg Sports Traumatol Arthrosc. 2006 Jan;14(1):76-81.

116. Jost B, Koch PP, Gerber C. Anatomy and functional aspects of the rotator interval. *J Shoulder Elbow Surg.* 2000; 9:336-41.

117. Joung HN, Yi CH, Jeon HS, et al. Effects of 4-week self cross body stretch ing with scapular stabilization on shoulder motions and horizontal adduction adductor strength in subjects with limited shoulder horizontal adduction. J Sports Med Phys Fitness. 2018; 37 (3): 108-114.

118. Kaltenborn FM. Manuelle mobilisation der extremitätengelenke. Olaf Norlis Bokhandel; 1985:25)

119. Karatas GK. Meray J. Suprascapular nerve block for pain relief in adhesive capsulitis: comparison of 2 different techniques. Archives of Physical Medicine & Rehabilitation. 2002; 83(5):593-597.

120. Kelley et al. Shoulder pain and mobility deficits: Adhesive capsulitis. Clinical practice guidelines linked to the international classification of functioning, disability, and health from the orthopedic section of APTA. J Orthop Phys Ther 2013;43(5):A1-A31

121. Khan KM, Tress BW, Hare WSC, Wark JD. Treat the Patient, Not the X-Ray - Clinical Journal of Sport Medicine. 1998;8:1-4.

122. Kibler WB. Biomechanical analysis of shoulder during tennis activities. *Racquet Sports.* 1995; 14: 79-85.

123. Kibler WB. Shoulder rehabilitation: principles and practice. Medicine & Science in Sports & Exercise. 1998; S40-S50.

124. Kibler BW et al. Electromyographic analysis of specific exercises for scapular control in early phases of shoulder rehabilitation. Am J Sports Med. 2008;36:1789-98.

125. Kibler WB, Sciascia A, Thomas SJ. Glenohumeral internal rotation deficit: pathogenesis and response to acute throwing.Sports Med Arthrosc.2012;20:34–38.

126. Kibler WB, Uhl TL, Maddux WQ, Brooks PV, Zeller B, McMullen J. Qualitative clinical evaluation of scapular dysfunction: A reliability study. J Shoulder Elbow Surg 2002; 11:550-6.

127. Kim K et al. Capsule preservation improves short-term outcome of hydraulic distension in painful stiff shoulder. J Orthop Res. 2011; 29:1688-1694.

128. Kim SH, Ha KI, Han KY. Biceps load test: a clinical test for superior labrum anterior and posterior lesions in shoulders with recurrent anterior dislocations. Am J Sports Med. 1999;27(3):300-3.

129. Kim DH, Murovic JA, Tiel RL, et al. Management and outcomes of 42 surgical suprascapular nerve injuries and entrapments. Neurosurgery. 2005; 57:120-126.

130. Kim SH, Ha KI, Ahn JH, Kim SH, Choi HJ. Biceps load test II: A clinical test for SLAP lesions of the shoulder. Arthroscopy. 2001 Feb;17(2):160-4.

131. Kim JM, Kim YW, Kim HS, et al. The relationship between rotator cuff tear and four acromion types: cross-sectional study based on shoulder magnetic resonance imaging in 227 patients. Acta Radiol. 2018; Aug 15:284185118791211. [Epub ahead of print]

132. LaBan, et al. Slip of the lip—tears of the superior glenoid labrum-anterior to posterior (SLAP) syndrome. A report of four cases. Am J Sports Med 1995; 74:448-52.

133. Lafosse L, et al. Arthroscopic release of suprascapular nerve entrapment at the suprascapular notch: technique and preliminary results. Arthroscopy. 2007;23:34-42.

134. Laroche M, Ighilahriz O, Moulinier L, et al. Adhesive Capsulitis of the Shoulder - An Open Study of 40 Cases Treated by Joint Distension During Arthrography Followed by an Intraarticular Corticosteroid Injection and Immediate Physical Therapy. Revue du Rhumatisme. 1998;65:313-319.

135. Lee BC, Yegappan M, Thiagarajan P. Suprascapular nerve neuropathy secondary to spinoglenoid notch ganglion cyst: case reports and review of literature. Ann Acad Med Singapore. 2007;36(12):1032-5.

136. Le Lievre HMJ, Murrell GAC. Long-term outcomes after arthroscopic capsular release for idiopathic adhesive capsulitis. J Bone Joint Surg Am. 2012;94:1208-16.

137. Leppala J, Kannus P, Sievanen H, et al. Adhesive Capsulitis of the Shoulder (Frozen Shoulder) Produces Bone Loss in the Affected Humerus, But Long-Term Bony Recovery Is Good. Bone. 1998; 22: 691-694.

138. Leschinger T, Wallraff C, Muller D, et al. In vivo analysis of coracoid and subacromial shoulder impingement mechanism during clinical examination. Eur J Orthop Surg Traumatol. 2017;27:367-372.

139. Leschinger T, Wallraff C, Muller D, et al. Internal impingement of the shoulder: a risk of false positive test outcomes in external impingment tests? BioMed Research International. 2017;2017:2941238.

140. Levine WN, Flatow EL. The pathophysiology of shoulder instability. Am J Sports Med 2000; 28:911-17.

141. Lewis A, Kitamura T, Bayley JIL. The classification of shoulder instability: new light through old windows!. Curr Orthop. 2004;18(2):97-108.

142. Lin A, Xue X, Chen Y, et al. The external rotation immobilisation does not reduce recurrence rates or improve quality of life after primary anterior dislocation: a systematic review and meta-analysis. Injury. 2014; 45:1842-1847.

143. Lintner S, et al. Glenohumeral translation in the asymptomatic athlete's shoulderand its relationship to other clinically measurable anthropometric variables. Amer J Sports Med. 1996; 24(6): 716-720.

144. Liu SH, Henry MH, Nuccion SL. A prospective evaluation of a new physical examination in predicting glenoid labral tears. *Am J Sports Med.* 1996;24(6):721-5.

145. Lombardi I et al. Progressive resistance training in patients with shoulder impingement syndrome: a randomized controlled trial. *Arthritis & Rheumatism.* 2008;59(5):615-22.

146. Ludwig PM, Phadke V, Braman JP, et al. Motion of the shoulder during multiplanar humeral elevation. J Bone Joint Surg Am. 2009;91:378-389.

147. Ludwig PM, Reynolds JF. The association of scapular kinematics and glenohumeral joint pathologies. J Orthop Sports Phys Ther. 2009;39:90-104.

148. Lunden JB, Muffenbier M, Giveans MR, et al. Reliability of shoulder internal rotation passive range of motion measurements in the supine versus sidelying position. JOSPT. 2010; 40(9): 589-594.

149. Malicky et al. Total strain fields of the antero-inferior shoulder capsule under subluxation: A stereoradiogrammetric study. *J Biomech Eng – Transactions of the ASME*, 2001; 123:425-31.

150. Maitland's peripheral manipulation, ed 4. Hengeveld E. Banks K. eds. Philadelphia PA 19103, Elsevier Butterworth Heinemann, 2005.

151. Manton GL. Schweitzer ME. Weishaupt D. Karasick D. Utility of MR arthrography in the diagnosis of adhesive capsulitis. Skeletal Radiology. 2001; 30(6): 326-330.

152. Mahaffey BL, Smith PA. Shoulder instability in young athletes. Am Fam Physician. 1999 May 15;59(10):2773-82, 2787.

153. McClure P, Balaicuis J, Heiland D. A randomized controlled comparison of stretching procedures for posterior shoulder tightness. *JOSPT.* 2007; 37 (3): 108-114.

154. McGrory BJ. Endrizzi DP. Adhesive capsulitis of the hip after bilateral adhesive capsulitis of the shoulder. [Journal Article] American Journal of Orthopedics (Chatham, Nj). 2000; 29(6):457-60.

155. McGough, et al. Mechanical properties of long head of biceps tendon. Knee Surg, Sports Traum, Arthr 1996; 3:226-229.

156. Miniachi A. Magnetic resonance imaging evaluation of the rotator cuff tendons in the asymptomatic shoulder. Amer J Sports Med. 1995;2:142-145.

157. Misamore GW, et al. Parsonage turner syndrome (Acute brachial neuritis). J Bone Joint Surg. 1996; 78A: 1405-1408.

158. Morgan B, Jones AR, Mulcahy KA, Finlay DB, Collett B. Transcutaneous electric nerve stimulation (TENS) during distension shoulder arthrography: a controlled trial. Pain. 1996; 64:265-267.

159. Moseley JB, Jobe FW, Pink M, et al. EMG analysis of the scapular muscles during a shoulder rehabilitation program. Am J Sports Med. 1992;20:128-134.

160. Needell SD, Zlatkin MB, Sher JS, Murphy BJ, Uribe JW. MR imaging of the rotator cuff: peritendinous and bone abnormalities in an asymptomatic population. Am J Roentgenol. 1996;166:863-867.

161. Nordt WE, Garrettson RB, Plotkin R. The measurement of subacromial contact pressure in patients with impingement syndrome. Arthroscopy: J Arthroscopy Rel Surg. 1999;15:121-125.

162. O'Brien SJ, Pagnani MJ, Fealy S, McGlynn SR, Wilson JB. The active compression test: a new and effective test for diagnosing labral tears and acromioclavicular joint abnormality. *Am J Sports Med.* 1998;26(5):610-3.

163. Okino S, Miyaji H, Matodba M. The quadrilateral space syndrome. Neuroradiology. 1995; 37: 311-312.

164. Ogilvie-Harris DJ, Biggs DJ, Fitsialos, DP. The resistant frozen shoulder-manipulation versus arthroscopic release. Clin Orth. 1995;319:238-248.

165. Ozaki J. Pathomechanics and operative management of chronic frozen shoulder. Ann Chir Gynaecol.1996; 85(2):156-8.

166. Paley KJ, Jobe FW, Pink MM, et al. Arthroscopic Findings in the overhand throwing athlete: evidence for posterior internal impingement of the rotator cuff. Arthroscopy. 2000; 16(1): 35-40.

167. Panni et al. Histologic analysis of the coracoacromial arch: correlation between age-related changes and rotator cuff tears. Arthroscopy. 1996; 12: 531-540.

168. Pap G, Liebau C, Meyer M, et al. Results of mobilization under anesthesia in adhesive capsulitis in relation to stage of the disease. [German] Zeitschrift fur Orthopadie und Ihre Grenzgebiete. 1998; 136(1): 13-17.

169. Parentis MA, Glousman RE, Mohr KS, et al. An evaluation of the provocative tests for superior labral anterior to posterior lesions. Am J Sports Med. 2006;34(2):265-268.

170. Patzer T, Kircher J, Lichtenberg S, et al. Is there an association between SLAP and biceps pulley lesions? Arthroscopy: J of Arthroscopic & Related Surg. 2011:27(5):611-618.

171. Paul TM, Soo Hoo J, Chae J, Wilson RD. Central hypersensitivity in patients with subacromial impingement syndrome. Arch Phys Med Rehabil. 2012 Dec;93(12): 2206-2209.

172. Pellecchia GL. Intertester reliability of the Cyriax evaluation in assessing patients with shoulder pain. J Orth Sports Phys Ther. 1996;1:34-38.

173. Pfahler M et al. The role of the bicipital groove in tendopathy of long biceps tendop. *J Shoulder Elbow Surg.* 1999;8:419-24.

174. Piatt BE, Hawkins RJ, Fritz RC, Ho CP, Wolf E, Schickendantz M. Clinical evaluation and treatment of spinoglenoid notch ganglion cysts. J Shoulder Elbow Surg. 2002; 11:600-604.

175. Pradhan et al. Superior labral strain during the throwing motion - A cadaveric study. Am J Sports Med 2001; 29:488-492.

176. Provencher MT, King S, Solomon DJ, et al. Recurrent posterior shoulder instability: diagnosis and treatment. Oper Tech Sports Med. 2005;13:196-205.

177. Quraishi NA et al. Thawing the frozen shoulder: a randomized trial comparing manipulation under anaesthesia with hydrodilatation. J Bone Joint Surg [Br] 2007;89-B:1197-1200.

178. Rathi S, Taylor NF, Green RA. The effect of in vivo rotator cuff muscle contraction on glenohumeral joint translation: an ultrasonographic and electromyographic study. J Biomech. 2016;49(16):3840-3847.

179. Rawat P, Eapen C, Seema KP. Effect of rotator cuff strengthening as an adjunct to standard care in subjects with adhesive capsulitis: a randomized controlled trial. J Hand Ther. 2017; 235-341.

180. Reddy AS, Mohr KJ, Pink MM, Jobe FW. Electromyographic analysis of the deltoid and rotator cuff muscles in persons with subacromial impingement. *J Shld Elbow Surg.* 2000;9:519-23.

181. Reinold MM, Wilk KE, Fleisig GS, et al. Electromyographic analysis of the rotator cuff and deltoid musculature during common shoulder external rotation exercises. J Orthop Sports Phys Ther. 2004;34:385-394.

182. Rose M & Noonan T. Glenohumeral internal rotation deficit in throwing athletes: current perspectives. Journal of Sports Medicine. 2018;69-78.

183. Savoie FH, Papendik L, Field LD, et al. Straight anterior instability: lesions of the middle glenohumeral ligament. Arthroscopy. 2001; 32(3): 457-461.

184. Sawyer EE, McDevitt AW, Louw A, et al. Use of pain neuroscience education, tactile discrimination, and graded motor imagery in an individual with frozen shoulder. JOSPT. 2018; Dec 19:1-29. doi: 10.2519/jospt.2018.7716. [Epub ahead of print].

185. Schlemmer B, Dosch JC, Gicquel P, Boutemy P, Wolfram R, Kempf JF, Sick Hhiroaki I et al. Three-dimensional relationship of the glenohumeral joint in the elevated position in shoulder with multidirectional instability. J Shoulder Elbow Surg 2002; 11:510-515.

186. Shishido H, Kikuchi S. Injury of the suprascapular nerve in shoulder surgery: An anatomic study. J Shoulder Elbow Surg. 2001; 10: 372-376.

187. Schulz CU et al. The mineralization patterns at the subchondral bone plate of the glenoid cavity in healthy shoulders. J Shoulder Elbow Surg 2002; 11:174-81.

188. Senbursa G et al. Comparison of conservative treatment with and without manual physical therapy for patients with shoulder impingement syndrome: a prospective, randomized clinical trial. Knee Surg Sports Traumatol Arthrosc. 2007;15:915-21.

189. Silliman JF, Hawkins RJ. Classification and physical diagnosis of instability of the shoulder. Clinical Orthoped & Related Research. 1993; 291: 7-19.

190. Simao MN, Noguera-Barbosa MH, Muglia VF, et al. Anterior shoulder instability: correlation between magnetic resonance arthrography, ultrasound arthrography and intraoperative findings. Ultrasound in Med. & Biol. 2012; 38: 551-560.

191. Simotas AC. Tsairis P. Adhesive capsulitis of the glenohumeral joint with an unusual neuropathic presentation: a case report. American Journal of Physical Medicine & Rehabilitation. 78(6):577-81, 1999.

192. Singh GK, Srivastava S, Kumar M, et al. Effects of selected rehabilitative exercises on external rotator muscles and trapezius muscles of masonry workers. Work. 2018;60(3):437-444.

193. Sofu H, Gursu S, Kockara N, et al. Recurrent anterior shoulder instability: review of the literature and current concepts. World J Clin Cases. 2014; 2(11): 676-682.

194. Soifer TB, Levy HJ, Soifer FM, Kleinbart F, Vigorita V, Bryk E. Neurohistology of the subacromial space. Arthroscopy. 1996;12:182-186.

195. Song KD et al. Indirect MR arthrographic findings of adhesive capsulitis. AJR:197, December 2011.

196. Suenaga, et al. Electromyographic analysis of internal rotation motion of the shoulder in various arm positions. J Shoulder & Elbow Surg. 2003;12:501-505.

197. Struyf F, Cagnie B, Cools A. Scapulothoracic muscle activity and recruitment timing in patients with shoulder impingement symptoms and glenohumeral joint instability. J Electromyogr Kinesiol. 2014;24:277-284.

198. Synder SJ, Banas MP, Karzel RP. An analysis of 140 injuries to the superior glenoid labrum. J Shoulder Elbow Surg. 1995; 4: 243-248.

199. Tanishima T, Yoshimasu N. Development and prevention of frozen shoulder after acute aneurysm surgery. Surg Neurol. 1997;48:19-22.

200. Taylor DC, Arciero RA. Pathologic changes associated with shoulder dislocations. Am J Sports Med. 1997;25:306-311.

201. Ticker JB, Beim GM, Warner JJ. Recognition and treatment of refractory posterior capsular contracture of the shoulder. *Arthroscopy* 2000; 16:27-34.

202. Townsend H, Jobe FW, Pink M, et al. Electromyographic analysis of the glenohumeral muscles during a baseball rehabilitation program. Am J Sports Med. 1991;19:264-272.

203. Turkel SJ, Panio MW, Marshall JL, et al. Stabilizing mechanisms preventing anterior dislocation of the glenohumeral joint. J Bone Joint Surg Am. 1981; 63: 1208-1217.

204. Uhl T, Smith-Forbes EV, Nitz, AJ. Factors influecing final outcomes in patients with shoulder pain: a retrospective review. J Hand Ther. 2017;30:200-207.

205. Umer M, Qadir I, Azam M. Subacromial impingement syndrome. Orthopedic Reviews 2012; 4:e18.

206. VandenBerghe G, Hoenecke H, Fronek J. Glenohumeral joint instability: the orthopedic approach. Semin Musculoskelet Radiol. 2009;43(4):259-264.

207. Van der Reis W, Wolf EM. Arthroscopic rotator cuff interval capsular closure. *Orthop* 2001; 24:657-61.

208. Vanderwindt DAWM, Koes BW, Deville W, et al. Effectiveness of corticosteroid injections versus physiotherapy for treatment of painful stiff shoulder in primary-care - Randomized trial. *Br Med J.* 1998; 317:1292-1296.

209. van Royen BJ, Pavlov PW. Treatment of frozen shoulder by distension and manipulation under local anaesthesia. Int Orthop. 1996;20:207-210.

210. Vermeulen HM, et al. End-range mobilization techniques in adhesive capsulitis of the shoulder joint: A multiple-subject case report. Phys Ther, 2000; 80:1204-1213.

211. Visser CPJ, Napoleon L, Coene JEM, et al. Nerve lesions in proximal humeral fractures. J Shoulder Elbow Surg. 2001; 10: 421-427.

212. Volpin G, Stahl S, Stein H. [Impingement syndrome following direct injuries of the shoulder joint]. Harefuah 1996;130:244-7; 295.

213. Walmsley S, Rivett D, Osmotherly P. Adhesive capsulitis: establishing consensus on clinical identifiers for stage 1 using the delphi technique. Physical Ther. 2009; 89(9): 906-916.

214. Warby SA, Pizzari T, Ford JJ, et al. Exercise-based management versus surgery for multidirectional instability of the glenohumeral joint: a systematic review. Br J Sports Med. 2016;50:1115-1123.

215. Warby SA, Watson L, Ford JJ, et al. Multidirectional instability of the glenohumeral joint: etiology, classification, assessment, and management. J Hand Ther. 2017;30: 175-181.

216. Watson L, Bialocerkowski A, Dalziel R, et al. Hydrodilatation (distension arthrography): a long-term clinical outcome series. Br J Sports Med. 2007; 41: 167–173.

217. Watson L, Warby SA, Balster S, et al. Treatment of multidirectional instability with an exercise program: part 1. Shoulder Elbow. 2016;8(4):271-278.

218. Watson L, Warby SA, Balster S, et al. Treatment of multidirectional instability with an exercise program: part 2. Shoulder Elbow. 2016;9(1):46-53.

219. Wiater JM, Flatow EL. Long thoracic nerve injury. Clinical Orthopaedics and Related Research, 1999; 368: 17-27.

220. Wilk KE, Hooks TR, Macrina LC. The modified sleeper stretch and modified cross-body stretch to increase shoulder internal rotation range of motion in the overhead throwing athlete. JOSPT. 2013; 43(12): 891-894.

221. Yamaguchi K, et al. Natural history of rotator cuff tears: a longitudinal analysis of asymptomatic tears detected sonographically. J Shoulder Elbow Surg. 2001;10: 199-203.

222. Yamaguchi K. Sethi N. Bauer GS. Postoperative pain control following arthroscopic release of adhesive capsulitis: a short-term retrospective

review study of the use of an intra-articular pain catheter. Arthroscopy. 18(4):359-65, 2002

223. Yang J, Chang C, Chen S, Wang S, Lin J. Mobilization techniques in subjects with frozen shoulder syndrome: randomized multiple-treatment trial. *Physical Therapy* . 2007; 87: 10, 307-315.

224. Yoldas EA, Faber KJ, Hawkins RJ. Translation of the glenohumeral joint in patients with multidirectional and posterior instability: awake examination versus examination under anesthesia. J Shoulder Elbow Surg 2001; 10:416-20.